Sources Of American Spirituality

Walter Rauschenbusch

SELECTED WRITINGS

Edited by Winthrop S. Hudson

PAULIST PRESS
New York ◆ Mahwah

Library of Congress
Catalog Card Number: 84-62136

ISBN: 0-8091-0356-7

Published by Paulist Press
997 Macarthur Boulevard
Mahwah, N.J. 07430

Printed and bound in the United States of America

CONTENTS

To
Leonard I. Sweet

PREFACE

I undertook this volume of the Sources of American Spirituality at the request of Dr. John Farina of the Paulist Press. A portrait of Walter Rauschenbusch graced the wall of my office, as the focal point of attention, throughout most of my teaching career. I thought I knew him well from the vantage point of a direct line of academic succession. But when I was called upon to view him from a fresh perspective, I discovered that I had not fully known him. There were aspects of his life and thought that were unknown to me, and I was much the poorer for my lack of exposure to them.

There are many friends who have aided me in the recovery of fugitive materials by Walter Rauschenbusch and fugitive information about him. I tried to work out a neat classification to list those to whom I am indebted in so many ways: friends and scholars, friends and librarians. But this wouldn't do, for there were librarians who were scholars, and scholars who functioned as librarians in knowing where to locate a missing item. And a minister who was also a scholar as well as a friend had copies of documents I had not located. A number of those who helped me were former students of mine, now my colleagues and mentors. The common denominator among them all is that they are friends and that they went far out of their way to help me to a better understanding of Walter Rauschenbusch.

The listing of those to whom I wish to express appreciation begins at random with Robert T. Handy of Union Theological Seminary in New York, who gave me helpful direction; and then Stephen Peterson of Yale Divinity School library, who sent me a copy of an

1

item, otherwise unobtainable, just when I needed it most; Leonard I. Sweet, provost of Colgate Rochester Divinity School/Bexley Hall/ Crozer Theological Seminary, who generously provided me with photocopies of many materials; Grant Wacker of the University of North Carolina at Chapel Hill, who gave the Introduction a perceptive critical reading; Carl Johnson, minister of the Ridge Road Baptist Church in Raleigh; Peter VandenBerge of Rochester; John Braund of the University of Rochester; Donn M. Farris of Duke Divinity School library; Frederic M. Hudson for his unheralded and unpublished dissertation on the Brotherhood of the Kingdom; William H. Brackney, executive director of the American Baptist Historical Society and its Samuel Colgate Historical Collection, and thus official custodian of the remarkable Rauschenbusch materials assembled in Rochester, New York; and also to the gracious help extended to me by the archivist, Susan M. Eltscher. Finally, I must express my appreciation to Larry L. Greenfield, president of the theological complex in Rochester, for his many courtesies to me while I was in Rochester pushing the project to completion. To all these friends I am grateful for many kindnesses. When the book is in print, I shall be equally indebted to John Farina and his associates at the Paulist Press.

WINTHROP S. HUDSON

INTRODUCTION

> In Rauschenbusch . . . the reign of Christ required con-
> version and the coming kingdom was crisis, judgment as
> well as promise. Though his theory of the relation of God
> and man often seemed liberal he continued to speak the
> language of the prophets and St. Paul.
>
> *H. Richard Niebuhr*[1]

Walter Rauschenbusch is chiefly remembered as the outstanding American exponent of social Christianity during the years prior
to World War I. He has been called "the real founder" of the "social gospel" movement in the United States and its most brilliant
representative.[2] The former contention crowds the truth, for it obscures the important pioneering role of others. Still, it does empha-
size the centrality of Rauschenbusch in the recollection of the past by
a later generation.

Although in the 1890's Rauschenbusch was well known for his
interest in social reform within his own Baptist denomination and, to
a lesser degree, among socially sensitive persons of other denominations in New York City, it was the unexpected acclaim which
greeted the publication of *Christianity and the Social Crisis* in 1907
that rocketed him into national prominence. "The social move-

---

1. H. Richard Niebuhr, *The Kingdom of God in America* (New York,
1937), 194.
2. Reinhold Niebuhr, *An Interpretation of Christian Ethics* (New York,
1935), preface.

ment,'' he later explained, ''had got hold of me just as the social awakening had got hold of the country. The book came out at the psychological moment, and was taken as an expression of what thousands were feeling.''[3] Henceforth for the remaining eleven years of his life, he was besieged with requests from all parts of the country to speak and to publish. His teaching schedule at the theological seminary in Rochester, New York, was rearranged to provide four-day weekends for his ''public work,'' and time was found during long summer vacations for him to continue to set forth his views in print.

A social prophet and social reformer may seem a curious choice to be included in a series of books exploring the Sources of American Spirituality. Social activists seldom have time for either reflection or the routine of spiritual discipline. Nor do social reformers tend to stress and to urge upon others the primacy of the inner life of the Spirit. But there have been exceptions, and Rauschenbusch was numbered among them. In conscious intent he sought more than merely to reform the social order or to initiate a social revolution. For any outward change to have meaning and to endure, Rauschenbusch insisted that attention must be given to the deep wells of personal religious life. In terms of his own understanding of his vocation, Rauschenbusch was an evangelist in the tradition of the great revivalists, seeking to win people to an experience of Christ and to put them to work in the interests of Christ's kingdom. He entered the ministry with a strong desire to ''save souls'' and this, in his own mind, continued to be a constant objective.

EARLY YEARS AND CHOICE OF VOCATION

Walter Rauschenbusch began his ministry in New York City on June 1, 1886, when he assumed his duties as pastor of the Second German Baptist Church. He was twenty-five years old, having just graduated from Rochester Theological Seminary. For six generations his direct forebears had been Lutheran clergymen of a pietistic stamp. This German pietism, however, had been diluted and dis-

---

3. *Rochester Democrat and Chronicle*, 25 Jan. 1913; reprinted in *Rochester Theological Seminary Bulletin* XIII (Nov. 1918), 53.

placed by American evangelicalism a full decade before Walter Rauschenbusch was born. His father, Augustus Rauschenbusch, had
come to the United States in 1846 as a Lutheran missionary, but four
years later became a Baptist. After a stint as an agent of the American Tract Society and then as a Baptist missionary among German
immigrants in Canada and the West, he devoted the rest of his life,
as head of the German department of the Rochester Theological
Seminary, to the training of a Baptist ministry for work among the
German-speaking population.[4] This commitment to American evangelicalism as interpreted by Baptists found full expression in the
home in which Walter Rauschenbusch was reared, and it was an important influence in shaping his life. Toward the close of young Rauschenbusch's high school years at the Rochester Free Academy, he
experienced his initial conversion. Later he recognized that there
was much that was "foolish" in this adolescent awakening, but he
also insisted that it was a very true religious experience. "It was of
everlasting value to me. It turned me permanently, and I thank God
with all my heart for it. It was a tender, mysterious experience. It influenced my soul down to its depths."[5]

The four years following Rauschenbusch's graduation from
high school were spent in Germany, where he graduated in 1883
with first honors in classical studies from the Gymnasium at Gütersloh. He had decided to enter the ministry, and he returned home to
pursue simultaneously work for an "arts" degree at the University
of Rochester and his theological preparation at Rochester Theological Seminary. A summer spent as supply pastor of a small German
Baptist church in Louisville, Kentucky, deepened his sense of vocation. He reviewed his experience in a letter to a former schoolmate
at the Free Academy, reporting that the church was

> a small flock but a very neglected one. . . . Everybody
> was sorely discouraged and very many were hungry—

---

4. Several seminaries had foreign language departments for developing
ministries to work with immigrants. Among Baptists there was a French (Canadian)
department at Newton, an Italian department at Colgate, a Swedish department at
Morgan Park (soon to be the Divinity School of the University of Chicago).

5. "The Kingdom of God," *Cleveland's Young Men* XXVII (9 Jan.
1913); reprinted in Robert T. Handy, *The Social Gospel in America, 1870–1920*
(New York, 1966), 264–67.

which was the best thing about the church. I began with the determination to raise the spiritual standard of every Christian among them as far as he or she would let me. I worked a great deal from house to house, poo-pooed and frowned on their backbiting stories, reconciled those who hated each other, and tried everywhere to awaken in their hearts the love of Christ as the only sure cure for their love of self and sin. Then I preached as well as I could and had the satisfaction of seeing the congregation almost double in three months. . . . I rejoiced in a number of conversions. I saw members united by their common affection for their common Master. . . . I don't write this with a boastful spirit. . . . How foolish I would be to attribute that to myself! . . . There is one behind me, I am but the instrument in his hand.

The experience of the summer left a marked impact on Rauschenbusch's thinking. He had thought of being a professor, but by now his goal had shifted. "It is now no longer my fond hope to be a learned theologian and write big books," he wrote Munson Ford. "I want to be a pastor, powerful with men, preaching to them Christ as the man in whom their affections and energies can find the satisfaction for which mankind is groaning. And if ever I do become anything but a pastor, you may believe that I have sunk to a lower ideal or that there was a very unmistakable call in that direction."[6] Later he summarized his feeling at this time with equal vividness.

The idea came to me that I ought to be a preacher and help to save souls. I wanted to go out as a foreign missionary. I wanted to do hard work for God. Indeed, one of the great thoughts that came upon me was that I ought to follow Jesus Christ in my personal life, and live over again his life and die over again his death. I felt that every Christian ought to in some way or other participate in the dying of the Lord Jesus Christ, and in that way help to redeem humanity.

---

6. Letter to Munson Ford, see below p. 53.

During his senior year in seminary, Rauschenbusch did volunteer for service in the foreign mission field, but was forced to abandon the idea for medical reasons. This was the report of F. W. C. Meyer, a fellow student and later a faculty colleague as well as a life-long friend, who stated that, "owing to a defect in hearing" which subsequently became near total deafness, Rauschenbusch "heeded his physician's advice to stay in this country."[7]

The die was cast. His vocation for the next eleven years was to be the pastorate. It is not surprising that he chose to serve a small mission church in New York City. He had received a call from a prosperous church in Ohio, but asked for time to give it some consideration, whereupon the church turned to someone more decisive. When the call came from New York City he had no such hesitation.

The church, located on West 45th Street, to which Rauschenbusch was called in 1886 had many similarities to the one in Louisville where he had served as a summer supply. Four weeks after he arrived he reported his first impressions: "The church is not large, about 125 members. . . . The building is old-fashioned, inconvenient, and rather ugly, situated in a tough west-side neighborhood. . . . There are many little splits and much big discouragement. With God's help we shall go ahead." There was much work to do, and he had not had time even to pick up a book. He hoped that later he would be able to "find some time for study and literary work," but he also hoped that he would have the grace and wisdom to "subordinate that to my work as pastor." His great desire was "to be useful to my fellow man." His first weeks in New York, he reported, "have again taught me that I can do so best by bringing them into living and personal relations with our Lord Jesus Christ."[8]

While this was true, Rauschenbusch did not neglect more mundane considerations. He set about raising money to erect a new home for his mission church of German immigrants with such success that within three years the congregation was able to move into roomier and much more attractive quarters on West 43rd Street. In this en-

---

7. *Cleveland's Young Men*, reprinted in Handy, *The Social Gospel*, 265. F. W. C. Meyer, "Rauschenbusch: Preacher, Professor, and Prophet," *The Standard*, 3 Feb. 1912, 662 (6).

8. Letter to Munson Ford, see below pp. 58–59.

terprise he solicited and received support from an old friend of the seminary in Rochester, John D. Rockefeller. Meanwhile the membership of the church had almost doubled, church activities had multiplied, and Rauschenbusch, while not neglecting his congregation, was in process of broadening the focus of his concerns.

INFLUENCE OF THE WILLIAMS FAMILY HERITAGE

Rauschenbusch arrived in New York City equipped theologically with the tradition of American spirituality which, in the first half of the nineteenth century, was associated with such representative figures as Lyman Beecher and Charles G. Finney. Although Beecher and Finney originally were at odds, they had made their peace and had joined forces to promote revivals and lend support to causes of social reform.[9] Beecher was more the organizer, Finney more the active revivalist, but both were intimately related to the "benevolent empire" of voluntary societies formed to carry forward their common concerns. By mid-century Finney had adopted an almost Wesleyan emphasis on Christian perfection or sanctification.

For Rauschenbusch, the Finney influence was more readily available. Rochester in 1830 was the scene of Finney's first great triumph and, with the rest of central and western New York, it remained Finneyite territory and a center of reform impulses. Augustus Hopkins Strong, for forty years (1872–1912) president and

---

9. Finney was preeminently a revivalist, but his encouragement of reform efforts is well known. Beecher was more a promoter of revivals. See, for example, his "The Necessity of Revivals of Religion to the Perpetuity of Our Civil and Religious Institutions," reprinted in part in W. S. Hudson, ed., *Nationalism and Religion in America* (New York, 1970), 105–9. Beecher's interest in social reform is spelled out in "The Memory of Our Fathers," where he insists that a precondition for the renewal of the world promised in Scripture is the abolition of "the monopoly of the soil" which leaves many "crushed" beneath the orders of society above them and living "on the borders of starvation." He also notes that "the same monopoly" has sent others into "manufacturing establishments to wear out their days in ignorance and hopeless poverty." Ibid., 100. Before Beecher invited Finney to Boston, their interests had long intersected in the activities of the voluntary societies.

professor of theology at the Rochester Theological Seminary, in 1856 had been converted by Finney as had his father twenty-six years earlier, in 1830. Equally important, for Rauschenbusch, was the Finney tradition as it found expression in the activities of Dwight L. Moody in the two decades following Moody's return from England and Scotland in 1875. Through student Christian associations, the Student Volunteer Movement, and the Northfield Conferences, few students of these years escaped Moody's influence. Rauschenbusch was no exception. In a scrapbook that covers the first years of his New York City pastorate, 1886 through 1890, there are copies of sixteen sermons by Moody.[10] In 1887 Rauschenbusch wrote for *The Inquirer* his "Impressions of the Northfield Conference." During this period and for two or three years thereafter, Rauschenbusch was busy translating Moody-Sankey gospel songs into German and in taking the initiative in having compilations of the songs Sankey used in Moody's revivals published in German.[11]

If one immediate consequence of Rauschenbusch's acceptance of a call to the pastorate of a small immigrant church in New York City was to reinforce his sense of vocation, a second consequence was to introduce him to the field of social problems. In the fall of 1886, Henry George was a candidate for mayor on a Single Tax platform, and Rauschenbusch was caught up in the excitement of the campaign. "I owe my first awakening to the world of social problems," he later commented, "to the agitation of Henry George in 1886, and wish here to record my life-long debt to this single-

---

10. Vernon P. Bodein, *The Social Gospel of Walter Rauschenbusch and Its Relation to Religious Education* (New Haven, 1944), 3–4. Only after 1888 did materials dealing with social issues begin to appear in the scrapbook, one of the first being an address by Richard T. Ely.

11. Ira Sankey was Moody's song leader. In 1889 Rauschenbusch edited and published *Neue Lieder*, a translation into German of Ira Sankey's *Gospel Hymns No. 5*. The following year he published a translation of Sankey's *Gospel Hymns No. 1*. In 1894 he published a translation of *Gospel Hymns No. 2*. In 1897 the latter two were combined and republished under the title *Evangeliums-Lieder, 1 und 2*. A sampling of the first 100 songs in the 1897 songbook indicates that, while translations by others were used, about one-third of the gospel hymns had been translated by Rauschenbusch himself, including eighteen by Fanny Crosby.

minded apostle of a great truth.''[12] He also attributed his social awakening to his encounter with personal distress in the neighborhood. ''There among the working people my social education began.''[13] Both explanations were true, but a more immediate influence and one of greater consequence for the future was a friendship that was established soon after his arrival in the city. It was a friendship which, among other things, heightened his social sensitivity, helped him see the intimate connection between religious and social questions, and provided a theological perspective that resolved for him the tension between his biblically grounded evangelicalism and the new ''scientific'' historical studies of the Bible and religion.

A few blocks away at the Amity Baptist Church, William R. Williams had just concluded a long and distinguished pastorate of fifty-three years from which the note of evangelical social concern had never been absent.[14] His son Leighton Williams, a graduate of Columbia University and of its law school, had decided to give up a promising legal career to continue his father's work. The year previous to Rauschenbusch's arrival, young Williams had become a member of the American Economic Association founded by Richard T. Ely. Ely was a major voice in the developing interest in social Christianity. Williams also was active in the Henry George campaign. Rauschenbusch and Williams found a third kindred spirit in Nathaniel Schmidt, fresh from the Baptist theological seminary

---

12. Rauschenbusch, *Christianizing the Social Order* (New York, 1912), 394. Rauschenbusch remained firmly committed to ''the single tax'' as a means of redistributing and preventing the accumulation of unearned wealth. While middle-class people responded to the idea as a non-revolutionary way of achieving social justice, Rauschenbusch was disappointed that it elicited little interest among working people.

13. *Rochester Democrat and Chronicle*, 25 Jan. 1913; reprinted in *Rochester Theological Seminary Bulletin* XIII (Nov. 1918), 51. See also *Cleveland's Young Men*, reprinted in Handy, *The Social Gospel*, 265.

14. William R. Williams was widely admired. Henry B. Smith, president of Union Theological Seminary, advised his students that, ''if undoubted piety, unexampled humility, wide acquaintance with history, unusual attainment in literature, together with a refined taste and rare genius as a writer'' are qualities you would emulate then William R. Williams is the person upon whom you should attend. Henry G. Weston, *An Address Delivered in the Madison Avenue Baptist Church, New York City, April 4, 1885* (Chester, Penna., 1907), 2.

(Colgate) at Hamilton, New York, and pastor of the nearby Swedish Baptist Church. All three had distinguished themselves in scholarly pursuits.[15] Schmidt was later to gain distinction as professor of Semitic studies at Cornell University. Rauschenbusch and Schmidt were within a few months of the same age. Williams was seven years older, but new to the pastorate. They were much alike in temperament and in the seriousness of their religious commitment. And now they faced similar situations in their struggling Baptist churches. Small wonder that such congenial spirits should be drawn together to share the concerns of a common vocation.

A half-century earlier, in 1838, William R. Williams had given an address on "The Jesuits as a Missionary Order" before the Society of Missionary Inquiry at Brown University. "The institution, on whose history we have dwelt," he told the students, "shows what a few resolute hearts may accomplish."

> When Ignatius[16] with his first companions bound themselves by a midnight vow . . . some three centuries ago, to renounce the world for the purpose of preaching the gospel wherever the supreme pontiff might send them, the engagement was one most momentous to the interests of our entire race. That company of seven poor students, with but zeal, talent, and stout hearts, and a burning enthusiasm, formed then a bond far more important to the after history of mankind than most of the leagues made by kings at the head of embattled squadrons.

Williams concluded the address with a moving exhortation.

> My young brethren in Christ, permit a stranger to hope that, among the honors of your Alma Mater . . . it may yet be recorded that hence went forth men, who, on the stock of a purer faith, grafted the zeal of Francis Xavier, and,

---

15. This was true of Rauschenbusch at Gütersloh and Rochester. Schmidt was a graduate of Stockholm University before pursuing his theological studies at Hamilton, being recalled there to teach the following year. Williams was immersed from childhood in a world of books, and his studies at Union Theological Seminary were preceded by graduation with honors from Columbia University.

16. Ignatius of Loyola, 1491–1556.

emulating his virtues, won a success more durable, because the means they employed were more scriptural—
men, who, sitting at the Master's feet, and reflecting his
image, and breathing his spirit, were recognized by an ad-
miring world and an exulting church as those who had
been much with Christ and learned of him, and who belonged on earth, and would assuredly through all eternity
continue to belong, of a truth and in the highest sense of
the words, to "the Society of Jesus."[17]

Almost fifty years later, the elder Williams' exhortation bore
unexpected fruit. By the late spring of 1887, the three young men
were meeting weekly for Bible study and discussion as well as
uniting each Sunday afternoon in a communion service. "I remember with special joy the communion services," Rauschenbusch later
commented. "A tranquil spirit of reverence and contemplation, a
deep reverence toward our Lord, a sense of his real presence, and
unusual joy in Christian fellowship invited the soul to rest and true
prayer."[18]

The three young ministers, encouraged by the reminder from
the past of "what a few resolute hearts may accomplish," in 1887
banded themselves together in a tightly knit group, a new society of
Jesus. "We had become impressed," said Williams, "with the evils
of cherishing individual ambition and became convinced that it was
our duty to work unitedly as far as fidelity to individual conviction
permitted us to do." The plan they had in mind was to form "a
union which should have the strength and cohesion of the Jesuit order without its danger to individual initiative." Through the discipline of weekly study, discussion, mutual criticism, and common
worship, they sought to clarify their thinking, deepen their devotion,
and chart a course by which they might exert a united influence.
"The idea was simply that [of] a band of men voluntarily associat-
ing themselves, with a devotion as great as that of the Jesuits but

---

17. William R. Williams, *Miscellanies* (New York, 1850), 191–92.
18. *The Examiner* 16 Jan. 1913, 89. Quoted by Frederic M. Hudson, "The
Reign of the New Humanity: A Study of the Background, History, and Influence of
the Brotherhood of the Kingdom," Columbia University doctoral dissertation
(1968), 26–27.

with clearer and juster opinions and greater freedom for individual action, who should be in a truer and higher sense a Society of Jesus, and who, without subscription to any creed, should endeavor to realize the ethical and spiritual principles of Jesus, both in their individual and social aspects, in their own lives and work, both individually and in cooperation with each other.'' This theme was stressed repeatedly. It was to be ''a true Society of Jesus in which individual ambitions should be subordinated to a common and lofty aim.'' It was to be ''a new society of Jesus, of the union and combination of Catholic devotion with Protestant faith in the service of Jesus as Lord and Master.''[19]

For the next twenty years, few positions on theological and social questions were adopted and few activities undertaken by any of the three men without prior consultation. Within little more than a year, of course, Nathaniel Schmidt had left the city to become associate professor of Semitic languages and biblical Greek at Colgate Theological Seminary. In some ways this was an advantage, Williams noted, for an active correspondence was maintained and this necessitated reducing their views to writing, a procedure which made for added ''clearness and depth.''[20] It also was arranged that

---

19. Leighton Williams, *The Brotherhood of the Kingdom and Its Work*, Brotherhood Leaflet No. 10, 2–3. See also Rauschenbusch's Brotherhood Leaflet, *Suggestions for the Organization of Local Chapters of the Brotherhood of the Kingdom*, and two items by Leighton Williams: a reprint of the above leaflet in *The Kingdom* I (Aug. 1907), published by the Brotherhood of the Kingdom, and ''The Reign of the New Humanity,'' op. cit. (Dec. 1907). There is no pagination to *The Kingdom*.

20. See Williams, *The Brotherhood of the Kingdom and Its Work*. The reduction of their views to writing was related to the production of a book to set forth their views. The drafting of it was left mainly to Rauschenbusch, although Schmidt wrote more than seventy pages of comments and suggestions. This certainly was part of the ''active correspondence'' necessitated by Schmidt's absence from New York City which Williams considered an advantage. Williams made marginal notes on the manuscript, raising points which he was able to discuss with Rauschenbusch in person. The book was never completed and put in final form, and the initial drafts of the various chapters were dispersed and scattered in different places in Rauschenbusch's files. The existence of the manuscript was unsuspected until Max Stackhouse stumbled upon an Introduction and Table of Contents and then pieced together most of its components, which he published as *The Righteousness of God*, ed. Max Stackhouse (Nashville, 1968).

the three members of the little society should spend some time together each summer at the Williams family farm at Marlborough-on-
the-Hudson. They met there first in 1888, just before Schmidt assumed his new post. In 1889 Rauschenbusch noted in the Visitors'
Book that "Christian fellowship is Jesus' own substitute for his bodily presence." The following year there was time only for a brief day
together, for Schmidt was sailing for a year's study in Germany.
But, wrote Schmidt, it was "a day full of spiritual blessings."
"Only an afternoon and evening," commented Rauschenbusch,
"yet enough talk to turn over the world and enough love to make any
heart happy."[21]

At the outset Leighton Williams contributed most to the relationship.[22] His leading role within the triumvirate was partly because
he was older, partly because he was full of ideas of projects to be undertaken, and partly because, as a native New Yorker, he was familiar with the city, its problems and resources. In addition he was
heir to a remarkable family tradition of ministry in New York City
which gave a sense of continuity to the concerns and endeavors of
the two younger men.

The Williams family tradition began in 1798 when John Williams came from Wales and established the Fayette Street (later
called the Oliver Street) Baptist Church, serving as its pastor for
twenty-seven years. The tradition was continued when his son, William R. Williams, abandoned a well-established law practice to
draw together some members of his father's former congregation to
form in 1832 the Amity Baptist Church. As was true of his father,
the son soon had a large and flourishing congregation composed, it
was said, of persons of wealth and fashion. The son was a man of
culture, widely traveled and widely read, deeply interested in both

---

21. The Visitors' Book is in the Samuel Colgate Baptist Historical Collection of the American Baptist Historical Society, Rochester, N.Y.

22. There is little reason to question Frederic Hudson's verdict that Williams was the "mentor" of the group. The closeness of the relationship is indicated
by Conrad H. Moehlman's later comment that by the time Rauschenbusch returned
to Rochester in 1897, Williams had become his "alter ego." See Hudson, "The
Reign of the New Humanity," iv, 29–30; 211–12. For relationship of Moehlman to
Rauschenbusch, see *Rochester Theological Seminary Bulletin* XIII (Nov. 1918),
17.

literature and history. By the time of his death he had accumulated a personal library of more than twenty thousand volumes.[23]

Apart from the polished eloquence of his sermons and the insight and inspiration he derived from literature and history, there was little in the first three decades of his ministry to distinguish William R. Williams from many contemporary evangelicals. He was an ardent supporter of missions, and of the voluntary societies organized to promote other worthy causes—education, temperance, peace, and the abolition of slavery. By 1845 he understood the saving of souls as a process through which justification and sanctification would lead to the transformation of society. In "The Church of Christ, the Home and Hope of the Free," he stated his fundamental contention. "The church seeks the universal illumination and emancipation and evangelization of the race. Its prayer is, Thy kingdom come; and the Messiah's kingdom is but another name for the liberty wherewith Christ maketh free. It would banish war and bondage, intemperance and ignorance, and oppression—all that can degrade, all that can exasperate, divide, or brutify the race." If the heart is left under "the bondage of selfishness and depravity," then neither "science" nor "the freedom of earth" can "make any change of circumstances" that will "heal the private and social miseries of the time." But, on the other hand, if people "seek first the kingdom of God," then one may expect that, ultimately, under its emancipating, enlightening, and peaceful influences, "the earth will become the suburbs of heaven."[24] Two years later, during the Mexican War, he preached a sermon against delighting in war which he thought of suf-

---

23. For his library, see Hudson, "The Reign of the New Humanity," 4, and the auction catalog, *Library of the Late William R. Williams, Part I* and *Part II* (New York, 1896).

24. William R. Williams, *Miscellanies*, 143, 145, 147. In an earlier sermon he had affirmed the God-given mission of America to be by its example "a national epistle to other lands." Ibid., 235. Later, in a sermon entitled "God Timing All National Changes to the Interests of His Christ," Williams sought to make sense of the Civil War by noting how God governs through two realms, the realm of providence and the realm of grace, a distinction the Puritans had made between the realm of nature and the realm of grace. Hudson, "The Reign of the New Humanity," 14. Williams had made the same distinction between the two realms in his *Lectures on the Lord's Prayer* (Boston, 1851), 52.

ficient significance to be included in his volume of *Miscellanies*, published in 1850.[25]

Williams interpreted the Civil War as part of God's providential activity, punishing the people as evidence of his displeasure and thus summoning them to repent and mend their ways that the nation might recover the initial vocation it had been designed to serve. At the close of the war Amity Baptist Church, belying its name, was beset by controversy. Williams submitted his resignation in 1865, but it was not accepted. He was now sixty-one and was to remain pastor of a dwindling congregation for the next twenty years. People were on the move and Williams' voice was failing and no longer possessed its former power. A large congregation could no longer be attracted from a distance. The congregation divided over the issue of erecting a new church building, the controversial feature being a proposal to relocate. One may surmise that Williams wished to relocate in an area more adaptable to the development of a neighborhood ministry, for this is what occurred. The new concept may have crystallized in 1859 when Williams was in England and visited, among others, F. D. Maurice who, with his concern for the poor, was developing a doctrine of Christian socialism. Perhaps Williams' considerably younger wife was the decisive influence, for she played a key role in implementing the neighborhood ministry and continued to do so after his death. But most likely the proposal to relocate was the culmination of Williams' long-held conviction that "all reformations must begin with the lower classes."[26] In any event, in 1867, William R. Williams led the remaining faithful members of the church to purchase a small abandoned Episcopal chapel on the east side of the city, a neighborhood already being infiltrated by new immigrants. Within a year a daily kindergarten had been established, a neighborhood missionary program inaugurated, a variety of recreational activities organized, and a Saturday industrial school opened to teach children Scripture, sewing, carpentry, and printing. Three years later the retired president of Columbian College (now George Washington University) was recruited to teach evening Bible classes for young men, an enterprise that later became

---

25. *Miscellanies*, 367–87.
26. "Christ, a Home Missionary," ibid., 229.

the Amity Theological School. This was the milieu into which Walter Rauschenbusch and Nathaniel Schmidt were introduced.

What use was made of this heritage?

The first concerted action of Rauschenbusch, Schmidt, and Leighton Williams was to deepen and strengthen their own devotional life. No one knows exactly the external resources upon which they drew beyond the words of Scripture, but from scattered intimations it is clear that they made much of their common memory of Augustine's *Confessions, The Imitation of Christ,* John Bunyan's *Pilgrim's Progress,* Richard Baxter's *The Saints' Rest,* and Philip Doddridge's *The Rise and Progress of Religion in the Soul.* At some point they appropriated Francis of Assisi as an exemplar much to be admired. They discovered Henry Scougal's *The Life of God in the Soul of Man.* They mined the insights they found in Giuseppe Mazzini's *Essays,* with their stress on community and association, organic relationships and human solidarity. Rauschenbusch, writing on the "Influence of Mazzini" for *The Colloquium* of November, 1889, called Mazzini's *Essays* a "book of devotion" and spoke of Mazzini as a prophet "to whom God has given an eye for the lessons of the past, and an ear which he has laid on the beating heart of his own generation, and who therefore is able to tell us what shall be."[27] They rehearsed the exploits of George Whitefield and the Wesleys, but seem to have been drawn even more strongly to the early Quakers with their appeal to the Spirit, to the Christ within. And at an early date, they had become acquainted with William Arthur, the Irish Methodist, whose book *The Tongue of Fire* had gone through repeated printings and editions since its first publication in America in 1856. Rauschenbusch called attention to Arthur's insistence that individual regeneration and social renewal go hand-in-hand, but the striking thing about Arthur must have been his constant stress on the power of the Spirit, upon its energizing force.[28] Although these clas-

---

27. Bodein, *The Social Gospel of Walter Rauschenbusch,* 6.
28. *For the Right* (Aug. 1890).

sics were all important resources, the focus of the group's Sunday afternoon meetings was not upon outward helps but upon the practice of an inward spiritual discipline: reflection, contemplation, and prayer, followed by communion.

Second, the neighborhood ministry was not neglected. Existing programs were supplemented by new forms of evangelical outreach into the community. But it was Mary Bowen Williams, Leighton's mother, who took the lead in augmenting the neighborhood ministry. Nathaniel Schmidt had returned to Hamilton by the time most of the new enterprises were launched. Williams and Rauschenbusch were supportive and provided leadership where appropriate, mostly in such programs as the Amity Missionary Conferences and the Amity Theological School, which were designed to reach beyond the local community. Moreover, several of the ministries, such as the Deaconess Home, were joint undertakings of the two congregations.[29] Still, most of these enterprises were almost incidental to the task the three young ministers had set for themselves. Their vision extended beyond the neighborhood in which their congregations were located. They were thinking in terms of a new age of the Spirit

---

29. In addition to the Deaconess Home, the new ministries established to provide further evangelical outreach into the neighborhood included a Working Women's Society, a Christian Working Men's Institute, a Heartease Home for Young ("fallen") Women, and the Amity Coffee Room for Working Girls. All had a major focus on evangelism. While the Coffee Room ostensibly provided a warm, clean, and quiet place where working girls could eat the food they brought with them, the lunch hour began with Bible study and closed with prayer. The deaconesses moved throughout the community, meeting many needs and providing many services, but two years of theological study was required of them before they could be ordained. Furthermore, the expense of providing the various ministries was kept to a minimum, since they were staffed by lay volunteers. Even fulltime deaconesses were given no salary. The Amity Theological School, which developed out of the Evening Bible Classes for Young Men and was designed to train lay workers, had a large enrollment but was taught on a volunteer basis by some of the ablest theological scholars and ministers of the city. In contrast to the $60,000 "institutional" budget of St. George's Episcopal Church, the Amity "institutional" program was operated on a budget of $4,000. The chief "angel" at Amity was presumably Leighton Williams' mother who instigated, organized, and supervised most of the activities. For further details, see Hudson, "The Reign of the New Humanity," 164–87. For a variety of reasons, first Rauschenbusch, and then Leighton Williams, became skeptical of the value of "institutional church" programs.

in which the whole of society, both at home and abroad, would be reconstituted to bring it into accord with the principles of Jesus. It was with this larger end in view that the banding together of the three men in a new "society of Jesus" was followed by a burst of activity. Three projects were adopted as joint endeavors by which their united influence could make itself felt.

The first project was the writing and publication of a book which would set forth their views. The initial draft of the manuscript was undertaken by Rauschenbusch with major assistance provided by Schmidt from his teaching post at Hamilton. It was never put in final form and published, however. Apparently their views were not sufficiently crystallized to permit them to be explicated in systematic fashion to the full satisfaction of each member of the group.[30]

A second project was the publication of *For the Right*, a monthly "people's paper" designed "to discuss from the standpoint of Christian socialism" such questions as "engage the attention and affect the life" of the working classes of New York City. Its "aim" was "to reflect in its pages the needs, the aspirations, the longings of the tens of thousands of wage-earners who are sighing for better things, and to point out . . . not only the wrongs that men suffer but the methods by which these wrongs may be removed." Walter Rauschenbusch and Leighton Williams were listed as editors, as was Elizabeth Post[31] who fulfilled the duties of managing editor, and J. F. Raymond, a young Baptist minister from Harlem who served as business manager. The editors made it clear that their brand of "Christian socialism," with its dual emphasis on "personal regeneration" and "social reform," was not to be equated with any doctrinaire socialist theory. They reported that they were giving their time and labor freely, "animated solely by the hope that their efforts may aid the advancement of that kingdom in which wrong shall have no place, but Right shall reign forever more." "God helping us,"

---

30. See above, note 19. For other abortive attempts by Rauschenbusch to set forth his views in a book, see *Rochester Theological Seminary Bulletin* XIII (Nov. 1918), 52.

31. Elizabeth Post may have been the sister of Louis Freeland Post (1849–1928), a journalist and social reformer, who was the publisher of *Truth* and a leading protagonist for Henry George. His mother's name was Elizabeth.

they declared, "we shall strive to speed the day when God's will shall be done on earth as well as in heaven."[32]

For the Right lasted only eighteen months, from October 1889 to March 1891 when its funds, perhaps supplied by one of its contributors, Grace H. Dodge, ran out.[33] The great disappointment of the editors was a failure to reach a working-class readership, the circulation being confined primarily to a small group of sympathetic middle-class Protestants. This was probably inevitable. The mortality rate of such endeavors is high, but a contributing factor was the lack of a clear focus. In an attempt to appeal to a variety of tastes the paper became a mélange. In addition to editorials and articles on religious, social, economic, and political issues, there were self-help essays, news items, statistical reports, poetry, and serialized chapters from novels. Another important reason may have been an unconsciously patronizing attitude of the young and inexperienced editors in some of the items they published. Rauschenbusch, for example, sometimes pitched his contributions to a level of readership less than that of the brightest and best of working-class leadership. This was not always true, but on occasion he wrote what amounted to children's stories to explicate the merits of a Single Tax, free trade, or the evils of monopolies. He was imitated in this tactic by other contributors, including J. F. Raymond. Also patronizing, at least in the eyes of a later generation, were Elizabeth Post's monthly columns on "A Charming Home," which gave helpful hints on homemaking, housekeeping, the buying of furnishings, cooking, diet, rearing of children, use of time, and the avoidance of gossip and harsh words both within and without the home. Grace Dodge made similar contributions which dealt with "Some Thoughts on Dress," "Hints about Food," "The Home Maker," and "Working Girls Clubs." Small wonder that *For the Right* attracted few readers beyond a select circle of humanitarian evangelicals.

---

32. *For the Right* (Oct. 1889), 1 and (Aug. 1890), 2.

33. Grace Hoadley Dodge (1856–1914), social worker and philanthropist, was heir of four generations of evangelical merchants who provided major financial support to evangelical causes. The family fortune had been augmented by profits from the mining concern of Phelps, Dodge and Co., and her own evangelical commitment was strengthened by contact with Dwight L. Moody. Later she was president of the national board of the Y.W.C.A.

From 1887, when they formed their little "Society of Jesus," the three men were operating on several fronts simultaneously, fronts which can better be described as concentric circles rippling out to wider areas of concern. At the same time that they were cultivating their inner devotional life, ministering to their own congregations and neighborhood, and seeking "to engage the attention and affect the life" of the working classes of New York City, they also were exploring possibilities of effecting changes in the wider life of the church and the nation. Indeed, they regarded the whole world as their parish. They were caught up in the enthusiasm generated by Josiah Strong in 1887 when, with twelve to fifteen hundred other delegates, they attended the Washington convention of Strong's rejuvenated Evangelical Alliance assembled to discuss how the churches could join forces to deal with current "National Perils and Opportunities." Although the focus was on the nation and much attention was given to the increasingly acute urban and social problems of the United States, the enthusiasm engendered by the convention was by no means parochial. As Strong was consistently to remind the Alliance: "My plea is not, Save America for America's sake, but Save America for the world's sake."[34]

Inspired by and responsive to the summons of the Evangelical Alliance to marshal the resources of the churches to deal with the urgent tasks posed by a changing America, the three young men who had bound themselves to collective undertakings knew that the place to begin to meet the challenge set before them by the Alliance was within their own Baptist denomination. The instrument they seized upon for this purpose was the Baptist Congress which had been meeting annually since 1882 to discuss issues of current concern. The Congress was an unofficial gathering, but the four-day sessions held in different cities did attract the prominent and intellectually alert leaders of the denomination. The calculated strategy of the New York trio was to infiltrate the Congress and to use it to begin the process of directing the attention of Baptists to social issues and social reforms.

The infiltration was successful. Williams secured the office of secretary in 1888 and continued to serve in this capacity until 1892,

---

34. Hudson, "The Reign of the New Humanity," 69–73.

when he was succeeded by Rauschenbusch who remained as secretary until 1897 when he returned to Rochester. Both men became members of the small executive committee, and all three—Rauschenbusch, Williams, and Schmidt—participated in the annual programs, beginning in 1888, usually as speakers, sometimes as commentators, commonly as both. And they also were in a position to participate in the choice of other speakers and of issues to be discussed. No votes were taken, but the Congress was an important forum to mold opinion and an occasion when friendships were formed.

FORMATION OF THE
"BROTHERHOOD OF THE KINGDOM"

At the same time Williams, Rauschenbusch, and Schmidt were seeking to exert influence through the Baptist Congress, they were being influenced by other participants, most notably by George Dana Boardman, pastor of the First Baptist Church of Philadelphia and son of a famed Baptist missionary to Burma. Boardman's great interest was Christian unity. He had spoken at the 1877 Baptist Congress on "Unity of the Churches; or, The Problem of Ecclesiastical Unity," an address which was printed in New York the following year. Deeply impressed by the doctrine of the Holy Spirit, Boardman proposed it as the basis for Christian unity. The emphasis on the Holy Spirit fit neatly into all the concerns of the young triumvirate as well as with what they had learned from William Arthur's *The Tongue of Fire*. Henceforth, believing that they were living in the midst of a new awakening, they began using a new vocabulary to express their views, speaking of "the new age of the Spirit," "the tuition of the Spirit," "the new apostolate," and "the new humanity."

Rauschenbusch spoke on "The Tuition of the Spirit" at the Second Annual Amity Missionary Conference, 5–6 April 1892, and four years later at the Sixth Annual Amity Conference, he emphasized the need for "a new apostolate," people "who have received their ordination not merely from men, but from God himself." What is the power of the new apostolate? "None can share that power except as inspired of the Holy Ghost. It cannot be got in books, but from the throne of God. Let us not talk about the Holy Ghost, but have it. Then will we truly understand the Bible."[35]

Leighton Williams set about the task of recasting Baptist history to bring it into accord with the new emphasis on the Spirit. He elaborated his argument in a series of articles in the Baptist *Standard* of Chicago, which were reprinted in the *Canadian Baptist*, and published in 1892 as a small book entitled *The Baptist Position, Its Experimental Basis*. While "Baptists cannot claim to be the sole evangelical church," wrote Williams, they do build their "entire system," properly understood, upon the "experience of the new birth." This stress is in accord with "the religious movement of the day" which "is toward experimental Christianity." It is not surprising, therefore, "to find in every church" a "growing demand" for "evidence of a real change of heart shown in the outward life, and that under all the rebellion against dogmatism and ritualism, there is real yearning after vital religion." There is much talk about the union of churches, but "it is evident that no such union is possible either on the basis of a ritual or of a creed." "It is just as evident that there is an actual movement toward union on the experimental basis," the inward experience. Let it be remembered, insisted Williams, that God is neither just a past memory nor a future hope. God is our contemporary, a present and "efficient power" at work in the world. Even when one speaks of the authority of Christ and of the Scriptures, one must not forget that "the life of Christ" is "revealed in Scripture by the Spirit, interpreted by the Spirit, and wrought in us by the Spirit." The Spirit is the authenticating authority.[36]

On the frontispiece of Williams' book there was an extract from

---

35. See the reports for the Amity Missionary Conferences for 1892 and 1896. "The New Apostolate" was given at the Brotherhood of the Kingdom session at the 1896 Amity conference. The manuscript of the address, from which Bodein quotes (*The Social Gospel of Walter Rauschenbusch*, 22–23) has been mislaid or lost. The 1896 Amity report provides a summary from which the present quotation is taken.

36. Leighton Williams, *The Baptist Position: Its Experimental Basis* (New York, 1892), 4–5, 13, 15.

a letter of John G. Whittier praising Boardman for rightly interpreting "the central thought of Quakerism." "It seems to me," Whittier wrote,

> that many of the Friends of our day are virtually abandoning this vital doctrine, while, on the other hand, in the best utterances of leading minds of other sects, I find the Quaker doctrine of the Spirit clearly and fully enunciated. I believe it will, in the end, be found the stronghold of Christianity against the critical and agnostic spirit of our age. No revelation of science, no destructive biblical criticism, can shake the faith of those who listen to the voice of God in their own souls.

The last point was important. This appeal to the Spirit, to the voice within, was an escape hatch by which tension between the inherited faith and the claims of historical studies and scientific investigations could be avoided.

Still, at the sessions of the Baptist Congress there were tensions. Opposition was voiced to new ways of thinking, to new tasks to be undertaken, and there were defenders of the old ways. Several of the friends of Rauschenbusch, Williams, and Schmidt began to feel the need of mutual support and reinforcement. The idea of a more formal relationship for those of like mind came to the fore in 1892. The Congress was held that year in Philadelphia immediately prior to the May meetings of the Baptist missionary societies. A small group met at that time in the office of H. I. Wayland, editor of *The National Baptist*, to discuss methods of "close cooperation" among themselves and other like-minded friends. A follow-up meeting was held in July at Rauschenbusch's home in New York City where it was agreed that they should "strike hands in the name of Christ, and by union multiply our opportunities, increase our wisdom, and keep steadfast our courage." A proposed constitution was drafted at a third meeting in December at Philadelphia to be presented for adoption in August 1893 when the group assembled for four days at the Williams' Marlborough farm.

Among those present in August when the Brotherhood of the

Kingdom[37] was formally constituted, in addition to Williams, Rauschenbusch, and Schmidt, were such key figures as George Dana Boardman; William Newton Clarke, professor of theology at Colgate whose *Outline of Christian Theology* was to become the most widely used text in liberal seminaries; S. B. Meeser of Crozer Theological Seminary; and Samuel Zane Batten, a pastor from suburban Philadelphia who was to become prominent as head of the denomination's social service commission. The number of brothers was never large. Most were pastors of Baptist churches, and some were women. In time members of other denominations were brought into membership.

The preamble to the constituting document ("Spirit and Aims of the Brotherhood of the Kingdom") of the Brotherhood was in effect a covenant:

> The Spirit of God is moving men in our generation toward a better understanding of the idea of the Kingdom of God on earth. Obeying the thought of our Master, and trusting in the power and guidance of the Spirit, we form ourselves into a Brotherhood of the Kingdom, in order to re-establish this idea in the thought of the church, and to assist in its practical realization in the life of the world.

Rauschenbusch set forth this purpose in greater detail in the initial Brotherhood leaflet:

> We desire to see the Kingdom of God once more the great object of Christian preaching; the inspiration of Christian hymnology; the foundation of systematic theology; the en-

---

37. Batten was credited by Williams with having supplied the name of the Brotherhood ("The Brotherhood of the Kingdom and Its Work," *The Kingdom*, Aug. 1907). It is possible that Williams and Rauschenbusch had thought of naming the group "The Knights of the Holy Ghost." Williams had used this phrase at Colgate (Hamilton) seminary in 1892, and Rauschenbusch at the 1893 Baptist Congress, prior to the formation of the group, suggested the need for a small but select "new order of chivalry," stressing the importance of standing together, of "uniting their counsels and their sympathy, supporting every man who bears hardship in the service of Jesus, and thus forming a new order of chivalry, the Knights of the Holy Ghost." See Hudson, "The Reign of the New Humanity," 92.

during motive of evangelistic and missionary work; the religious inspiration of social work . . . the object to which
a Christian man surrenders his life; the common object in
which all religious bodies find their unity; the great synthesis in which the regeneration of the Spirit . . . and all
that concerns the redemption of humanity shall be embraced. To this task, God helping us, we desire to dedicate
our lives.

What was involved in this dedication was enumerated in what
amounted to a "rule" or "discipline" for a community in disper-
sion.

1. Every member shall by his personal life exemplify obedience to
   the ethics of Jesus.
2. He shall propagate the thoughts of Jesus to the limits of his ability—in private conversation, by correspondence, and through
   pulpit, platform, and press.
3. He shall lay special stress on the social aims of Christianity and
   shall endeavor to make Christ's teaching concerning wealth operative in the church.
4. On the other hand, he shall take pains to keep in contact with the
   common people, and to infuse the religious spirit into the efforts
   for social amelioration.
5. The members shall seek to strengthen the bond of Brotherhood
   by frequent meetings for prayer and discussion, by correspondence, exchange of articles written, etc.
6. Regular reports shall be made of work done by members, in such
   manner as the Executive Committee may appoint.
7. The members shall seek to procure for one another opportunities
   for public propaganda.
8. If necessary they shall give their support to one another in the
   public defense of the truth; and shall jealously guard the freedom
   of discussion for any man who is impelled by love of the truth to
   utter his thoughts.[38]

---

38. "The Spirit and Aims of the Brotherhood of the Kingdom" served as a
frontispiece to each annual report. Rauschenbusch's leaflet, *The Brotherhood of the
Kingdom*, was reprinted from the *National Baptist*. See below pp. 74–76.

In spite of its loose organization, the Brotherhood was a tightly knit and disciplined body, a sort of Protestant Third Order dedicated to demonstrating once again "what a few resolute hearts may accomplish." The central feature of the life of the Brotherhood was the time spent together each year for study and devotion at Marlborough. Here, high above the Hudson River, they knew the "ecstasy" of their Master's presence as they gathered for morning prayers and for the "twilight evangelistic service" on "the consecrated hilltop."[39] They were knit together as they shared a "fellowship meal," made their reports of activities undertaken and tasks completed, and planned their strategy for the advancement of the Kingdom: the writing of essays, the publication of tracts, and other means of propaganda. But above all, through the presentation and discussion of papers at Marlborough, the members of the Brotherhood clarified their thinking and hammered out a common position to undergird their manifold activities. All the leading members of the Brotherhood were men of unusual ability and scholarly insight. What was required of them was a ready willingness to subject themselves to the disciplines of group discussion, criticism, and direction.

Within the matrix of the Brotherhood of the Kingdom, Rauschenbusch's thinking continued to develop. It is difficult to say to what extent he shaped or was shaped by the thinking of the Brotherhood. It was a heady experience, as Rauschenbusch acknowledged in 1909 in the Marlborough Visitors' Book: "Only where mind touches mind does the mind do its best work. Where love and confidence draw back the bars and bolts of caution and distrust, thought passes readily from heart to heart. . . . So we grow. . . . God bless this hilltop of the Spirit. . . . May it do for others in the future what it did for me in the past."

THE APOSTOLATE OF THE SPIRIT

Given Rauschenbusch's understanding of the human situation, it was inevitable that he should regard evangelism as the primary

---

39. For a description of what must have been a typical closing "twilight service" with informal remarks, interspersed with prayers and singing, see the 1895 annual report of the Brotherhood of the Kingdom.

task of the church. One of his most revealing statements as to why this was so was made in 1892 in an address on "Conceptions of Missions."[40] In discussing the current conceptions, he insisted that interest in educational and philanthropic work must not be allowed to obscure the central aim of missions, which is "the extension of faith in the crucified and risen Christ, who imparts his Spirit to those who believe in him and thereby redeems them from the dominion of the flesh and the world and their corruption, and transforms them into spiritual beings, conformed to his likeness and partaking of his life." It is this inward spiritual experience that provides "the only solid and trustworthy basis" for anything else that may be attempted. "We are inclined to forget this," he said.

In this address, Rauschenbusch almost intuitively seemed to have anticipated the charges of superficial optimism, moralism, and altruism that were to be brought against advocates of the social gospel in the 1930's. He proceeded to explain why people are apt to forget that an inward spiritual experience is indispensable to the transformation of the social order: "One reason why we forget is because many of us, through ease of life and the exceeding pleasantness of this present world, are prone to sag down from evangelical religion to humanitarian morality, from spiritual fervor to altruistic earnestness." A second reason is that "the spread of the idea of evolution has created an optimism among us which is not warranted by the facts." He went on: "We have heard so much about the progress of civilization that a serene faith has come over us that the cart is slowly but surely rolling up the hill, and that all that is necessary is to clear away the obstacles by education and reform, and leave play to the inherent upward forces of humanity."

Rauschenbusch acknowledged that he was "once of this opinion" and "found it comforting," but "observation and the study of history" compelled him "to part with it sadly."

> However evolution may work in the rest of creation, a new element enters in when it reaches the ethical nature of man. Ethically man sags downward by nature. It is ever easy to follow temptation and hard to resist it. The way that leads to destruction is always broad and its asphalt

---

40. *The Watchman*, 24 Nov. and 1 Dec. 1892. See below pp. 64–70.

pavement is kept in perfect order, with toboggan slides at either side for those who prefer a steeper grade . . . . Let us not be beguiled by that seductive devil who tells us that man will walk into the millennium, if only you will point out to him where the millennium is and clear away the worst obstacles for him. Man was never built that way. If he is to get in, he will have to be lifted in.

Valuable as all secondary concerns may be, the inward spiritual experience comes first, for without it "education will turn into a striving after a wind, culture into lasciviousness, social reformation into social unrest, philanthropy into a sprinkling of rose-water over the carcass."[41] Later, Rauschenbusch was to comment: "If the new interest in social questions crowds out the old interest in evangelistic work, it is a reaction from an old one-sidedness into a new one-sidedness."[42]

Rauschenbusch was frequently contemptuous of the professional evangelists among his contemporaries, but he was not contemptuous of the older evangelism which had nourished his own spiritual life. The older evangelism, he readily acknowledged, was one-sided, but it was not superficial. What dismayed him was what so many of the contemporary professional evangelists were doing to it—stripping it of all profound emotion and rendering it devoid of significant content. In his final book, he commented: "To one whose memories run back to Moody's time, the methods now used by some evangelists seem calculated to produce skin-deep changes. Things have simmered down to signing a card, shaking hands, or being introduced to the evangelist."[43] The nub of the problem was what he called the substitution of "proselyting" for "discipling." The difference, he said, is this: "Discipling produces a real change for the better in the inward character, while proselyting leaves the man as it found him."[44]

---

41. See below p. 70.

42. "Social Motives in Evangelism," an unpublished manuscript, as quoted in Dores R. Sharpe, *Walter Rauschenbusch* (New York, 1942), 395.

43. Rauschenbusch, *A Theology for the Social Gospel* (New York, 1917), 96–97.

44. "Discipling versus Proselyting," *Report of the Third Annual Amity Missionary Conference*, August 3–4, 1893.

There was a deeper problem than mere superficiality. Even Moody had recognized that the older evangelism was becoming increasingly ineffective, and in his final years he had cast about for a more promising alternative.[45] In 1904 Rauschenbusch reported that the "waning power" of the old evangelism was "generally conceded," but "there is as yet no new evangelism before us which we might adopt; we are only wishing that there might be." In an article on "The New Evangelism,"[46] he diagnosed the malady and indicated the direction the new evangelism must take.

Rauschenbusch's basic assumption was that, while "the gospel of Christ is one and immutable," the "comprehension and expression" of the gospel in history has been of "infinite variety."

> No individual, no church, no age of history has ever comprehended the full scope of God's saving purpose in Jesus Christ. Neither has any proclaimed it without foreign admixtures that clogged and thwarted it. A fuller and purer expression of the evangel has therefore always been possible and desirable. It is on the face of it unlikely that the gospel as understood by us is the whole gospel or a completely pure gospel. It is a lack of Christian humility to assume that our gospel and *the gospel* are identical.

Consequently our understanding of the gospel must be subject to constant reconstruction, and this becomes an urgent task in a transitional age when all categories of life and thought are silently changing.

> The gospel, to have power over an age, must be the highest expression of the moral and religious truths held by that age. If it lags behind and presents outgrown conceptions of life and duty, it is no longer in the full sense the gospel. Christianity itself lifts the minds of men to demand a better expression of Christianity. If the official wardens of the gospel . . . refuse to let the spirit of Christ flow into the

---

45. Winthrop S. Hudson, *The Great Tradition of the American Churches* (New York, 1953), 145, 150.

46. Published in *The Independent*, 12 May 1904. See below pp. 136–44.

larger vessels of thought and feeling which God himself had prepared for it, they are warned by finding men turn from their message as sapless and powerless.

Since we are "passing through an historical transition as thorough and important as any in history," it would scarcely be surprising to discover that "the message of the church has failed to keep pace with a movement so rapid," nor should it be regarded as strange that "humanity, amid the pressure of . . . new problems, fails to be stirred by statements of truth that were adequate to obsolete conditions."[47]

Evangelism, to be effective, declared Rauschenbusch, must do two things. It "must appeal to motives which powerfully seize men," and it "must hold up a moral standard so high above their actual lives that it will smite them with conviction of sin." If it fails at either of these two points, "if the motives urged seem untrue or remote, or if the standard of life to which they are summoned is practically that on which they are living, the evangelistic call will have little power."[48]

Rauschenbusch recognized that "motives urged at any time will vary with the preacher and the audience, and there will always be a large measure of truth and power even in the most defective preaching that touches human nature at all." Nevertheless, there are changes of emphasis from age to age, and the motives which sway men in one age may be less powerful in another. "Within our own memory," he continued, "the fear of hell and the desire for bliss in heaven have strangely weakened even with men who have no doubt of the reality of hell or heaven."[49] On the other hand, other motives have become much stronger. "Past Christianity has developed in us a love for our fellows and a sense of solidarity so strong that they demand to be considered in every religious appeal." While people

---

47. Ibid, see below, pp. 137–38.

48. In "Social Motives in Evangelism," Rauchenbusch noted that "there is nothing distinctly Christian either in the fear of hell or the hope of heaven. Other religions have them even more strongly." Too often, he said, the response to this motivation is simply "a higher form of self-seeking." Sharpe, *Walter Rauschenbusch*, 398.

49. "The New Evangelism," see below, pp. 139–40.

"give less thought to their personal salvation than our fathers . . . their sympathy for the sorrows of others is more poignant." Furthermore, in a transitional age, there is an anticipation of "great coming changes" and an awareness of "the plastic possibilities" of the future. People are motivated by "a hope for humanity such as has long existed only where the millennial hope was a vital thing." Thus, while some motives are dropping away, "larger and more truly Christ-like motives are offering themselves," but they are motives to which the church has been making no adequate appeal.[50]

"The moral standard held up by the church in its teaching and in its collective life" is equally inadequate. It has been largely individualistic in its ethic, dealing primarily with private and family life, and it has been largely successful in this teaching. "In general, the community has risen toward the level of the church in private and domestic virtue, and the church has drifted toward the level of the respectable community in regard to amusements." As a result of this twofold movement, the gap between church and community has narrowed. "The morality of the church is not much more than what prudence, respectability, and good breeding also demand." When the church says, "Repent and become like me," there is little either in her teaching or example that is sufficient to convict people of sin and summon them to repentance. The plain fact is that, in terms of the most critical issues of life, the church "lacks an ethical imperative which can induce repentance."[51]

Rauschenbusch confessed, however, that a new evangelism which shall "again exert the full power of the gospel cannot be made to order nor devised by a single man," but if we are to have a part in shaping it, we must be "open to two influences and allow them to form a vital union in our personalities."

> We must open our minds to the Spirit of Jesus in its primitive, uncorrupted, and still unexhausted power. That Spirit is the fountain of youth for the church. As a human organization it grows old and decrepit like every other human organization. But again and again it has been rejuvenated by a new baptism in that Spirit.

---

50. Ibid., see below, p. 140.
51. Ibid., see below, pp. 140–41.

> We must also keep our vision clear to the life of our
> own time. Our age is as sublime as any in the past. It has
> a right to its own appropriation and understanding of the
> gospel. By the decay of the old, God himself is forcing us
> on to seek the newer and higher.

The forging of a new evangel, Rauschenbusch acknowledged, will
be a slow process, but he had "full faith" that it would be accomplished. "A new season of power will come upon us . . . . Our bitter need will drive us to repentance. The prophetic Spirit will
awaken among us. The tongue of fire will descend on twentieth-cen-
tury men and will give them great faith, joy, and boldness, and then
we shall hear the new evangel, and it will be the Old Gospel."[52]

While recognizing the need for a restatement of the gospel,
Rauschenbusch's retention of the phrase "the tongue of fire" (the
gift of the Spirit) indicates that, as yet, he was not contemplating any
sharp break with his past understanding of the gospel as it had been
shaped by discussions within the Brotherhood. What he seems to
have had in mind, in the light of conditions prevailing in the modern
world, was no more than a reexamination of the motives to which
appeal can most successfully be made, and a rephrasing of moral
standards in ways sufficiently compelling to induce repentance.

IMPORTANCE OF THE LABORING CLASS

By 1904 when Rauschenbusch wrote the article on the necessity for a "new evangelism," he already had spent eighteen years
seeking to identify the "stronger motives" and to work out the
"wiser methods" which he regarded as indispensable components
of a new evangelism. When he arrived in New York City he had
been convinced that he could be most useful to his fellow men by
"bringing them into living and personal relations with our Lord Jesus Christ." What he discovered, however, was that the old evangelistic appeal did not work. Those who stood within the church, to
be sure, did "respond joyfully to the ideas in which their Christian
life was nurtured and in which their holiest memories" were "en-

---

52. Ibid., see below, pp. 143–44.

shrined,'' but as soon as the ''evangelistic efforts'' were extended beyond the young people of the church family, the ''evangelistic call strikes an invisible wall and comes back in hollow echoes.'' The few who could be persuaded to come to church once did not return because they heard nothing to which they could respond.[53] How was he to reach these working people in whose midst his little church was set?

The first answer, worked out in conjunction with Williams and Schmidt, was to identify himself with the struggles and aspirations of the working class. He and Williams had tried to do this with the publication of *For the Right*, but were not successful. What they learned was that the gospel had to be so presented that it would touch the emotions, for only as the emotions were profoundly stirred was there the possibility of leading people to a ''new birth.''

Rauschenbusch was insistent upon the importance of emotion. Speaking before the Baptist Congress in 1893, he declared: ''Being saved without emotion is unthinkable. Imagine a man being born again without being stirred to the bottom of his nature.'' ''If I had to choose,'' he continued, ''between intellect and emotion in religious work, I would rather have genuine emotion with little intellect than the reverse,'' for a religion without emotion is ''valueless'' and ''has no saving power.''[54] This is not to say that Rauschenbusch was advocating any contrived emotionalism. ''Emotion,'' he was later to affirm, ''is good only when it is spontaneous, only when it rises naturally in the soul in response to a great thought or in view of some entrancing object.'' If it is contrived, it cannot be either ''genuine or lasting.''[55]

Rauschenbusch explored various possibilities for speaking to people in ways that would stir their deepest emotions. He identified several, including the sense of compassion which was the product of

---

53. Ibid., see below, pp. 140, 141.

54. ''Emotionalism in Religion,'' *Proceedings of the Baptist Congress, 1893*, 33. A similar stress on the importance of emotion is present in Rauschenbusch's account of the Welsh revival in *The Examiner*, 15 June 1903. See below, pp. 106–11.

55. Rauschenbusch, ''The Freedom of Spiritual Religion,'' a sermon preached as a session of the Northern Baptist Convention, 8 May 1910.

a long-term Christian penetration of American society, and also the emotional power resident in an emphasis on the "plastic possibilities" of the future for either good or ill, and used them in a Thanksgiving sermon in 1898.[56] Three months later he drew another lesson from the signs of the time: "The sooner we learn that this earth is a very small planet and getting smaller every year, and that our welfare is bound up with all the other passengers, the better it is for us."[57]

Socialism, however, was his most momentous discovery. Rauschenbusch refused to regard socialism "as a red-hot lava eruption from the crater of hell," insisting instead that it was "a river flowing from the throne of God, sent by the Ruler of history for the purification of the nations."[58] It was a judgment on the churches and their unsocial Christianity, and there was much of Christ in its deepest concerns. But one of its most important features to Rauschenbusch was that it represented a point of contact with the working classes; it symbolized their aspirations and it was a word which had powerful emotional connotations. Thus, while Rauschenbusch was not a socialist in the accepted doctrinaire sense of the term,[59] he was quick to claim the name "Christian Socialist" for himself.

The word "socialism" spoke to contemporary man in a way few other words could speak. It conveyed a sense of social sin, a feeling of complicity in and responsibility for the sins of society in which all have shared. Thus it served as "shorthand" for a moral standard which extended beyond a purely individualistic ethic and it could be utilized as a clear-cut summons to repentance. But the use of the word "socialism" did more than this. It appealed to the mo-

---

56. *Rochester Post-Express*, 28 Nov. 1898. See below, pp. 134–35.

57. *Rochester Democrat and Chronicle*, 13 Feb. 1899.

58. "Ideals of the Social Reformers," *American Journal of Sociology* II (Sept. 1896), 202.

59. For the points of "conscious antagonism" to the prevailing tendencies of socialism, see Rauschenbusch's article, "Christian Socialism," *A Dictionary of Religion and Ethics*, eds. Schailer Mathews and G. B. Smith (New York, 1921). See also "The Ideals of the Social Reformers," op. cit.; "Practical Measures of Socialism," *The Treasury* (Jan. 1901); and especially his address before the Labor Lyceum in Rochester, *Rochester Democrat and Chronicle*, 25 Feb. 1901. For a more complete text of the last item, see Sharpe, *Walter Rauschenbusch*, 203–16.

tive of compassion for the downtrodden. It emphasized the necessity for fraternal association in common tasks. It quickened the feeling of kinship between nations and races. It bespoke a new age pregnant with promise. It was, in brief, a word that could be captured and utilized for a more powerful presentation of the gospel.[60]

Still there was more to it than symbolic value. In his exposure to socialist literature, Rauschenbusch became more and more impressed with the importance of social forces in shaping the course of history and producing changes in the social order. Such observation of the course of historical development could be read as a disclosure of God's intentions within the realm of his providential activity. God was not necessarily restricted to the influence exerted through regenerated individuals. God also operated within and through the structures of society. The significance of this insight apparently came to Rauschenbusch following his call for a "new evangelism." It was an insight which he incorporated in his first book, *Christianity and the Social Crisis* (1907).

In the last chapter of the book, where Rauschenbusch discusses "What To Do," little consideration is given to the reciprocal relationship of personal regeneration and social reform. "We must not blink the fact," he asserts, "that idealists alone have never carried through any great social change." Truth may be mighty,

> but for a definite historical victory a great truth must depend on the class which makes that truth its own and fights for it. If that class is sufficiently numerous, compact, intelligent, organized and conscious of what it wants, it may drive a breach through the intrenchments of those opposed to it and carry the cause to victory. If there is no such army to fight its cause, the truth will drive individuals to a comparatively fruitless martyrdom and will continue to hover over humanity as a disembodied ideal.

---

60. See "Ideals of the Social Reformers," op. cit., 203–10, and "Contributions Socialism Has Made to Social Feeling," *Rochester Democrat and Chronicle*, 13 Dec. 1909.

Consequently, "the splendid ideal of a fraternal organization of society cannot be realized by idealists only. It must be supported by the self-interest of a powerful class," by a "class whose economic future is staked on the success of that ideal." The corollary is that those who are interested in the fraternal ideal of society will have to "enter into a working alliance" with the rising and upward moving industrial working class to secure a victory for the "gradual equalization of social opportunity and power."[61]

Rauschenbusch was confident that the excesses of the class struggle could be tempered and mitigated by what he variously referred to as religious sentiment, the religious spirit, the Christian spirit, the Christian temper of mind, and Christian principles.[62] This would be especially true if Christians among the professional class, and even some members of the business class, could be persuaded by "religious and ethical motives" to "overcome their selfish interests" and to champion social justice and give their support to the cause of the laboring class. "Their presence and sympathy would cheer the working people and diminish the sense of class isolation . . . . No other influence could do so much to prevent a revolutionary explosion of pent-up forces."[63]

THE GOSPEL AND THE SOCIAL CRISIS

When *Christianity and the Social Crisis* was published in 1907, Leighton Williams responded with an article on "The Reign of the New Humanity" in *The Kingdom*. Williams noted that "our contentions" have now been set forth "in a systematic way," adding that the book may be regarded as "a finished exposition of our opinions."[64] Except for the last chapter, the book was indeed largely a stitching together of papers which Rauschenbusch had presented be-

---

61. Rauschenbusch, *Christianity and the Social Crisis* (New York, 1907), 400–401, 409, 414. See below, pp. 150–51, 156.
62. Ibid., 397, 398, 399, 409, 413, 418.
63. Ibid., 402, 409–10. See below, p. 157.
64. *The Kingdom* (Dec. 1907), no pagination.

fore members of the Brotherhood over a period of fourteen years. Thus, to a major extent, *Christianity and the Social Crisis* could be called a group product, for most of the chapters were written within the context of earlier discussion and reshaped as the result of subsequent discussion.

Williams' gracious comment, however, was a gentle way of introducing a mildly expressed but major rebuke. He immediately proceeded to point out that the book was an exposition of only one aspect of the Brotherhood's concern. After asking, is "our gospel fully made known, our testimony ended, and our work accomplished?" Williams responded, saying, "We think not." There is "a still deeper work to be done." Our gospel "has its Godward as well as manward side, and this men have not seen, nor have we yet fully declared it."

> The heart of our movement is a deep, personal experience, mystical in its nature, which forever makes us different men from what we were before we received it, and puts a gulf between us and the world that has it not . . . . Can you analyze our economic and political opinions and discover the genesis and power of our movement apart from this inner impulse and the loving fellowship begotten of it? Our opinions on social and economic questions were not original with us . . . but we affirmed them as true because we recognized their necessary and eternal validity by a kind of insight and certitude which we felt ourselves to possess . . . . All our opinions were verified for us by this inner light.

While "we have felt the presence of economic need and realized the bitterness of the 'bread and butter question' with so many of the suffering and oppressed of our brethren," still "we have continued to realize the truth of our Lord's words, 'Man doth not live by bread alone, but by every word that proceedeth out of the mouth of God.' "[65] Preaching, as we have, "as high a standard of individual

---

65. Mt 4:4.

and social morality as was made known to us," we have "not forgotten the fountain of living waters and confounded morality with
religion."

> We may rejoice that many are now uniting with us in urg-
> ing the need of a high ethical standard . . . . But when it is
> asserted that this ethical element constitutes the whole or
> the essential content of Christianity, we must part com-
> pany with these new allies. When they affirm righteous-
> ness to be the great word of the New Testament, we demur
> . . . . We believe that morals are the efflorescense of true
> religion and its fruitage, but never let us confound the
> fruits with the roots . . . . My father used to say: "Morals
> apart from the religion are like cut flowers. They may re-
> tain their form and fragrance for a time after they are sev-
> ered from the parent stem, but their life is gone and they
> must soon wither and decay." And with reference to
> Christian morals, it is most clearly evident that they are the
> outgrowth of the faith of the believer, and of his experi-
> ence of the grace of Christ.

In conclusion, Williams announced that his aim was to point out that
the Kingdom of God cannot be thought of from "an exclusively political and economic standpoint" and that hence "our Brotherhood
should maintain its witness for the evangelical experience as the basis of its social propaganda."

No evidence survives of any specific response by Rauschenbusch to Williams' criticism, but it was noticed, and in his next
book, *Christianizing the Social Order* (1912), the balance was re-
stored. "Spiritual regeneration," Rauschenbusch wrote,

> is the most important fact of any life history. A living ex-
> perience of God is the crowning knowledge attainable to a
> human mind. Each one of us needs the redemptive power
> of religion for his own sake, for on the tiny stage of the hu-
> man soul all the vast world tragedy of good and evil is re-
> enacted . . . . No material comfort and plenty can satisfy
> the restless soul in us and give us peace with ourselves. All

who have made the test of it agree that religion alone holds the key to the ultimate meaning of life, and each of us must find his way into the inner mysteries alone.

Later, in the same volume, Rauschenbusch affirmed: "It is not this thing or that thing our nation needs, but a new mind and heart . . . . We want a revolution both inside and outside."[66]

If Rauschenbusch was ready to give more attention to the necessity for personal religion, he was satisfied that *Christianity and the Social Crisis* did not leave people untouched religiously. "People told me," he reported in 1913, "that it gave them a new experience of religion and a new feeling about Christ."[67] Rauschenbusch was pleased with the reception accorded his *Prayers of the Social Awakening* (1910), and his two little books *Unto Me* (1912) and *Dare We Be Christians?* (1914). He also was pleased with the reception of *The Social Principles of Jesus* (1916), a study book for college Christian fellowships and other groups sponsored by the North American Christian Student Movement and the Sunday School Council of Evangelical Denominations. This volume had, in fact, the largest circulation of any of his books.

Rauschenbusch's final work, *A Theology for the Social Gospel*, was first given as the Nathaniel W. Taylor lectures at Yale University. It was intended as a serious scholarly study, but nothing could suppress the vividness and moving power of his words. Indeed, it was not a full systematic study as he himself acknowledged. But it was a beginning. Many aspects of theology were scanted, for the focus of the book (six chapters) was on the stubborn fact of sin, its transmission from generation to generation, and its incorporation into an almost intractable "kingdom of evil." Theology has dealt with the transmission of sin, he said, "in the doctrine of original sin." Whereas "many modern theologians are ready to abandon this doctrine," I "take pleasure" in "defending it."[68] His analysis at this point was the major theological contribution of the volume.

---

66. Rauschenbusch, *Christianizing the Social Order* 104, 459. See below pp. 168, 183.

67. *Rochester Theological Seminary Bulletin* XIII (Nov. 1918), 53.

68. *A Theology for the Social Gospel* (New York, 1918), 57.

Time, for him, was running out. He did not have a chance to do the full-orbed study he knew was needed.

Spirituality is an intangible quality that is easy to recognize but difficult to define, describe, and characterize. This is doubly true of Walter Rauschenbusch, whose theology was complex, changing, and evolving, and thus provided no stable foundation as a basis for analysis. He was devout, charming, and eloquent. Many have echoed H. Shelton Smith's verdict that he was "the foremost molder of American Christian thought in his generation."[69] Copies of his books in college and university libraries and in used-book stores testify to his influence, for they are well worn from much use and heavily marked and underlined. Apart from the piety he radiated through personal contact with his students, friends, and casual acquaintances, and the intimate rapport he established with members of the audiences to which he spoke, his primary continuing influence was his emphasis on human need and social reform as integral to any adequate theology. This was the debt to Walter Rauschenbusch acknowledged by Martin Luther King. "I came early to Walter Rauschenbusch's *Christianity and the Social Crisis*," he reported, and it "left an indelible imprint on my thinking by giving me a theological basis" for "my social concern." "It has been my conviction ever since reading Rauschenbusch," he continued, "that any religion which professes to be concerned about the souls of men and is not concerned about the social and economic conditions that scar the soul is a spiritually moribund religion."[70] King's comment was typical of most who came under the influence of Rauschenbusch's writings. The continuing popularity of Rauschenbusch's *Prayers of the Social Awakening*, however, is evidence that the impact of his piety and life of prayer is not to be minimized even when mediated through the printed page.

---

69. H. Shelton Smith, *Changing Conceptions of Original Sin* (New York, 1955), 199.

70. Martin Luther King, Jr., *Stride Toward Freedom* (New York, 1958), 91. See also King's *Strength To Love* (New York, 1963), 138.

I.

THE GATE AT THE END OF THE ROAD

Walter Rauschenbusch died of cancer ("sarcoma of the brain") on July 25, 1918, during the last bloody fighting of World War 1. His body was cremated and the ashes scattered on the waters of Sturgeon Lake in Ontario where he had spent so many happy summers with family and friends.

The war years had been difficult. He was not a pacifist but he hated the blood-letting savagery of war. It was foreign to all his deepest impulses and to his hopes for humanity. Rauschenbusch had been born in America, and the American ideals of democracy dominated so much of his thinking.[1] Yet such was the temper of the time that anyone with a German name was subject to the suspicion of being a "slacker," and it was not uncommon for yellow paint to be splattered on the door, porch, or steps of one so suspected. Old friendships were strained.

In the midst of this tension, Rauschenbusch became the victim of a mysterious illness. He called it "a subtle case of 'pernicious anaemis'," in a letter to Leighton Williams on March 18, 1918. A month earlier he had written Clarence A. Barbour, president of Rochester Theological Seminary:

I am not getting better. The condition of nerves in hands and feet is about the same . . . . The sinuses of the face carefully examined, but with negative results. Blood tests of various kinds have

---

1. See letter of May 1, 1918, to Cornelius Woelfkin, pastor of the Fifth Avenue Baptist Church in New York City and former faculty colleague of Rauschenbusch, printed in Sharpe, *Walter Rauschenbusch*, 385–88.

been made and no pus germs found. It was thought perhaps the marrow of the long bones which produces blood cells was affected, but new radiographs showed nothing. Liver, kidneys, and spleen seem all right . . . . The digestive tract is yet to be explored, but *evidently the doctors have come to the place where the road ends at a board fence.*

Common sense would dictate that I quit work . . . . I only want you to understand that I am traveling an uphill road at present. Work and effort come hard . . . . Family cares and questions do not grow less in these dark times. So I plod along like Christian[2] before his load dropped off, looking to the Lord. . . .

In May he went to Johns Hopkins hospital in Baltimore where, as he put it gently, he began to wonder "if God is not intending to be very kind to one of his servants."[3]

It may seem strange to begin a collection of readings selected to illumine the spiritual pilgrimage of Walter Rauschenbusch at the end rather than at the beginning. The reasons are simple enough. Throughout his life Rauschenbusch was working his way through the complexities of a rapidly changing society and rapidly changing ways of thinking. In the midst of many ambiguities it should be helpful to keep in mind the glimpse one has of him just as the final curtain was about to fall. A more pragmatic reason is a fear that Rauschenbusch's poem, "The Little Gate to God" might be left unread if it were appended at the end instead of being given a place of prominence at the beginning.

LETTER TO LEMUEL CALL BARNES[4]

On 10 May 1918 Rauschenbusch dictated a letter to Dr. Lemuel Call Barnes of the American Baptist Home Mission Society in response to a suggestion that a word from Rau-

---

2. Bunyan's *Pilgrim's Progress.*

3. The letters are in the archives of the Colgate Rochester Divinity School or in the Samuel Colgate Baptist Historical Collection of the American Baptist Historical Society, Rochester, New York. Most of them appear in Sharpe, *Walter Rauschenbusch.* The italics have been added by the editor in the letter to Barbour.

4. Both the letter to Lemuel Call Barnes and the poem "The Little Gate to God" are from the *Rochester Theological Seminary Bulletin* (Nov. 1918), 38–40. The poem was circulated as a "separate" by the Federal Council of Churches of Christ in America.

schenbusch would be much appreciated at a conference on personal religion and evangelism being held at Atlantic City. Rauschenbusch used the request as an occasion to recall his own religious experience and to give an account of his mature faith.

My dear Dr. Barnes:

You ask me to say a word from my heart about personal religion. Perhaps I can state my convictions most effectively by a testimony of my personal experience.

I learned to pray as a little boy at my mother's knee. When I was leaving boyhood behind me, and the seriousness of life began to come over me, I felt the call of God, and after a long struggle extending through several years, I submitted my will to his law. Henceforth God was consciously present in my life, and this gave it a sense of solemnity and worth. This gave a decisive reinforcement to my will, and turned my life in the direction of service and, when necessary self-sacrifice; so salvation came to me.

But this was only the beginning of my personal religion. It had to connect with all the chief tasks of my life.

When I came to intellectual maturity I had a second great struggle for salvation, perhaps of equal spiritual importance. During my theological education I was confronted with the choice between the imposing authority of human traditions and the self-evidencing power of God's living word. The former offered a restful dependence on outward authority; the latter brought a never-ending quest for a holy light that always moves forward. This was the personal religious problem of faith applied to intellectual duty. I now had to lean back on the living Spirit of God for support in my intellectual work, and felt his cooperation. This extended the area of personal religion in my life. I am inexpressibly grateful that I made the choice aright.

In my efforts to secure more freedom and justice for men I acted under religious impulses. I realized that God hates injustices and that I would be quenching the life of God within me if I kept silent with all this social iniquity around me.

My life has been physically very lonely[5] and often beset by the

---

5. Rauschenbusch's physical loneliness was due to his deafness.

consciousness of conservative antagonism. I have been upheld by the comforts of God. Jesus has been to me the inexhaustible source of fresh impulse, life, and courage.

My life would seem an empty shell if my personal religion were left out of it. It has been my deepest satisfaction to get evidence now and then that I have been able to help men to a new spiritual birth. I have always regarded my public work as a form of evangelism, which called for a deeper repentance and a new experience of God's salvation.

Pardon me if this narrative is too personal. I put my name to every statement in it.

Faithfully yours,
Walter Rauschenbusch

THE LITTLE GATE TO GOD

Sometime during the spring, perhaps at about the same time he wrote the above letter, for spring in Rochester would be May and June, Rauschenbusch composed the following poem. Nothing could express more beautifully, in the midst of personal pain and of a world where rivers were running red with blood, the solace he found in intimate communion with God.

The Little Gate to God

In the castle of my soul
Is a little postern gate,
Whereat, when I enter,
I am in the presence of God.
In a moment, in the turning of a thought,
I am where God is.
This is a fact.

This world of ours has length and breadth,
A superficial and horizontal world.
When I am with God
I look deep down and high up.
And all is changed.

The world of men is made of jangling noises.
With God it is a great silence.
But that silence is a melody
Sweet as the contentment of love,
Thrilling as a touch of flame.

In this world my days are few
And full of trouble.
I strive and have not;
I seek and find not;
I ask and learn not.
Its joys are so fleeting,
Its pains are so enduring,
I am in doubt if life be worth living.

When I enter into God,
All life has a meaning.
Without asking I know;
My desires are even now fulfilled,
My fever is gone
In the great quiet of God.
My troubles are but pebbles on the road,
My joys are like the everlasting hills.
So it is when I step through the gate of prayer
From time into eternity.

When I am in the consciousness of God,
My fellowmen are not far-off and forgotten,
But close and strangely dear.
Those whom I love
Have a mystic value.
They shine, as if a light were glowing within them.
Even those who frown on me
And love me not
Seem part of the great scheme of good.
(Or else they seem like stray bumble-bees
Buzzing at a window,
Headed the wrong way, yet seeking the light.)

So it is when my soul steps through the postern gate
Into the presence of God.
Big things become small, and small things become great.
The near becomes far, and the future is near.
The lowly and despised is shot through with glory,
And most of human power and greatness
Seems as full of infernal iniquities
As a carcass is full of maggots.
God is the substance of all revolutions;
When I am in him, I am in the Kingdom of God
And in the Fatherland of my Soul.

Is it strange that I love God?
And when I come back through the gate,
Do you wonder that I carry memories with me,
And my eyes are hot with unshed tears for what I see.
And I feel like a stranger and a homeless man
Where the poor are wasted for gain,
Where rivers run red,
And where God's sunlight is darkened by lies?

II.

FORMATIVE YEARS

As is true of most persons, information about Rau-schenbusch's early life (the years prior to the formation of the Brotherhood of the Kingdom) exists in bits and pieces, scattered references, and later recollections. By a stroke of good fortune, Rauschenbusch's letters to a former school-mate have been preserved. They provide us with an intimate and fascinating first-hand account of Rauschenbusch's formative years at seminary and in the pastorate. Brief items from For the Right, *the monthly paper which was a project of the little "society of Jesus" which preceded the Broth-erhood of the Kingdom, provide insight into his developing social views, while the article "Conceptions of Missions" serves to place him within the context of the contemporary theological climate.*

LETTERS TO MUNSON FORD

Few documents provide clearer insight into Walter Rauschenbusch's early feelings and motivations, aims and ambitions, than his letters to Munson Ford.[6] Ford was Rau-schenbusch's schoolmate and friend at the Rochester Free Academy, and the intimacy of their friendship continued

---

6. Munson Holt Ford graduated from the University of Rochester in 1883. He had won the freshman prize in mathematics, and after graduation accepted for a brief period a job as a bookkeeper in Rockford, Illinois, before entering the insur-ance business.

during the years that followed their graduation. Although Rauschenbusch's letters from Germany when he was pursuing his collegiate studies in the Gymnasium at Gütersloh are interesting, they primarily reflect the excitement of his experiences and travels as a student far from home. The subsequent letters deal with some of the more fundamental issues of his life.

Louisville, Ky., June 14, 1884

My dear Munson,

"Well, I'll be kicked"! I hear you exclaim, "a letter from Walter R——sch dated Louisville Ky."! You see my dear fellow, it's this way. I deliberated a while whether it were better for me to stay at Roch. and make love to our librarian at the Sem., or to go off and do some active work. My friends all urged me to do the latter and as I felt myself becoming (by a retrograde process of evolution unheard of by Darwin) a regular bookworm fit for nothing but devouring books and anti-dyspeptic remedies, and as moreover I had considerable desire to *do* something, I decided to go off. I was offered a situation here to supply the small German B.[7] church and have accepted. Now you can hear me hold forth twice on Sunday and twice a week, and much do I enjoy it for I can work to an end now.

I am very pleasantly located. The Germ. Bapt's have an orphan asylum in this beautiful city and I have a very nice room in it. I enjoy the children and I think they enjoy me. Only last night I tore a nice pair of trousers trying to teach them "double ghoul" (I suppose that is the way it is written).

I did not care much to stay to the College Commencement. I suppose you will get all the news about it. Strong[8] wrote me that he and Coe[9] had pulled through the Senior prize examination very

---

7. German Baptist.

8. Charles A. Strong, son of Augustus Hopkins Strong, attended Gütersloh Gymnasium with Rauschenbusch, married Bessie Rockefeller in 1889, taught at Cornell and Chicago before becoming professor of psychology at Columbia, and retired in 1912 to reside in Italy and devote himself to writing.

9. George Albert Coe taught first at Northwestern and then became professor of religious education and psychology at Union Theological Seminary in New York.

cheerfully; their only opponent, the redoubtable Hodgeman,[10] having withdrawn. I saw Williams[11] and Pratt[12] just before leaving and gave them your regards transmitted by your letter of May 26. Pratt is going into business I believe, William is going to enter a seminary in Pennsylvania, he thinks a change of air etc. would be beneficial to him.

Our Sem. Commencement was a very nice one, I think. The examinations were, as far as I could judge, quite as hard as they will be likely to be given in any Sem; I hope I passed. The graduating orations were very good, much abler in every way than those at the great Seminary[12a] here, which indeed reminded me painfully of our R. F. A[13] productions. I am very well satisfied with my first year in Seminary, I think I advanced in knowledge somewhat, and in my life with God a good deal.

Now I have talked so much about myself, I want to talk about you. I guessed when I looked at your handwriting that you had been in one of those business schools that succeed so well in substituting for God-given individuality their man-given uniformity. You are indeed passing through a series of metamorphoses, but I don't feel inclined to believe that your latest development as assistant bookkeeper is the final appearing of the butterfly within you. Just let me talk roughly to you for once Munson, as an old friend. You see there are some natures with such lofty possibilities and ambitions, that they could never be squelched in any position. You will not, I know, claim such a one for yourself. I tell you, my friend, I have often admired you for the fine intellect and the noble character that God has given you and that you have developed. But look to yourself! You are able to fill high positions well, if you are put into them, but you will neither aspire after them nor make them. I know you love to dabble in figures, but I fear that the sing-song of the day-

---

10. Thomas Morey Hodgman, Jr., was later professor of mathematics at the University of Nebraska and then president of Macalester College.

11. Elmer E. Williams graduated from Crozer Theological Seminary and was ordained to the Baptist ministry.

12. Charles Frederick Pratt worked for Sherwin Williams Paint Company in Cleveland, and then became president and general manager of the Jewell Carriage Company and Ohio Motor Car Company in Cincinnati.

12a. Southern Baptist Seminary in Louisville.

13. Rochester Free Academy.

book and ledger will be the lullaby to your finer capacity. I have no high respect for addition and subtraction etc., they are about the only operations of the brain that machines can do as well. There is nothing of the higher life of man in them, none of the glow and throb of heart that makes man man. If you settle down to book-keeping you will probably stay there all the days of your life unless you get an ambitious wife that will stick a pin into you, and when you die of a ripe old age, the newspaper will tell of the death of the chief bookkeeper of X. Y. Z. and Co., trusted by his employers, respected by all that knew him and beloved and admired by the smaller circle of friends that etc. No Munson, aspire to something higher; if you must stay in business, get a clerkship where you can get into the business itself. But I would rather see you occupied differently, ministering to the higher wants of man, if not a general yet a captain in the onward marching army of our people. Think about it whether God may not have given you the powers that you have that you should employ them in His service. Don't tell me that you can't because you are not brilliant; it's not the brilliant speakers that do the work of God, but the quiet pastors of small churches, whose work is not broad but deep. Or if God has not called you to that, I know none among my friends who is more adapted to teaching than you are with your clear analysis and calm demonstration.

Think it over, my boy, and don't be angry at me. My kindest regards to your parents.

Your old friend,
Walter R——sch.

Rochester, Dec. 21, '84

My dear Munson,

Your letter of July 15 and your postal of Nov. 15 are both before me. So is the new year. I write. In fact, I don't know any earthly reason why I did not write long ago. I thought of you often. I had time enough. I like you as well as I ever did, and if you were here at this moment I should enjoy a talk with you immensely. So the only reason that I did not write to you at all seems to be that I did not write to you at any single time.

I see in your letter you wish to know more about my first pastorate in Louisville. Well, that seems very far in the past now, but it forms a very pleasant remembrance indeed. It was only a very small flock but a very neglected one. Sins of pastors and sins of members had created distrust and contempt among outsiders. Internal dissensions had banished the spirit of brotherly love. Everybody was sorely discouraged and very many were very hungry—which was the best thing about the church. I began with the determination to raise the spiritual standard of every Christian among them as far as he or she would let me. I worked a great deal from house to house, poopooed and frowned on their backbiting stories, reconciled those who hated each other, and tried everywhere to awaken in their hearts the love of Christ as the only sure cure for their love of self and kin. Then I preached as well as I could and had the satisfaction to see the congregation almost double in 3 months. I organized the young people, gave Bible readings, in short I pitched in. As for externals I lived on the hospitality of one family and got $20 a month; when I left the place I was as thin as a ghost, but I rejoiced in a number of conversions. I saw the members again united by their common affection for their common Master, I saw them deeply affected when I said farewell to them at the little social they gave me, and I was satisfied. I don't write this with a boastful spirit, Munson; I am proud of my diligence and application, for of that any man may be proud, and I got a better opinion of myself in that respect than I had before. But as for the success and the blessing, I am not proud of that. Again and again I said to myself this summer: "How foolish I sh'd be, were I to attribute this to myself! This is beyond my vainest imaginings about my own powers; there is One behind me, I am but the instrument in his hand."

You can imagine that three months of such work have an influence on one's ideas and ideals. It is now no longer my fond hope to be a learned theologian and write big books. I want to be a pastor, powerful with men, preaching to them Christ as the man in whom their affections and energies can find the satisfaction for which mankind is groaning. And if ever I do become anything but a pastor, you may believe either that I have sunk to a lower ideal or that there was a very unmistakeable call to duty in that direction.

My studies here are progressing quietly. I don't mean to fall in my standing, yet I no longer regard them as an end in themselves, if

I ever did. I look more for the great thoughts that shake mankind than for certainty in regard to a disputed date in Acts or an obscure root of a Hebrew verb.

From Ed Hanna[14] I had a letter dated August 17, but it was so full of a compendium of Roman Catholic systematic theology that it fairly squelched me for a time and I have not had the cheek to answer him with my low gossip. He has received all the orders, has the "character indelebilis" as priest, is bound to eternal virginity, etc. Should you ever write to him you would have to address him now with Rev. He will finish there about the time that I do here.

I called on Miss Page in the beginning of this term and found a young gentleman by the name of Hawthorne visiting her. The other day I called again and lo he was still there. In other respects she seems to be well. Last night I went to see Miss Davis and had a very good time with her. There is an air of purity and childlikeness about her which is very charming compared with the self-possession of the average American girl. Her oddity only makes it the more piquante so that I find her in spite of her oblique stare and undeniable home-liness a much more pleasing companion than Miss Page with all her natural and acquired "smartness." Don't imagine, however, because I have mentioned several calls to young ladies that I have any habits tending in that line. I enjoy them when I do make them but on the whole I find myself better without.

Now I have talked a great deal about myself. Do thou likewise, that is to say talk about yourself for that is what I want to know most. How are you getting on in business? How does your place look? How are your parents? Have you got as handsome a pair of burn-sides and such a charming moustache as I have? Well, write soon, old fellow, and we'll start the carts into a trotting match. My mother sends kind regards. My father is in Cleveland. Remember me to your father and mother.

Yours,
W. Rauschenbusch

---

14. Edward L. Hanna, a close friend of Rauschenbusch and Ford at the Rochester Free Academy, pursued studies for the priesthood at Rome and elsewhere abroad before teaching theology at St. Bernard's Seminary in Rochester. Subsequently he became archbishop of San Francisco.

Louisville, Ky., May 30, 1885

Dear Munson,

I was sorry to see from your letter of Feb. 7, that you were sick and out of employment. I can sympathize with you in the former calamity, because I have been sick myself several times last Winter; the sensation of having nothing to do has so long been a foreign one to me that it has rather a delightful glamour about it. I hope however that you soon succeeded in obtaining another position and that you are again as deep in figures as a drowning fly in molasses . . . .

As you have seen by the superscription of my letter I am once more in Lou. Ky. It was very hot here last summer and I get worked very hard, so that I got home in Sept. last quite fagged out and thin. My parents wanted me to take a vacation this year and go to the country somewhere, but the church here, which is still without a pastor, asked me to come again and I did not have it in my heart to say no. The people here seem to be attached to me and I certainly am to them according to the mysterious law that we love those from whom we have had much trouble.

Altho' it was a very great strain on me, I enjoyed the work here very much. I had a chance to do something for others and I believe true happiness is proportioned to the degree of unselfishness which enters into any act or state. Unselfishness and self-sacrifice seem to me the idea of Christ's life and therefore the expression of God's character. In proportion as they become the dominant facts of our own life, are we conformed to his image. I tell you I am just beginning to believe in the gospel of the Lord Jesus Christ, not exactly in the shape in which the average person proclaims it as the infallible truth of the Most High, but in a shape that suits my needs, that I have gradually constructed for myself in studying the person and teachings of Christ, and which is still in rapid process of construction. I don't believe that believing any doctrine will do a man any good except so far as it is translated into life. I don't believe that when a man believes in the vicarious death of Christ that death will be imputed to him; how can it be? But if he begins to live a Christ-like life, he will find that tho' there is no cross for him to be nailed to, he will die piecemeal by self-sacrifice just as Christ did even before his crucifixion and then he is at one with Christ and placed by God into the same category.

I must stop now; to-morrow is Sunday. Remember me most kindly to your parents. My address for the next 10 weeks will be: Care of Mrs. P. Kratz, 723 Gray St., Louisville, Ky.

Your friend,
Walter R——sch.

Rochester, Feb. 20, 1886

My dear Munson,

It's a crying shame the way I have neglected you and I ought to be kicked. So I ought (but I'd like to see the feller that w'd undertake the job). I ought to treat the few friends I've got better, esp. when they use me as Solomon, Solomon Levi. I sold your vest to an excellent pious young fellow who didn't have any vest to pull down at all, at all; and your coat to a man who unites goodness of character to brilliance of mind. I gave them the bargain cheap, sold 'em for the price I paid myself—a goose-egg.

It is 11:02 P.M. I have finished the writing of my chapel sermon tonight; wrote a letter in my father's name to a man that wanted to know whether it was right to substitute water or milk for wine in communion (poor fellow! thinks he's got the clear wine of an old man's wisdom and gets the must[15] of a young fool's conceit); wrote another letter to a young lady in my own name, and now am scribbling to a fellow whom I haven't seen for I don't know how long, and whose molecules have all changed since that time. Why do I write? I don't know except that I used to know him and liked him and w'd probably like him as well as ever if I got within eye-shot (?) of him.

Yes, it's quite true what your mother is just remarking, that I ought to be in bed and preparing for the sermon I have to preach to-morrow night and of which I know nought but the text, but what is a man to do that has a letter written last July rubbing and chafing his unluckily tender and quivering conscience?

O say, let me whisper to you that I have a call from Springfield, Ill. I looked forthwith to see how far that is from Rockford and was grieved. However, we'll be neighbors anyway.

---

15. Pulp.

Ed Hanna will prob'ly return in summer next, and be at the beck and call of the bishop here in town, under whose jurisdiction he is. Becky Sharp—I mean Carrie A. Page—is teaching the youthful ideas of the Free Academicians to shoot, and you bet (I beg pardon, I forgot) she'll explode sometimes in making them shoot. I haven't called on her for $x + y^2$ years. Twice in succession I met a young fellow there by the name of Hawthorne and I concluded my path was thorny enough without picking quarrels with promiscuous young men.

I am struggling thro' this last term as well as I can; there are no honors to be gained and so my food is not spiced with laurel leaves. And how is it with you? Still making the ledgers crawl as if a certain one of the plagues of Egypt were come upon Rockford? Still hanging on the parental bough too? How do you expect the young fry like yours respectfully to do the square thing in addition, duplication, and multiplication if you don't set them a better example? And you're the man that lectured me for not delighting in the society of the ladies enough! Well I can't help it when they get scared at the permanent scowl hovering over my brow like the thunder-cloud of Jupiter-torians; but a ladies' man, that sings, etc., etc., has no excuse at all. Let me hear better things concerning thee.

Really a letter to you is very exhausting, one has to put so much sense in it. I'm always afraid of the genus homo mathematicus(s). Either they've got some superfluous clicking side-arrangement in their head that ought to be amputated, or else, if they are normal, I'm the other thing and it isn't pleasant to have my sister's assertion verified that there is a vacuum in my head somewhere.

I enjoyed the visit from your mother, or rather my visit to her, greatly; it carried me back to my few but delightful visits in Pittsford when you promised to treat Ed and me on watermelons and had them frozen for us when we came. You owe us them yet.

Now write soon, tell me how you are all faring, how your health is etc. Don't say a word about me. I know all about that coon, but tales of Munsoon Ford, Esq. Kind regards to your mother and father.

Your old friend,
Walter R——sch.

Finished 11:41 P.M., so that you'll not think I wrote on Sunday.

N.Y. City, 30–VI–86

Dear Munson,

Your letter of Apl 14th rec'd in due time, but all the exams and
commencement duties tho' not so pleasant, were more imperative
than the answering of your welcome letter. You will prob'ly have
seen an acc't of the Commencement in one of our denominat'l papers. At any rate I am not going to entertain you with what belongs
now to medieval church histy. They were not willing to give me time
for consideration at Springfield, so that matter collapsed and I accepted a call rec'd later from the 2nd Germ.[16] Church in N.Y.C. I
came here June 1st and leave tomorrow on a 2 month's vacation,
having engaged a student to fill my place. This month I spent in
learning the ropes and giving my people a chance to get acquainted
with me. The church is not large, about 125 members; congregation
about 150–200. The building is old-fashioned, inconvenient, and
rather ugly, situated in a tough West Side neighborhood. The church
has had bad experiences with my predecessors who have left an un-
savory reputation behind them. The consequence is that there are
many little splits and much big discouragement. But they have
picked up splendidly this month and a very helpful feeling obtains.
With God's help we shall go ahead; there is room for work. My salary is $900; about $300 of this am't will be consumed in rent, which
is enormously high. $25 a month will get a decent flat of 5 rooms or
so.

I hope your change from in-door to farm work will do you
good. I can sympathize with you in your catarrhal troubles, tho' I am
prob'ly not bothered as much as you are. You were sadly mistaken
when you tho't I w'd puzzle for 15 minutes about your trigonometri-
cal problem about the square of the sandiness of Ill. soil and the in-
verseness of its productiveness. I have been in a Bapt. Sem. for 3
years and have learned to take things on authority.

I had a letter from Carrie[17] the other day asking for information
about the "boys" of '79. She hinted that some day she w'd be my

---

16. German Church.
17. Carrie A. Page.

neighbor in N.Y. It will be under the alias of Mrs. Hawthorne I suppose. How are the mighty fallen! Eddie Hanna is still in Rome and will not return, prob'ly, till next Spring. His folks tell me that he is not a Jesuit at all. He admires them and may become one hereafter.

My work here will be very laborious: 2 Sunday services and a young men's class in S. S.[18] (at present merely a project of mine); 2 regular prayer-meetings and one young people's meeting take away 3 nights of the week, and a fourth night is almost invariably taken up with something. During this month I have not taken up a *book* for reading except the Bible, and Anderson's Fairy Tales while waiting in a doctor's ante-room. I hope that after I have the things well in hand, I shall find some time for study and literary work, tho' I hope I shall have grace enough to subordinate that to my work as pastor. God knows I have a little desire to be useful to my fellow-men and these few weeks have again taught me that I can do so best by bringing them into living and personal relations with our Lord Jesus Christ.

Give my kind regards to your parents and write soon, to the old address at Rochester.

Your friend,
Walter R——sch.

"FOR THE RIGHT"

For the Right, *a monthly "people's paper" for the working classes of New York City, published from October 1889 until March 1891, may have lacked editorial focus but there was no lack of clarity of purpose and intention as is made evident by Rauschenbusch's brief essay which appeared in the August 1890 issue, accompanied on another page by an extract from William Arthur's* The Tongue of Fire *(1856), a "holiness" volume which continued to be reprinted constantly throughout the remaining decades of the nineteenth and the early decades of the twentieth century.*

---

18. Sunday School.

Good Men and Good Government[19]

One of the peculiarities which distinguishes *For the Right* from many other papers akin to it, is that it stands for a combination of personal regeneration and social reform. Most of the social reformers claim that if only poverty and the fear of poverty could be abolished, men would cease to be grasping, selfish, overbearing, and sensual. We do not see it so. We acknowledge that evil surroundings tempt to evil actions and strengthen evil character, and we go as far as any in the earnestness of our protest against any social institution which makes null the prayer: "Lead Us Not Into Temptation." But we can conceive of a state of society in which plenty would reign, but where universal opulence would only breed universal pride and wantonness. Mankind rolling in material wealth with no moral earnestness and spiritual elevation would only be something worse than swine champing in a full trough or maggots burrowing in a carcass. We believe in God and in the law of God. And we believe that every individual soul ought voluntarily to subject itself to the law of God and obey it because it loves it. Only if the number of such God conquered souls is great and increasing in any nation will the progress of that nation in material wealth be of real benefit to the people! This is the point on which we differ from many with whom we are at one in the plans for social reform.

On the other hand, we differ from many Christian men and women in our insistence on good institutions. They believe that if only men are personally converted, wrong and injustice will gradually disappear from the construction of society. It does not appear so to us. Revivals in the South were not directly followed by a general freeing of slaves. Revivals in the North do not ease the pressure of competition in a community or stop speculation in land. Special work and hard work has to be done in pointing out a social wrong and thinking out its remedy, before the righteous purposes of a community can be brought to bear upon it. This is essentially a function of those who profess to know and love God's will, and we raise the charge of negligence and sloth against the church of God in suffering injustice to be incorporated in the very construction of society.

---

19. *For the Right* (Aug. 1890).

We are not alone in this protest. One voice after another is being uplifted, and they are some of the sweetest and noblest voices on God's earth. Men whose spiritual fervor is undoubted consider it no descent from their high plane to discuss the social question. We print on another page an extract from one of the finest and most notable books on spiritual religion, *The Tongue of Fire*, by William Arthur. Our Christian readers can read his words with the assurance that he is an orthodox and spiritually minded man, and that they will not cease to be good Christians if they should entertain views like his.

Walter Rauschenbusch

From The Tongue of Fire[20] *By William Arthur*

In the words, "continued steadfast in the Apostles' doctrine and fellowship, and in breaking bread, and in prayers," we see the effect of the regeneration of individuals on the character of a community. From a number of good men at once arose a united and fraternal society. Statesmen and philanthropists, occupied with the idea of forming happy nations, frequently look to good institutions as the means of doing so, but find that when institutions are more than a certain distance in advance of the people, instead of being a blessing, they become a snare and a confusion. The reason for this is obvious. Good institutions to a certain extent presuppose a good people. Where the degree of goodness existing in the people does not, in some measure, correspond with that presupposed in the institutions, the latter can never be sustained. As the organ, embodiment, and conservators of individual goodness, the value of good institutions is incalculable; and he is one of man's greatest benefactors who makes any improvements in the joinings and bearings of the social machine. But as a means of regeneration, political instruments are impotent. Good institutions given to a depraved and unprincipled people end in bringing that which is good into disrepute. The only way to the effectual regeneration of society is the regeneration of in-

---

20. The extract published in the Aug. 1890 issue of *For the Right* was probably taken from a later edition, but, if so, it is identical with the material in William Arthur, *The Tongue of Fire* (Nashville, Tenn., 1856), 142–46.

dividuals. Make the tree good and the fruit will be good. Make good men and you will easily found and sustain good institutions. Here is the fault of the statesmen, they forget the heart of the individual.

On the other hand, have not those who see and feel the importance of first seeking the regeneration of individuals, too often insufficiently studied the application of Christianity to social evils? When the result of Christian teaching long addressed to a people has raised the tone of conscience, when a large number of persons embodying true Christianity in their own lives are diffused among all ranks, a foundation is laid for social advancement. But it does not follow that, by spontaneous development, the principles implanted in the minds of the people make to themselves the most fitting and Christian embodiment. Fearful social evils may co-exist with a state of society wherein many are holy and all have a large amount of Christian light. The most disgusting slave-system, base usages fostering intemperance, alienation of class from class in feeling and interest, systematic frauds in commerce, neglect of workmen by masters, neglect of children by their own parents, whole classes living in sin, usages checking marriage and encouraging licentiousness, human dwellings which make the idea of home odious, and the existence of modesty impossible, are but specimens of the evils which may be left age after age, cursing a people among whom Christianity is the recognized standard of society. To be indifferent to these things is as unfaithful to Christian morals on the one hand, as hoping to remedy them without spreading practical holiness among individuals is astray from the truth on the other.

The most dangerous perversion of the Gospel, viewed as affecting individuals, is when it is looked upon as a salvation for the soul after it leaves the body, but not salvation from sin while here. The most dangerous perversion of it, viewed as affecting the community, is when it is looked upon as a means of forming a holy community in the world to come, but never in this. Nothing short of the general renewal of society ought to satisfy any soldier of Christ; and all who aim at that triumph should draw much inspiration from the King's own words: "All power is given unto me in heaven and earth." Much as Satan glories in his power over an individual, how much greater must be his glorying over a nation embodying, in its laws and usages, disobedience to God, wrong to man, and contamination to morals! To destroy all national holds of evil, to root sin out of institutions, to hold up to view the Gospel ideal of a righteous nation, to confront all unwholesome public usages with mild, genial, and ardent advocacy of what is purer, is one of the first duties of those whose position or mode of thought gives them an influence on general questions. In so doing they are at once glorifying the Redeemer by displaying the benignity of his influence over human society, removing hindrances to individual conversion, some of which act by direct incentive to vice, others by upholding a state of things the acknowledged basis of which is "Forget God."

It Shall Be[21]

> *Walter Rauschenbusch, on 14 March 1891, sailed for an extended period of study and observation in Britain and Germany. His departure coincided with the demise of* For the Right, *and he left for publication in the final March issue a parting word of faith and confidence entitled "It Shall Be."*

Some day it shall be! All the far-off visions of the seers shall take form and substance. All that the prophet's fire-touched lip has spoken shall be true; no clash of sword, no tramp of armed men, but the glad click of scythes in the harvest field and the happy song of maidens going to their common task. No longer shall the groaning of creation rise to touch the heart of God, but peace shall be on earth, and glory shall rise to the Giver of good like the rising of the tinted morning mists.

Where once the city of Satan stood shall stand the city of God. No pall of smoke shall hang above with feeble lights to pierce it from beneath; for the glory of the Lord shall rest upon it and the Lamb shall be the light thereof. There shall be no temple there, no sacred spot or hallowed time, for all time shall be God's and all life shall be a sacrifice. Then knowledge and wisdom shall not be the heritage of few, but all men shall know, and the knowledge of the Lord and his works shall cover the earth like the rolling waters of the sea. And when the men meet on the streets of that city, they shall clasp hands

---

21. *For the Right* (March 1891).

and say: "My brother, God is good," and the only tear that flows there is the tear of joy and adoration.

It shall be, for God reigns. It shall be, for humanity feels it afar off, and the soul of humanity is prophetic. "Watchman, what of the night?" Is thy soul awake and thine eye clear to discern the coming of the Lord? Is thy soul purified to meet his gaze? Is thy heart loving and thy brow meek? Is thy heart firm in faith and tranquil in hope?

It shall be. The Kingdom of God is coming. Shall it come with or without thy help, O my brother?

"CONCEPTIONS OF MISSIONS"[22]

Rauschenbusch was always interested in foreign missions. Perhaps it appealed to his spirit of adventure. More likely it was his desire to do "hard work for God" that led him on graduating from seminary to seek appointment to a mission post in India. This venture was aborted by his physician who warned him that he would be too far removed from the medical care he required. In 1894 his sister Emma married John E. Clough, a veteran missionary among the Telegus in India, and this family tie kept his interest alive on a very personal basis. The view of missions set forth in the following article, published in The Watchman, *24 November and 1 December 1892, is especially interesting for its rejection of any notion of automatic progress, a view that he maintained throughout his life, and for his cautious attitude toward "secondary" conceptions of missions. "Faith in the power of the risen Christ," he insisted, was "the central conviction" of mission work.*

There is need for emphasizing the evangelical conception of missions. There are so many things that call themselves missions nowadays. It is one proof that the missionary idea is victorious. Any effort to reach out beyond an established circle in the spread of ideas or in the extension of practical help is called a mission.

This is well. It is well that all unselfish impulses in humanity

---

22. *The Watchman*, 24 Nov. and 1 Dec. 1892.

should range themselves under the missionary banner of Christ and obey his command to "go." It is well that the missionary impulse to save humanity is branching out in many directions. If a field is to be irrigated, it will have to be done by a multitude of tiny channels and noiseless rivulets. And if the whole of human life is to be penetrated by the saving health of Christianity, it will have to be done by a multitude of movements and a variety of endeavors.

The danger is that in the minor aims, the central aim is forgotten; that in designing the ornaments for the front of the edifice the architects are forgetting to lay a solid foundation; that in seeking the applications of the power of Christianity, the source of that power is neglected.[23] Hence I wish to lay stress on the evangelical conception of missions as distinguished from secondary conceptions.

By secondary conceptions of missions I mean especially the work of secular education, of philanthropic effort, and of denominational propaganda.

Christian people are taking an interest in the spread of education for its own sake. Our interest in Zenana work[24] and in the school of the Pandita Ramabai[25] is based not so much on the hope of seeing individuals converted, as on the hope that the crippled intellect of Hindu women will be straightened to healthy life, their horizon extended, and the heritage of humanity be secured for them. We feel that the light of intellectual knowledge and the zest of mental activity are blessings in themselves, and that it is really missionary work to pass the torch of knowledge on to those who sit in intellectual dark-

---

23. The same caution with regard to churches in the United States was voiced by Rauschenbusch in 1897. "Increasing social distress . . . has led to the establishment of the so-called institutional churches. . . . Scarcely any churches have entirely escaped the influence of this tendency. It has modified them all. This is greatly to the credit of the churches . . . . But that does not do away with the fact that a fearful burden has thus been imposed on the churches. . . . There is always the danger that the distinctive spiritual work will be crowded to one side. . . . The people ought to be able to provide for themselves what the churches are trying to provide for them. Make social life healthy and you can simplify church work." *American Journal of Sociology* III (July 1897), 25–26.

24. Zenana work was education carried on by missionaries among secluded high-caste women in India.

25. Pandita Ramabai, a female convert, focused on educational work among low-caste girls in South India.

ness. We take a keen interest in the educational movements of Japan and China. The intellectual life of the West is touching these nations with a quickening touch. The laborious erudition of the learned classes in China, their fruitless studiousness and slavish subjection to the classics of their past are exactly like the learning of Europe in the age of scholasticism and of the undisputed reign of a supposed Aristotelian philosophy. Something is going on there similar to the revival of learning in the fifteenth century through the rediscovery of Greek literature. Now we, who live an intellectual life ourselves and appreciate the blessings of virile and unhampered thought, cannot help being deeply interested in what is going on there, and we justly regard any effort to hasten the incoming of intellectual light as truly a missionary effort.

We have the same feeling about the growth of philanthropic work among the heathen. Here at home there is a growing effort in the direction of practical philanthropy. We are becoming more and more sensible that social misery lies as guilt at the door of churches. We are responding to the pressure exerted by the growth of the social movement. All this makes every effort for the alleviation of pain and the abolition of wrong very important and very dear to us. We take a lively interest in the abolition of the C. D.[26] Acts, in the raising of the age of marriage in India, in the undermining of the caste system by railroad travel and the commercial mingling of the people, in the spread of humane sentiments and the awakening of social compunction in the higher classes of the Orient, in Lady Dufferin's fund for extending medical aid to the women of India,[27] in the first dawn of parliamentary representation for the people of Japan. In the last ten years, there has been a new factor in our home mission work. We have felt as never before the greatness of the disintegrating forces at work in our national life and the need of a quickened and effective Christian life, if our country is to be saved. The remarkable sale of Dr. Strong's[28] little book on *Our Country*[29] has been both a symptom

---

26. Civil Disobedience.

27. Wife of the viceroy of India who enlisted the aid of missionary doctors to administer the government hospital and training school for nurses in Rangoon.

28. Josiah Strong (1847–1916).

29. *Our Country: Its Possible Future and Its Present Crisis* (1885) was reprinted as one of the Harvard "classics," edited with an introduction by Jurgen Herbst (Cambridge, Mass., 1963).

and a cause of the spread of these ideas. This element in home missions has made us more hospitable to similar ideas on the foreign field.

A third conception, which even more emphatically deserves the name of secondary, is the conception of missions as a propaganda of our denomination. We all would probably repudiate the insinuation, if it were charged, that we considered the extension of our own denomination as important for its own sake. We should insist that we love our denomination because it stands for certain truths and principles, and we desire its extension only because we desire the extension of the truths with which it is identified. But let us be candid. Human nature seems to be built on a very finite model. We have a special love for our own family, our own profession, our own political party, our own denomination, which we do not give to the whole of humanity. These enlarged egotisms are perhaps necessary and inevitable but they ought not to be elevated to the dignity of a principle to be acknowledged and deferred to. We ought not to grow enthusiastic in outstripping some other denomination, while we remain apathetic in saving men. It ought not to be the clinching argument with the givers among us that, if we do not do such and such a thing, the other fellows will. The welfare of our denomination may be important, but our denominational principles are more important far. And something else is more important than our denominational principles. And what is that? The fact and power of Christianity. The tendency of the natural man is toward denominationalism. We should direct our efforts to lift up the interest in Christianity and to keep down the interest in the denomination. If we do not, the latter will come up like the lean kine of Pharaoh and swallow everything, and God will not like it.

First of all and above everything comes evangelical Christianity. And what do I mean by that? I mean by that, not any particular type of doctrine, but the extension of faith in the crucified and risen Christ, who imparts his Spirit to those who believe in him, and thereby redeems them from the dominion of the flesh and the world and their corruption, and transforms them into spiritual beings, conformed to his likeness and partaking of his life. That is the primary aim of Christian missions, first in the order of importance, first in the order of time.

It is first in the order of importance because nothing can exceed in value the regeneration of individual souls who shall become dwelling places and instruments of the Holy Spirit on earth, and here and hereafter members of the eternal kingdom of God. To save men from sin and death and see them become brethren of Jesus Christ must ever remain the first and mightiest motive of Christian missions.

And this conception of missions is also the first in order of time because it is the only solid and trustworthy basis on which to build up all the secondary work of education and reformation.

We are inclined to forget this. One reason why we forget it is because many of us, through ease of life and the exceeding pleasantness of this world, are prone to sag down from evangelical religion to humanitarian morality, from spiritual fervor to altruistic earnestness. Another reason is that the spread of the idea of evolution has created an optimism among us which is not warranted by the facts.

We have heard so much about the progress of civilization that a serene faith has come over us that the cart is slowly but surely rolling up the hill, and that all that is necessary is to clear away obstacles by education and reform, and leave play to the inherent upward forces of humanity. I was myself once of this opinion and found it comforting. Observation and the study of history have compelled me to part with it sadly. However evolution works in the rest of creation, a new element enters in when it reaches the ethical nature of man. Ethically man sags downward by nature. It is ever easy to follow temptation and hard to resist it. The way that leads to destruction is always broad, and its asphalt pavement is kept in perfect order, with toboggan slides at either side for those who prefer a steeper grade. The way to life is always a climb, and every toiling traveler on it feels that asthma clogs his lungs. Moral gravitation is downward. It is accelerated in us by years of sin and by the swirling rush of centuries of wrong which pushes us from behind.

Let us not be beguiled by that seductive devil who tells us that man will walk into the millennium, if only you will point out to him where the millennium is and clear away the worst obstacles for him. Man was never built that way. If he is to get in, he will have to be lifted in. There will have to be a force from above strong enough to overcome all the downward gravitation of flesh and world, and to conquer the devil in addition. It is this force on which the evangelical conception of missions insists and which evangelical Christianity transmits.

Education has not brought salvation. There was intellectual keenness and light enough among the ancient Greeks, but they rotted just the same. Their wisdom degenerated into hair-splitting and their philosophy into the building of inverted pyramids. There is education and culture enough in France. What a refinement of taste, what an exquisite delicacy of workmanship in the products of their intellectual work. And how that nation is rotting. It is the same thing with political and social changes to some extent, and with the works of philanthropy. It is all a shifting about of what is already in society, and not the introduction of a new force into it. And yet a new force is needed. Salvation came by the coming of the Son of God into humanity, initiating the new humanity with a force not previously among us. It came by the coming of the Spirit of the risen Christ, transforming individuals, fusing them into a new society inspiring new thoughts, impelling to new undertakings, making all things new. They became the salt that stopped the putrefaction of society. They became the bits of leaven mixed into the flat lump of humanity. They furnished the basis for every work of education and reform. To attempt the salvation of heathen nations without that basis to build upon, is to mold statues of soft butter; to build houses with untempered mortar. It is an attempt foredoomed to failure. Such an edifice will slump together as soon as it is to bear any serious pressure.

The secondary conceptions of missions are just and necessary. We *must* educate. The Christ-life is incompatible with darkness of any sort. Any religion, be it Romanist or evangelical, which does not tend to enlightenment in all things, is to that extent not of the Christ. It is a most significant fact to me that the man who is confessedly the greatest evangelist of the East today, our own Dr. Clough,[30] is also the one who has labored to get the endowment for the seminary at Ramapatam, and to build the high school at Ongole, and who is now—and in my judgment not a day too soon—endeav-

---

30. John E. Clough (1836–1910), who was to become Rauschenbusch's brother-in-law in 1894, was noted for the mass movement among the Telegus to Christianity. His headquarters were at Ongole.

oring to found the college there. We must also seek the transformation of political and social life. To be indifferent about any question of justice and love is to fall under the condemnation of Christ. Where his saving health comes, all proud flesh will have to be cut down and all withered muscles will have to distend with a new current of life-blood.

All these things are good, just, indispensable. But spirituality is first. Without it, education will turn into a striving after a wind, culture into lasciviousness, social reformation into social unrest, philanthropy into a sprinkling of rose-water over the carcass.

What was Paul's conception of missions? He believed that God had in Jesus Christ worked a great deed of salvation whereby remission of sins and a life of grace was possible. He believed that the risen Christ was enthroned as the Son of God with power and that his Spirit was indwelling in the hearts of believers, transforming them, neutralizing and turning back the power of sin and death in man and in humanity, and overcoming every spiritual power working in a contrary direction. Faith in the power of the risen Christ—that I take to be the central conviction in the evangelical conception of missions. And on that foundation it will be well for us to build whatever edifice Christ has called us to erect in this generation.

III.

THE BROTHERHOOD OF THE KINGDOM

Walter Rauschenbusch was the chief publicist of the small but influential group formally constituted in August 1893 as the Brotherhood of the Kingdom.[31] At the outset he wrote brief articles to explain the Kingdom of God as the chief focus of the Brotherhood's concern. Some of these articles were reprinted for distribution as Brotherhood tracts. In 1896, when the spread of millenarian ideas was gaining increased momentum and creating misunderstanding, Rauschenbusch wrote an extended article for The Examiner *on "Our Attitude Toward Millenarianism" to explain in greater detail how the view of the Brotherhood was related to the most vigorously espoused millenarianism of the time.*

"A CONQUERING IDEA"[32]

"Since the second century nothing has less guided the church in its efforts for moral renewal than the idea of the kingdom of God in the sense in which Christ used the words." These are the words of

---

31. "The Ideals of the Social Reformers," *American Journal of Sociology* II (July 1896), 202–19, has an appended editorial note which states that Rauschenbusch is "corresponding secretary of 'The Brotherhood of the Kingdom,' and this paper is written from the viewpoint of that organization." The same would be true of "The Stake of the Church in the Social Movement," published in the same journal, III (July 1897), 18–32, and would also be true of articles published in *The Biblical World* and elsewhere.

32. *The Examiner*, 31 July 1892.

71

Albrecht Ritschl,[33] the great theologian, who has himself done more, perhaps, than any other man to rehabilitate that idea in the theological thought of Germany.

It is strange, and yet it seems true, that the leading conception in the teaching of Jesus, at once its historical basis, its logical center, its ethical aim, and its religious impulse, has almost dropped out of the Christian vocabulary. But the conception expressed by it has been so pruned and so tangled up with other conceptions that its original force has been largely lost.

In the first place, the realization of the Christian hope of perfection has been transferred to the life after death. The kingdom of the heavens has become the kingdom which is in heaven. Our hope is that we may go hence to the kingdom, and not that the kingdom may come upon earth. Those who have taken pains to draw out the ideas of our plain church members find that they almost always misunderstand the phrase, "the kingdom of heaven," in that way.

In the next place, the idea of the kingdom has been replaced by the idea of individual salvation. The kingdom is a collective ideal. It takes account of the race as a great unity. We are individuals in religion. We have lost the corporate ideal. Paul's profound doctrine of the sin of the race in the first Adam floats upon the mill-pond of our systematic theology like the bowsprit of a sunken ocean vessel. It has become a joke to many because they understand nothing but individualism.

In the third place, the idea of the kingdom has been swallowed up in the idea of the church. That substitution began with the apostolic writings. It was elaborated by Augustine in *De Civitate Dei* . It has become one of the dominant ideas of the Catholic Church. It underlies all the mistaken efforts for the realization of the theocracy on the part of Catholics and Puritans. It is also the common thought with us today.

Now all these things are true. Heaven is a truth; individual salvation is a truth; the church as the body of Christ is a tremendous truth. But none of these, neither singly nor combined, make up the full idea of the kingdom of God. When taken as parts of that larger idea, and recognized in their relation to it, they are good and indis-

---

33. Albrecht Ritschl (1822–89), German theologian.

pensable. When taken as a substitute for it, they work mischief. The substitution of heaven for the kingdom of God on earth has pushed Christianity from an offensive to a defensive attitude, has substituted asceticism for a revolutionary movement. The domination of individualism has fostered religious selfishness and crippled the missionary impulse. The substitution of the church for the kingdom has made Christianity one-sided, has made philanthrophy a side-show, and has left the bulk of human life unsanctified even in theory. We need it as the all-powerful impulse to missionary effort, as Dr. Northrup has pointed out again and again. We need it as the basis for that work of social regeneration to which our generation has been called in the providential march of history. Ideas precede facts. We cannot have the kingdom of God unless we first seize intellectually, and with the vigor of faith, the idea of the kingdom.

If anyone should regard it as strange and improbable that one of the main ideas of the Bible should be lost, only to turn up again after nineteen centuries, he may be reminded that the leading conception of Paul, the doctrine of justification by faith, was also lost to be rediscovered by the Reformation. Perhaps our generation is called to go back to the synoptic Christ as Luther's generation was called to go back to Paul. And perhaps that ideal of Christ is large enough to include in one tremendous synthesis all the terms that are crowding into the life of this second age of renaissance. Perhaps it alone contains the latest fire to kindle anew into a blaze the now smouldering fires of Christendom.

It may be called a conquering idea because it is apparently spreading on all hands and moving to victory. One can hardly take up a religious newspaper without encountering somebody who is trying to spell out that idea. At a single session of the Missionary Union in Philadelphia,[34] three speakers had hold of it. Dr. Murdock implied it. Dr. Northrup proclaimed it. Mr. Faunce defined it.

The Millenarians have hold of one end of it. They have it in a bizarre form often, but they have it. And whatever of peculiar hopefulness and vigor there is in them, is due to this. Socialism has hold of another end of it. It often has the kingdom of God with God left out. Yet that fractional part of the idea of the kingdom which they

---

34. American Baptist Missionary Union.

have got casts a halo about their aims, and puts a religious enthusiasm into their propaganda. In theological thought the idea of the kingdom gains ground as fast as the study of Biblical theology gains ground. Any one who has begun to study the Bible along these lines cannot shut his eyes to the doctrine of the kingdom. Even systematic theology is feeling the victorious march of the idea, and some day we may see a new configuration of its table of contents dominated by that idea.

The reconception of the kingdom, the application of this idea to ethical questions and to the practical aims of Christianity, and especially its popularization in the general thought of the church, will not be the work of a few men. It calls for investigation in every pastor's study, and for discussion wherever Christian men may meet. It is a large task, but there is none more fruitful.

"THE BROTHERHOOD OF THE KINGDOM"[35]

The recent announcement of the formation of the Brotherhood of the Kingdom has awakened considerable interest, if we may judge by the number of questions asked concerning it. Perhaps a brief statement concerning its origin and purpose will be welcome.

The Brotherhood has taken shape very gradually, naturally, and, as we believe, under the guidance of God. It began in the friendship of a number of us who had been drawn together by kinship of spirit and similarity of convictions. As we exchanged our thoughts about the Kingdom of our Master, our views grew more definite and more united. We saw the Church of Christ divided by selfishness; every denomination intent on its own progress, often at the expense of the progress of the Kingdom; churches and pastors absorbed in their own affairs and jealous of one another; external forms of worship and church polity magnified and the spirit neglected; the people estranged from the church and the church indifferent to the movements of the people; aberrations from creeds severely censured, and aberrations from the Christian spirit of self-sacrifice tolerated.

---

35. Brotherhood Leaflet No. 2. Rauschenbusch Scrapbook in the Colgate Rochester Divinity School library.

As we contemplated these blemishes of the body of Christ, and sorrowed over them in common with all earnest lovers of the church of Jesus, it grew clear to us that many of these evils have their root in the wrongful abandonment or the perversion of the great aim of Christ: the Kingdom of God. As the idea of the Kingdom is the key to the teachings and work of Christ, so its abandonment or misconstruction is the key to the false or one-sided conceptions of Christianity and our halting realization of it. Because the Kingdom of God has been dropped as the primary and comprehensive aim of Christianity, and personal salvation has been substituted for it, therefore men seek to save their own souls and are selfishly indifferent to the evangelization of the world. Because the individualistic conception of personal salvation has pushed out of sight the collective idea of a Kingdom of God on earth, Christian men seek for the salvation of individuals and are comparatively indifferent to the spread of the spirit of Christ in the political, industrial, social, scientific, and artistic life of humanity, and have left these as the undisturbed possessions of the spirit of the world. Because the Kingdom of God has been understood as a state to be inherited in a future life rather than as something to be realized here and now, therefore Christians have been contented with a low plane of life here and have postponed holiness to the future. Because the Kingdom of God has been confounded with the Church, therefore the Church has been regarded as an end instead of a means, and men have thought they were building up the Kingdom when they were only cementing a strong church organization.

As these thoughts took shape through observation and the study of Scripture and church history, and grew hot through prayer, and as we felt in our personal efforts the magnitude of the task of removing these evils, we determined to strike hands in the name of Christ, and by union to multiply our opportunities, increase our wisdom, and keep steadfast our courage. So we formed ourselves into a "Brotherhood of the Kingdom," in order "to reestablish this idea in the thought of the church and to assist in its practical realization in the world."

We desire to see the Kingdom of God once more the great object of Christian preaching; the inspiration of Christian hymnology; the foundation of systematic theology; the enduring motive of evangelistic and missionary work; the religious inspiration of social work and the social outcome of religious inspiration; the object to which a Christian man surrenders his life, and in that surrender saves it to eternal life; the common object in which all religious bodies find their unity; the great synthesis in which the regeneration of the spirit, the enlightenment of the intellect, the development of the body, the reform of the political life, the sanctification of industrial life, and all that concerns the redemption of humanity shall be embraced.

To this task, God helping us, we desire to dedicate our lives. We invite others, ministers and laymen, to join us in it. We are not a proselyting body. We care little for numbers. We care much for the spirit. If anyone has cherished the same prayerful longings and feels that he is in substantial agreement with our aims, and if, moreover, he is willing to render service that may not bring honor or profit, we heartily invite him to put himself in communication with our secretary, Rev. S. Z. Batten (197 Green Lane, Manayank, Philadelphia, Pa.), or with any of our members. Pastors who desire to have their people come in contact with the ideas for which we stand, will find us ready to serve them in the pulpit or on the platform, so far as other duties permit. As far as our efforts will reach in the churches, in the religious press, in the social movements, and in our personal relations, we hope to carry the thoughts and the spirit of the King whose bondservants we are, and to hasten with all our strength the time when the kingdoms of the earth shall be the kingdom of the Christ.—*Reprinted from The National Baptist.*

"THE KINGDOM OF GOD"[36]

An organization has recently been formed by Christian believers called "the Brotherhood of the Kingdom." Its members believe that the idea of a kingdom of God on earth was the central thought of Jesus, and ought ever to be the great aim of the church. They are convinced that this aim has largely dropped out of sight, or has been misunderstood, and that much of the social ineffectiveness of church life is due to this misunderstanding. Therefore, they have organized

---

36. Brotherhood Leaflet No. 4. Rauschenbusch Scrapbook in the Colgate Rochester Divinity School library.

"in order to reestablish this idea in the thought of the church, and to assist in its practical realization in the world."

The idea of "the Kingdom of God" has gone through many changes in the history of Christianity. At present we can distinguish five different senses in which the term is used.

1. The common people generally understand by the "Kingdom of God," or the "Kingdom of Heaven," the blessed life after death—heaven. It is a condition to which they expect to go, and not a condition which they expect to come to them. Perhaps the most vivid proof for the prevalence of this conception of the "Kingdom" is the fact that the description of the New Jerusalem, in the Book of Revelation, is popularly supposed to describe heaven, while the author meant to describe the perfect city to be established on earth at the return of Christ.

2. Men of a mystical mind have usually seized on the idea of "the Kingdom of God" to designate that inner life of the Spirit which to their minds constitutes the highest gift of Christianity. Men of that turn of mind frequently slight the questions of dogma and of ecclesiastical organizations which absorb others, and they need some term not stamped with a technical sense by church usage. Their favorite passage is "The Kingdom of God is within you."[37]

3. Men of ecclesiastical temper use the term synonymously with the "Church." The church sums up the total of divine forces in the world to their minds, and so they can make the kingdom coterminous with the church.

4. Men with whom the second coming of Christ is a living hope have restricted the term to the reign of Christ to be established after his return.

5. Men who are interested in movements that extend beyond the existing work of the church, and are pushing out under religious impulses into new fields of Christian activity, have seized on this term as one large enough to include everything else *plus* the work to which they are giving themselves. So at the beginning of foreign missionary activity its pioneers loved to speak of "the enterprise for the extension of the Redeemer's Kingdom." And at present those

---

37. Lk 17:21.

who labor for a righteous social order under religious impulses always raise the standard of "the Kingdom of God."

Which of these ideas is right? We reply: they all err by defect. The Kingdom of God is larger than anything contained in any one of these ideas. It stands for the sum of all divine and righteous forces on earth. It embraces all pure aspirations God-ward and all true hopes for the perfection of life. It is a synthesis combining all the conceptions mentioned above, and if we could combine them in such a synthesis, it would prove to be like some chemical compounds, more powerful than the sum of all its parts.

1. In the common conceptions of the Kingdom as heaven, we must recognize the truth that we have here no abiding city. Life at its best is transitory and unsatisfactory. The perfection of our personality is not attained on earth. Even if humanity lives on and marches toward the golden city of the Ideal, the weary toiler to whom its progress is due drops by the wayside and his feet never enter the city of his longings. An ideal which is to satisfy all the desires of the human heart and is to embrace perfect man as well as the perfect Man must include a heaven beyond death.

2. In the mystical conception of the Kingdom as the inward fellowship with God, we must recognize the justice of human yearning for the living God. A righteous and happy intercourse with our fellowmen, in a true human society, will not satisfy the heart completely. Deeper than the hunger and thirst for the justice of God lies the hunger and thirst for God himself. It would be a mistake on the part of those who labor for a perfect humanity to rule out the efforts of religion to bring men into personal intercourse with the living God.

3. We must recognize the importance of a living church within the Kingdom. It must not dwindle. It is the channel through which ethical impulses pour into humanity from God. Yet the church and the Kingdom are not identical. We are the church as we worship together; we are the Kingdom as we live justly and lovingly with one another.

4. We must recognize the justice of the millennial hopes. They stand for the force of cataclysms in human history; for the direct interference of God in the life of nations; and for the ultimate victory of right and love in the conflict of the ages.

5. But finally, we must insist that the Kingdom is not only in

heaven but is to come on earth; that while it begins in the depths of the heart, it is not to stay there; that the church does not embrace all the forces of the Kingdom and is but a means for the advancement of the Kingdom; that while the perfection of the Kingdom may be reserved for a future epoch, the Kingdom is here and at work. The Kingdom means individual men and women who freely do the will of God, and who therefore live rightly with their fellowmen. And without a goodly number of such men and women, no plan for a higher social order will have stability enough to work. But the Kingdom also means a growing perfection in the collective life of humanity, in our laws, in the customs of society, in the institutions for education, and for the administration of mercy; in our public opinion, our literary and artistic ideals, in the pervasiveness of the sense of duty, and in our readiness to give our life as a ransom for others.

With most social reformers, it is the former aspect which needs emphasis; with most religious people, it is the latter.—*Reprinted from the City Vigilant, May, 1894.*

"OUR ATTITUDE TOWARD MILLENARIANISM"[38]

I. The Importance of the Topic

1. It is a necessity to the human mind to inquire into the whence and whither of any object to which it gives its interest. We do not fully understand a thing until we know what causes have brought it into being and have shaped it as it is; and, on the other hand, what its final end is to be and for what destiny it has been brought into existence. The question has special importance in regard to the end and destiny of the human race, because right or wrong views on that will shape our actions and hasten or retard the attainment of our goal. Whether he has sighted the light-house that marks the entrance to the harbor, or whether he has mistaken a promontory on a treacherous coast for it, is certainly no idle question to the man at the tiller.

2. A second reason why the study of the topic is important is

---

38. *The Examiner*, 24 Sept. and 1 Oct. 1896. Rauschenbusch Scrapbook in the Colgate Rochester Divinity School library.

that a large body of Scriptural teaching bears on last things. In the prophetic writings of the Old Testament, in the parables and discourses of our Lord, in the passing allusions and set discussions in the epistles, and in the entire Apocalypse the coming of the Lord, the judgment and the reward, bulk up with unmistakable importance. The faithful student of Scripture is constantly being called out of the dear but narrow grooves worn by his own thinking to face some less congenial question, and is rewarded by the rounded fullness of completer knowledge. Wide and mature thought on eschatology is especially desirable for all who are called to guide religious thought, because so many of our brethren have an intense but one-sided interest in eschatology. They try to round this Cape Horn of theology with all sails set, but little of the ballast of historical knowledge in the hold. And so they often run into vagaries that lame their practical usefulness, or into fanaticism which does damage to their Christian character and to the cause of Christ.

3. Finally, the question is especially urgent for those of us to whom the kingdom has become once more the great aim of Christianity and the synthesis of all divine forces in humanity. When Jesus began his public ministry he encountered his chief obstacle, not in the men who cared nothing about the kingdom and knew nothing of a coming Messiah, but in men who cared for both most earnestly, and were sure they knew all about the manner of their coming. We also feel the Spirit of the Lord upon us, and are lifting up our voices with the old cry: "The kingdom of God is at hand! Repent and believe in the glad tidings!" And we also encounter men whose eyes brighten at the word "kingdom," but who, when they hear our message, turn from us in pity or in anger and say: "Your kingdom is not the kingdom, but a counterfeit of it; your repentance is no repentance, and your glad tidings are a mockery and a snare." It is a condition of our usefulness to our generation that we clear the ground and find out where we agree and disagree.

II. The Two Views in Contrast

We are all more or less familiar with the questions involved, but a brief reminder will bring the matter before us with freshness.

There is substantial agreement among Christians on the fact that at some time there is to be a great day of the Lord, an end of the world, and a final settling of accounts. There is no doubt of the fullness of Scriptural teaching on that; and, indeed, it is only natural to suppose that this planet and the race that sucks sustenance from its crust will not last forever. Some may spiritualize the dramatic prophecies of the Bible more than others; to none of us, perhaps, is the end so real and pressing a fact as to the early Christians. But that there will be an end we can, I think, take for granted. The question that divides men is on the way we approach that end.

Some hold that the world will continue in its present course of development. Through the missionary activity of the church there will be a gradual extension of Christianity. In heathen nations, where the work is now progressing tediously, like the drilling of blast holes in a great tunnel, there will come a collapse of heathenism by and by and a very general conversion to Christ. In the Christian nations also the proportion of regenerate persons will increase, and by their example and personal influence they will make goodness easier and wrong-doing harder. Some of those who hold this view, and who regard society not as a sand heap of individuals but as a great organism, and as a compound personality which learns and acquires habits, place stress on the penetration of public opinion by Christian standards of judgment, on the incorporation of Christian principles into the customs, institutions, and laws of the nations, and on the restraint of the instincts of self-interest by the conviction of duty and by the collective sense of fellowship. Thus humanity will gradually emerge like a mountain chain from the darkness of the night and the clinging mists of the dawn into the brightness of Christ's day. There will be no absolute cessation of evil. The wheat and the tares will grow side by side till the end. But there will be an increasing and victorious power of truth and goodness overcoming evil and steadily answering the prayer, "Thy kingdom come! Thy will be done on earth!" The progress will be due not to the inherent powers of humanity, but to the spiritual and redemptive forces implanted in humanity by Christ.

Finally, the end will come. Christ will judge the quick and the dead. There will be a new heaven and a new earth. God will dwell among his people and we, seeing him as he is, shall be like him.

This view contrasts with the other in presenting little that is definite; only a gradual development, the events of which are unknown and the length of which is quite conjectural, and then the end; that is all. It is one of the attractions of the other view, to many minds at least, that it presents a definite plan of the ages, precise in detail, constantly tempting its adherents to draw it up in the form of a map. It is, in fact, a map with some blank tracts and some dotted lines, but on the whole about as complete as a map of Africa was twenty years ago. Its advocates differ remarkably on the details, but with the details we are not now concerned. The view of almost anyone among them will serve as a sample to characterize the school. Perhaps I shall best put us *en rapport* with them if I give the substance of an interview I recently had with a careful and able student of both the American and German literature of Millenarianism, and state the plan of the future as he mapped it out. He said in substance:

The course of humanity will continue during the present era much as at present. The church will extend by missions and increase in wealth and influence, but only a part of it will really stand in the faith. The world will improve externally, but new evils will arise to counterbalance the improvements.

Then, when all nations have had witness borne to them, the really living Christians will one day, without warning to anyone, disappear from the earth and be with the Lord. About fifty per cent of our church members will have part in this rapture, for five out of the ten virgins were prepared for the coming of the bridegroom.[39] Simultaneously all the dead who died in the same spiritual condition will be raised and will also be with the Lord in the clouds, clothed with their glorious bodies. This double event is the beginning of the coming of the Lord.

On earth the disappearance of the saints at first makes a deep impression, but this soon wears away, and now that the salt is taken away, humanity rapidly deteriorates during the period of forty years which follows. Evil culminates in the reign of Anti-Christ and the false prophet during the last three and a half years of this period. On the other hand, many of the half-hearted Christians who were left behind at the rapture of the saints are aroused to zeal and are persecuted and beheaded. This period is the great day of the Lord.

During this time Israel gathers in Palestine. The Old Testament

---

39. Mt 25:1–13.

cultus is reorganized and the Messiah is expected, but without faith in Jesus as the Messiah. But owing, perhaps, to the persecution of the saints, or to the testimony of the two witnesses, or to some special revelation of God, Israel as a whole, though not without exception, is converted to Christ. One hundred and forty-four thousand is symbolic of totality. Anti-Christ also makes his throne in Jerusalem, but cannot conquer Israel encamped on Mount Zion.

Then comes the visible return of Christ. Anti-Christ and the false prophet are imprisoned in hell. Satan is not put in hell, but bound or restrained from activity. Christ moves about on earth as he did after the resurrection, visible now here and now there. The saints snatched away at the beginning of the forty years, those who were then raised, and those who were beheaded during the persecutions and who are now raised, dwell among men and reign over them. Through their moral influence and through the absence of Satan's temptations a very righteous condition of life ensues. Nature grows fertile as before the Fall. The wild beasts become tame. Men live long as before the flood so that a death at one hundred is like the premature death of a boy. Jerusalem, with the Jews, is the center of humanity. Israel is the bride. The other nations are the bridesmaids. This lasts for a thousand years and is the Millennium. Some believe that this will be a period of great missionary activity, and that many will be converted. My informant believes that we are at present in the era of the Church, and that the conversion of individuals will cease with the close of the present era at the coming of the Lord.

At the end of the thousand years Satan is let loose. A spirit of apostacy and rebellion possesses the nations. Satan gathers the army of Gog and Magog[40] to war against the Lord and the elect. But, just before the accomplishment of his design, fire falls from heaven and consumes the army. Satan is cast into the pit where Anti-Christ and the false prophet await him. Then follows the judgment. All the dead are raised, including the wicked and those Christians who were not worthy to share in the first resurrection. The great separation is made. The wicked are cast into hell. The good receive their glorified bodies. The earth is purified by fire and glorified and becomes the

---

40. Rv 20:8.

habitation of the saints. The new Jerusalem descends and the last two chapters of the Apocalypse are fulfilled. Israel occupies the city and is still the center, but the nations have the freedom of the city.

III. Our Attitude

This latter view is a sample of Millenarianism, diverging in detail from many other expositions of it, but fairly characterizing it in method and spirit. Now, what attitude shall we take toward it? It is easy to dismiss it with a sneer. There are many points in it which especially lay themselves open to exclamations of surprise. For instance, I inquired in my conversation with my Millenarian friend, what the final use of the Millennium is anyway, if none are converted in it, if all its results go to pieces again at the unloosening of Satan and, in the net results, the *status quo ante* reappears. Why not have the final separation take place at once and heaven begin? He replied that he thought the purpose was to prove to Satan the superiority of Christ. It gave him one last chance to test the saints and he would find himself baffled. I told him I thought there was a good deal to be said from Satan's point of view. I could imagine Satan saying: "Now I will give Christ one last grand chance. I will cease from activity for a thousand years. I will let him come personally and bring with him all his faithful ones of all ages. I will give them a free field. I will let them entrench themselves in all the institutions of life. And then, at the end of the thousand years, I will come back and my own will flock back to me. The work of ten centuries will be undone. The superiority of evil over good will be demonstrated, and it will take the application of violence to keep me from complete victory."

Arguments like that might be multiplied, but they would not make us wiser. Let us try to understand not only the letter but the spirit of Millenarianism, according praise as well as recording dissent. I shall mention first the points to which we can agree.

1. First, we should recognize the service of Millenarianism in emphasizing that Christianity is not yet exhausted.

It was one of the most remarkable traits in the religious life of Israel, and an evidence of its divine origin, that it not only did not claim finality but expressly disclaimed it. It pointed forward to revelations yet to come, to a great act of forgiveness, to a mightier outpouring of the Spirit, to a time when righteousness would cover the earth as the sea covers its bed. It was not the vague hope of the East for a new avatar. It was always connected with contemporaneous events. Christianity from the first bore the same expectant character. Christians were looking for another age to come. They were tasting its powers by faith. When they gathered to Christ's meal of fellowship, it was "till he come."

There has been danger that the church would lose this sense of the incompleteness of what we have, and of the need of new revelations of truth and power from on high. We have often been taught to look for the mighty manifestations of the Spirit in the past and not in the future. We are led to think that the faith has once for all been delivered to the saints to be guarded like water in a cistern, and not like seed-corn to be scattered on the ground for a richer harvest. It is orthodox to believe that the age of miracles has ceased and that inspiration stopped with the closing of the New Testament canon. Millenarianism has put in its protest against this merely reminiscent attitude of the church, and bids us lift up our eyes and behold the coming Christ.

2. In the next place we owe gratitude to Millenarianism for preserving to the church the collective ideal of Christianity.

In the Old Testament the nation and its salvation were nearly everything. The individual was saved or lost with the nation. In the New Testament that attitude is still maintained to some extent. There is distressingly little said about the destiny of the single soul that dies before the day of general salvation has come. With some of the church fathers, on the other hand, forgiveness and the gift of personal immortality came to mean almost the whole of Christianity. The future of the race, the salvation of the collective life of humanity, the fulfillment of the theocratic hope receded from view. It was still more so after the Reformation, especially with the Calvinistic branches of Protestantism. It is a common dictum that the material principle of the Reformation was justification by faith; its formal principle was the Scriptures. But the material principle in the teaching of Jesus was the kingdom of God; and the formal principle in Pauline theology was the Spirit. On the one side is an almost purely individual ideal; on the other, a collective ideal. Almost the only two forms in which this collective ideal has been preserved have been on the one hand the idea of the church organized, universal, and dominant; on the other hand the idea of a God-governed humanity in the Millennium, obeying in its collective life the will of the Lord.

3. In the third place we owe it to Millenarianism that we have rescued anything of the sweet hope of Israel, to see the hills and valleys and cities of its dear native land in the old familiar outlines and yet bathed in the dew and the light of a new morning. It is a very human hope and longing. Even after Christ, our great companion, has gone before and awaits us, the land beyond the river is an unknown country to us. The hope for it is largely dear to us by reason of the sorrows that we are to get rid of there. But if he were honest, I dare say many a Christian would confess that the burdocks in his own backyard are dearer to him than the trees of heaven and that the moss-grown paths he has trod with some dear one on earth are sweeter than the singing crowds of heaven. I love this dear old earth. I love the hills of the Hudson. I love New York Bay. It would be a comfort to me to know that even if I do not live till then, the slimy trail of selfishness will one day cease to disfigure the handiwork of God; that the earth will not forever stand like a queen in a filthy mob that is filching her jewels, tearing her robe, and even plucking the golden hairs from her head. Asceticism has tapped the blood from the Christian hope till it stands pale and almost haggard. It is too other-worldly for human nature to bear. Millenarianism has held up a hope that is connected with this world and with the life we now live, and that is a living and attractive hope.

4. In the fourth place, Millenarianism deserves credit for preserving to the church the social ideals of Christianity.

They have been in constant danger of oblivion. In the school of Origen the vine and fig-tree were spiritualized. The instinct of caution in political ecclesiastics who sought for favors from the rulers of this world or who wielded secular power themselves, the abstraction of the speculative theologians who were not sufficiently in contact with the world to have social interests, and the satiated condition of those who had the good things now and did not like to hear that they ought to share them with others; all these causes tended to suppress the social aspects of Christianity. Millenarianism has kept them alive. In the form of millenarian hopes they lived on among the lower classes. The pictures of the millennium are the utopias of Christianity and all their details are social, though to this day they remind one by their exclusively pastoral character of the age when they originated. They are more akin to Mr. Morris's "News from Nowhere" than to Mr. Bellamy's picture of future Boston.[41]

5. Finally, Millenarianism has kept alive the revolutionary spirit of Christianity. That such a spirit lived in early Christianity ought not to require proof. Jesus refused to bring the revolution to pass in the way others expected it to come. But he did come to bring, not peace, but the sword; he did come to reverse values and make the first last and last first, and that is done only by turning things bottom-side up. His chief conflict was with the chiefs and representatives of the present order, and he warned his disciples that their conflict would lie in the same direction. Even Paul, who is nearly as conservative in social matters as he is radical in theology, has plenty of passages which show, often under covert language, his deep hostility to the powers of this world and an exultant expectation of seeing them overthrown. The entire New Testament distinction between the *aion houtos*[42] and the *aion mellon*,[43] which finds its most militant expression in the Apocalypse, was a revolutionary expectation.

When the persecutions of the church died away and the church approached its external victory, this revolutionary protest began to hush its voice. Augustine was so well satisfied with things as they were going that he taught the organized church is the kingdom and that the millennium had begun with the first coming of Christ. The general expectations of the approaching end to the world about 1000 A.D. show how his view had taken root. Eusebius[44] tickled the fancy of the imperial table-round at Byzantium by the proposition that perhaps the gilded hall in which they were banqueting was the new Jerusalem of the Apocalypse.

Of course the revolutionary leaven of Christianity could not be hidden entirely. It broke out in a multitude of minor movements, some within the pale of church orthodoxy, others allied with heresies. But what concerns us now is that Millenarianism showed its affinity for these movements by appearing as an ingredient in most of them. It allied itself to church democracy, to the ideal of apostolic

---

41. The reference is to Edward Bellamy's *Looking Backward* (Boston, 1888).

42. The present age.

43. Age to come.

44. Eusebius of Caesarea (c. 260–c. 339), church historian.

poverty, to the protests against the secularization of the church. It is probably fair to say that wherever it has been more than an academic opinion of Biblical students, wherever it became a living conviction of the people, it is an indication that the people were suffering under the pressure of secular governments and were despairing under the deadness of the established church.

But now we must pass from praise to censure, and in this also I shall try to get below the surface and deal with the spirit of Millenarianism and not with its external features. It has been assailed on many grounds. . . . I intend to take up none of these points, though I think there is ground for most of them. I shall confine myself to three practical charges.

1. First, I charge that Millenarianism is based on and apparently inseparable from a narrow and unhistorical system of interpreting Scripture.

Its advocates are professedly very jealous for the absolute authority of the Bible, and the view is seldom held by any one who does not also hold high doctrine on inspiration. Yet, in reading their writings, I cannot help feeling that their reverence is not of the highest order. It is not the reverence of a good and loving man for another living personality, whose higher ability and goodness he recognizes, and on whose words he feeds, but whose mannerism of speech and oddities of behavior he smiles at and lovingly makes allowance for. It is rather the reverence of an Italian peasant woman for the Bambino, before which she prostrates herself at one moment, and which the next moment she takes down to put a new robe on it or give it a more becoming position.

The best known instances of their method of interpretation are their arithmetical calculations of the future. Not only Daniel and the Apocalypse are ransacked for chronological hints, but Canticles and the numerical value of the Jewish alphabet are pressed into use. One is often reminded of rabbinical and even cabalistic methods in following their discussions.

But the arithmetic is only a symptom. Their whole method is unhistorical. They are always quoting Scripture. But they do not say: "It was the conviction of Ezekiel that the sacrificial cultus was to be re-established on a larger scale," or "it was the cherished belief of Paul that the fullness of Israel would yet be gathered in." "The Scriptures say so," that is all. Daniel or Paul, Peter or the Apocalypse—it is all one. The passages of Scripture are to them not portions of a living organization of thought, belonging to one man of a certain age and a certain nation, to be handled reverently and to be understood only in connection with the other thoughts of that man and his time. They are rather adamantine pieces of dead matter, bits of glass distributed in boxes, which are to be arranged in a mosaic by the cunning workman in prophecies who has found the key, as if it was all a gigantic puzzle devised by the Almighty. They do not train themselves to discern the different trends of thought among Biblical writers. They make no allowance for the imperfections and crudities through which every great idea must pass in its earlier stages of development. Because the hope of the world's salvation was first nurtured in Israel, because those who saw its perfections in their visions were Jewish patriots to whom a handful of Jewish earth was more than all the lands of the Gentiles, because the swaddling clothes of Christianity were Jewish; therefore Jerusalem, and not London or New York, remains the focus of the world's forces to the end. And even after this earth has been consumed by fire and a new earth arises from its ashes, there is still a distinction between Jew and Greek, and Israel still is the bride of the Lamb while all other nations are but the bridesmaids. Is it that way in which the God of history works? Consider the prophecy contained in a caterpillar. You know that it will undergo further developments and you try to forecast them. You count his legs, and you find that there are six in front and ten behind. You reason that, whatever becomes of the creature, it will always have sixteen legs. And you refuse to accept the butterfly as the legitimate fulfillment of the caterpillar prophecy because it has only six legs. And if the developments in the embryology of the lower forms of life cannot be followed with any such crude rules, how shall the course of the most complex of all organisms, humanity, be forecast thereby?

Occasionally, also, we meet with a lamentable readiness to twist the backbone of a text in order to fit it into the exigencies of a closely wrought system. For instance, the Lord's parables of the leaven, of the mustard seed, and of the seed growing secretly, are justly used to prove that Christ expected a steady and organic growth of his kingdom through the development of germinal forces implanted by him in humanity. Millenarians find that an uncomfortable argument. So they have very generally ruled out the parable of the leaven, asserting that since leaven stands for evil in every other allusion in the Bible, it must signify the growth of evil here. But to any one with any literary sense the parables of the leaven and of the mustard seed move and turn together like two ships lashed bow to bow. Some, like Dr. Pierson,[45] have felt this and so he says of the growth of the mustard seed that "it signifies a worldly expansion of the church, attracting to its shadow the very birds which catch away the seed of the kingdom."

It would be unjust to charge Millenarians with the whole guilt of these sins of interpretation. They share them with many others. The turns and shifts by which Post-Millenarians have often tried to break down the manifestly Pre-Millenarian sense of Revelations 20 are just as distressing as anything we have alluded to. Yet I fear that this system of interpretation is not the rough nap of Millenarianism which can be singed off, but is woven into the cloth.

As men who desire the Scriptures to be honored and used to spiritual edification, we must set ourselves against a method of interpretation which dishonors the Bible while claiming to honor it, which misunderstands the nature of the Spirit of prophecy while making a hobby of prophecy, and which by teaching men to use the Bible as a puzzle book blinds them to its true and important uses.

2. My second objection to Millenarianism is its pessimism and world-flight.

Millenarianism refuses to believe that the world is getting better. It refuses to believe that the spread of intelligence, the growth of mechanical inventions, the progress of democracy, the increase of the church in numbers and wealth, are really an improvement in the net quantity of God-fearing righteousness on earth. Some of its adherents believe that things remain about even, every increase in good being counter-balanced by an equal intensifying of evil. Others believe that there is progress, but that it is from bad to worse, and that the world will never be so wicked as when Christianity has run its full course.

Now this view is not to be put aside quite as lightly as our American optimism would prompt us. Our first impulse naturally is

---

45. A.T. Pierson was a prominent pastor, evangelist, and editor of the *Missionary Review of the World*, who adopted premillennialist views in 1878.

to believe that the world is getting better. But the facts of history do not work out that way with the "slickness" of the problems in our school arithmetic which left no remainder. The evil of the world today is appalling in amount. The way in which the devil gets a hold of the products of civilization, for instance, of the public press and of democratic institutions and uses them after his own heart is enough to make a Thanksgiving orator pause in his figures.

We should have no quarrel with Millenarianism if it held that the world, *minus* the redemptive forces of Christianity, sags downward instead of rising upward, that society naturally decays, that the increase in material wealth only hastens the rotting, and that the spread of intelligence but makes evil more malignant. But when Millenarianism asserts the same things concerning humanity, *plus* the redemptive forces of Christ, we feel in our hearts an impassioned protest, and that protest issues, not from unsanctified optimism, but from sanctified faith in Jesus Christ. Did Jesus put his shoulder against the weight that is crushing the world, and was he too unable to stay it? Did the Lord Christ cast the full weight of his historic personality and the glorious power of his spiritual influence into the scales of history, and does the scale of wrong still continue to fall, and the scale of right continue to mount? Must we write on the book telling of the conflicts and prayers and agony of the Son of Man, as the verdict of history, the words, "Weighed and found wanting for the task?" It is true, Jesus tells us himself that good and evil will remain side by side to the end, that there will be affliction and opposition to the last, and that he is blessed who perseveres to the end. It may be true too that a great final struggle will take place, and that the old serpent will coil itself for a last spring. But for all that, we cannot cease to believe that Christianity is gaining inch by inch and that there is Scripture for that too.

In surveying the historical facts of the contention we must remember that joys taste sweetest in the recollection of them, while evil hurts most in the present endurance of it. In thinking of the past, its glories stand out and its worries are forgotten, while today the pebble in our shoe engages our attention more than the delectable mountain we are crossing. The men who draw such sombre pictures of our present condition are right enough when they compare them with the sunlight of our ideal, but their ignorance of the history of morals leads them astray when they try to prove that all things are degenerating. There is a large and useful field for us in the minute investigation of the changes that have actually been wrought in humanity through Christ, in its private life, its standards of manners and taste, its art and literature, its canons of public opinion, its laws and institutions, etc.

Now, if these pessimistic opinions of Millenarians were merely speculative, if they insisted that the chess-board is not white but black, but bravely played the game all the same, it would not matter so much. But the consequences flowing from their opinions are of the most practical sort. When I first became interested in social questions I found that there were two classes that were impervious to persuasion. The men who are making money fast are hotly opposed, the men who hold Millenarian views are cooly indifferent. "It is no use," they say, "every improvement you secure will be captured and twisted by the Devil. Thorough improvement is impossible in this era of the world; that will come when Christ returns. All we can do now is to be faithful and live soberly in this present world, waiting for Christ and gathering others into the church who will also wait."

This is a practical abdication from the task of conquering the world in all its relations for Christ. It is a shrinking back into the defensive attitude. And to take the defensive attitude toward the world is the essence of monkishness. Monasticism and its flight from the world were at bottom due to the feeling that the world without is stronger than the new life within us; that when the two meet, it is more likely that the world will destroy our faith than our faith will conquer the world. That attitude I feel we must condemn as lack of faith and partial apostasy. Millenarianism shares the despair of monasticism without braving its self-denials. It cultivates the attitude of separation while mingling with the world, and the consequence is frequently a life in two sections, the one expecting the Lord, the other conformed to the laws of the world. The best way to remain different from the world in all portions of life is to labor for the renewal of life in all its portions. The best method of keeping ourselves intact from the Devil is to keep charging down on him. Millenarians have themselves helped to make true their assertion that the world cannot be changed. They have been the section of the church which has held the belief in a renewal of social life but, by denying its present possibility, they have turned away the force of

Christianity from its task, and then they say: "There, you see, we told you it could not be done."

We must protest against the pessimism of Millenarianism as a partial surrender of our faith, and against its defensive attitude toward the world as a partial desertion of our Christian task.

3. The third point at which we must oppose Millenarianism is its faith in catastrophes and its consequent disjointing of faith and action.

Millenarianism presents much the same ideal of humanity that we hold: a community of men who love God and therefore serve their brethren, universal prosperity and peace, the lessening or abolition of suffering, the spread of good will and mutual helpfulness. These are all features of Millennial hope. Yet Millenarians refuse to take a vigorous part in measures that will bring at least an approximate realization of these blessings. They believe that in the Millennium every man is to sit under his own vine and fig-tree, but they refuse to touch the land question, or to interest themselves in public parks, which would at least give us a public vine and fig-tree to sit under. They believe that there is to be great longevity in the Millennium, but they are indifferent about child labor and the tenement-house question which brings the average of human life down at present.

Whence this curious contradiction between faith and works? One reason we have discussed—the laming power of pessimism. Another cause is apparently just the reverse—too great hopefulness. They believe that everything will be done at one stroke. Why then trouble to do it in many little strokes? They believe in salvation by catastrophe, and hence their lack of interest in salvation by development. They are much akin to socialists twenty years ago who staked their faith on the great social revolution, the beneficent topsy-turvy from which the new order would arise, like Venus, from the sea. Socialists in England have generally come to the conclusion of the Fabian Society that revolutions are not to be despised but that the main work will have to be done by taking measure for measure, and step for step, working socialist ideas into the social structure of England and learning at every step where next they can best plant the foot of progress. Christians have never yet, as a body, taken that attitude. They have either not believed in a social Christianity at all, or they have believed in its coming by a heavenly catastrophe. There is no telling what the result would be if they should take the attitude to which the thousand failures of the Millennial hope point them.

Faith in catastrophes, brought about by men, makes action spasmodic and feverish. Faith in catastrophes worked by the Lord discourages action entirely. For protracted effort human nature needs the sense of causation and continuity. It wants to see every step count, and the next step grow out of the preceding one. Millenarians justly point to their zeal for foreign missions as a reply to the charge of inaction. Their claim is just, but it only proves our point. They believe that the Lord has conditioned his return on that one point, that all nations must first have witness borne to them. Hence they are zealous to bear witness. It is the one means by which human action can hasten the catastrophe. If the Lord had said, "First must the last tenement-house disappear, and then will come the end," they would be zealous about tenement-houses. But has he not said it?

Faith in salvation by catastrophe cuts the nerve of action, but only in the unselfish pursuits of life. In the common affairs of life which press with directness on our love for self and love for family, and twinge the nerve of self-preservation, common sense gets the better of theory. I have yet to see proof that those who believe in the imminence of Christ's coming are indifferent to the security of real estate titles, the length of leases, the education of their children, and other things that involve a long look ahead. It is claimed that the sense of the shortness of this life, the possibility of being called at any moment to meet Christ, loosens a man's hold on this world. I do not doubt that it is often so. Anything which will make a man realize vividly that God is alive, and that he stands, or will stand, face to face with him is sure to have that effect. The question is, will this influence endure? With some it does. But I doubt if average human nature can endure the strain of constantly expecting something to happen which in fact never does happen. At first the thought, "Christ may come today," thrills the nerve of action, but as the years of life roll by, the thrill grows weaker. The doctrine is still held, but it is merely a doctrine and not a living verity. The question is, which will do more to make our lives spiritual and to release us from the tyranny of the world, the thought that we may at any moment enter into the presence of the Lord, or the thought that every moment we are in the presence of the Lord?

IV.

THE LAITY AND THE SPIRITUAL LIFE

Spiritual experience was boldly set forward again and again by Rauschenbusch as the one great thing in religion. The gift of the Spirit was to be sought, received, cultivated, and encouraged to grow to ever greater maturity in service to others. This was the ministry of the laity upon which, Rauschenbusch contended, all else depended. The three items included in this section—"The Culture of the Spiritual Life," "The Workers," and "The Welsh Revival and Primitive Christianity"—each is addressed to a different audience and thus provides a different perspective from which to view the role of the laity.

"THE CULTURE OF THE SPIRITUAL LIFE"

Rauschenbusch returned to Rochester in the autumn of 1897 to begin his teaching career at the theological seminary. Apart from the formal ceremony of welcome, he was introduced to the Baptist community by his front-page article in the November, 1897, issue of The Rochester Baptist Monthly. *The subject was "The Culture of the Spiritual Life."*

Life is full of noble aims to strive for. Bodily strength is one of them. A young man in the pride of his youth, with a body clean, chaste, and hardy, is a sight to gladden God and man. We may well rejoice that the spirit of athletics and physical culture is broad. But

95

there is a higher strength than that. We shall never equal the flying leap of the tiger or the tireless trot of the wolf. Most animals are our superiors in physical suppleness. Yet we are their masters. We hold the kingship of the earth by the sway of intellect. Men admire the wrestler and runner, but they reserve their higher homage for the man of thought, the poet, artist, orator, statesman. The culture of the mind is more important than the culture of the body.

But there is a realm superior to body and mind, a greatness that excels even intellectual genius. To do right is greater than to be strong. To be good is worthier than to be clever. The spiritual life is highest and its culture most important of all. It does not matter that there are many who do not recognize or acknowledge this. There are many to whom Tennyson or St. Gaudens are unknown names, while they know every man on their local baseball team and all his points. The fact that the intellectual life is dormant in some does not impugn its superiority; just so the absence of a relish for spiritual things in others does not impugn the superiority of the spiritual life or diminish the value of its culture.

The spirit outlasts the body and outlasts the mind. It shines in an old saint like the gleam of the sword in a wornout scabbard. It gives promise of a day of glorious unfolding like the bud of a flower in which the rosy tints of the corolla is just showing through the green leaves of the calyx. It is the one thing in life that lasts; the sifted grain of all our labor and weariness, the one thing God will ask for.

And this spiritual life needs culture, conscious and careful tending, for it is like a flower in sterile soil and under a hostile climate. Compare the powerful push of our sensuous impulses, with the fragile growth of our Godward aspirations. How alert we are when our selfishness spurs us, and how very feebly we stir when love or pity or unselfish love of right demands our action. Whether we have fallen and have been corrupted by ages of sin, as the Bible says, or whether we are slowly mounting from the purely animal life to the spiritual, as the doctrine of evolution asserts, in either case it remains true that the spiritual life is as yet very feeble in humanity. If it is to grow, it must not be left to the rude conflict with hostile forces of the flesh and the world, but must be consciously fostered.

Perhaps a few simple suggestions as to the culture of the spiritual life may be of service to some one who longs for more spiritual strength and does not know how to gain it.

First, realize often the presence of God. In Jeremy Taylor's "Holy Living"[46] that is the most important of all his counsels, "to practice the presence of God." It is the first article of religious belief that there is a living God. It is the first act of religious life to realize him and come in contact with him. It is a mighty act of faith every time. If this visible world fills your horizon, if you live for its pleasures and riches, bow to its laws, and are swayed by its desires, you are in that measure a child of the world, whatever your creed or your church relations may be. If your thoughts are often of the living God, if his fatherly care is your trust, if his will is your final law, if his communion is your joy, you are living as a child of God, as a possessor of the spiritual and eternal life. Therefore practice the presence of God. Bring him to mind in prayer. Just turn from the world a moment and think of God. Do so especially when you are anxious and worn with care. Turn to him and leave your troubles with him. Many of them will shrink and look foolishly small when his light falls on them. You will find, like the man in the fairy tale, that the devil has been leading you on by making you believe that withered turnips were gold. Turn to God in your moments of joy and gratitude too. Share them with him. Apply the social instinct to the best companion of all, to your Father.

Secondly, seek the fellowship of God's people in past and present. There is a dry atmosphere of unbelief in the world in its conversation, its aims, its literature. It saps our faith. Men live as if there were no God. To counteract that we must associate with those to whom God is a living reality. We can associate with men of God in past ages by reading their thoughts in the Bible or in the books of devotion they have left us. We can associate with people who are distinctively spiritual in our acquaintance and encourage them to talk to us of the deeper experiences of their faith. There is wonderful strength in such fellowship of the saints.

Third, we must constantly correct our purposes in life. Even if

---

46. Jeremy Taylor (1613–67) was an English devotional writer, chaplain to Charles I, and later a bishop in Ireland. *Holy Living* was published in 1650, and *Holy Dying* in 1651.

we have surrendered ourselves to the obedience of God, there will be a sagging downward. We begin by seeking first the kingdom of God, and end by taking the glory for ourselves. Our selfishness and pride steals insidiously into everything we do. We can do the most pious things, the most unselfish actions, and appropriate them all to ourselves and take all the holiness out of them. There are distinctions there too fine for the judgment of others, too fine too for our unaided eye. But when we bring them before God in prayer, we can see how things are. Therefore we need often to place our sins and motives before God for his scrutiny, praying him to cleanse us from our secret sins. Now and then, too, we ought to consider our life as a whole to see if it is not unconsciously deflecting from the straight line of God's will.

Fourth, it is a necessary part of spiritual culture that we put from us the things that hurt or imperil. Christ speaks of cutting off things as dear as a hand or an eye, and everyone who has fought for his spiritual existence will know some application of that principle. "Quench not the Spirit," it is quenched by refusing obedience to its promptings. "Grieve not the Spirit," it is grieved when we hold fast to things which it hates, books that sully, companions that scathe. Plants must be nurtured by securing for them sunshine and rain, but also by ridding them of the weeds and thistles that absorb the nourishment of the soil. The spiritual life too is fostered by removing the obstacles to it. They are different in every life, but not one need remain in doubt as to what they are in his own life. He need only pray about it sincerely and he will know.

But the main thing is to have God; to live in him; to have him live in us; to think his thoughts; to love what he loves and hate what he hates; to realize his presence; to feel his holiness and to be holy because he is holy, to feel his goodness in every blessing of our life and even in its tribulations; to be happy and trustful; to join in the great purposes of God and to be lifted to greatness of vision and faith and hope with him—that is the blessed life. Let us not grieve if it is faint in us as yet. When the young moon is filling its slender crescent, the astronomer can watch little points and rings of light on the surface that is still dark. The sunrise has struck the mountain tops of the moon. Those points and rings will widen and soon the silvery light will rest on it all.

"THE WORKERS"

The influence represented by The Tongue of Fire
*(1856), by the famous Irish Methodist William Arthur, con-
tinues to be evident in Walter Rauschenbusch's call to youth
in the 26 February, 5 March, and 12 March 1898 issues of*
The Baptist Union *of Chicago. The theme is the inaugura-
tion of the era of the Spirit at Pentecost, a democracy of the
Spirit when the gift of the Spirit becomes available to all and
when all who receive it are called, equipped, and empow-
ered by the Spirit to share a common ministry for the advancement of the Kingdom of God.*

I. The Democracy of the Spirit

One of the sublimist chapters in the Bible is that in which Isaiah
tells of the vision which called him to the prophetic ministry. He saw
the Lord sitting on his throne and the Seraphim above him, crying:
"Holy, holy, holy is Jehovah of hosts, the whole earth is filled with
his glory!" But instead of being lifted up by the vision, Isaiah was
smitten down with an overwhelming sense of his own uncleanness
and the uncleanness of his nation. He was cleansed by the painful
touch of holy fire, and then—after that experience—he heard the
voice of the Lord: "Whom shall I send, and who will go for us?"
and was able to reply in the true spirit: "Here am I! Send me!"[47]

There are a number of such scenes narrated in the Bible, moments when the Most High laid his consecrating hands on one of his
chosen ones. These prophets of the Old Testament were a spiritual
aristocracy. They rose among their generation like mountain peaks.
And as mountain summits are flooded with the golden fire of the
coming dawn while the plain still lies in darkness, so these princes
of the spiritual house of God received the baptism of the Spirit alone
among their fellows.

But one of them foretold that the time would come when God
would pour out his Spirit on all flesh, so that sons and daughters, and
servants and handmaidens should prophecy. No longer a few—but

---

47. Is 6:1–8.

all flesh; not only the aged and wise—but the young; not only men of rank and learning—but servants and handmaidens.[48]

With the fulfilment of that prophecy at Pentecost a new era began: the Democracy of the Spirit. The possession of a chosen few has become a possibility for all. We know by experience that he is ready to enter into every lowly heart and become there the Source and Creator of a new and heavenly life. But he is also willing to become a power equipping for service. Such are the gifts of the New Covenant which has lifted up the least to be greater than the greatest that came before. The Spirit who gave Daniel his wisdom, and Isaiah his eloquence, and Jeremiah his tenacity, and Amos his holy indignation, can equip us with power, even you and me, for there is no exception.

But if the possibility of the gift is universal, the obligation it carries with it is universal too. When God gave his Spirit to few, he called few to his service. Now that he offers his Spirit to all, he calls all to his work. It is a holy duty and we shirk it at our peril. If even a single good action, which we knew how to do and which we left undone, is counted as sin, how much more will God so consider a lifetime of service which we knew was asked for and which we refused? I think God will more easily pardon many a hot sin of commission, than that cool, life-long, damning sin of omission.

A life of service is a holy duty. Yes, and a blessed privilege too. How swiftly life spins away! I count myself among the young men, yet half of the allotted three score and ten is gone for me. And sometimes as I listen to the racing of the years, I feel a terrible catch of the heart, not at the coming of death, but at the passing of life. So much to be done, and as yet so little accomplished. I want to work, to serve in the redemption of the world from wrong, to help my Master save humanity. It is a glory, a privilege, and I want much of it. I fear lest my life pass away and I have not slaked my thirst for the service of God. This life can be so full, so noble, so blessed to us, so useful to others. And so often it is empty, vapid, trivial, discontented, useless. Which is the real privilege, to serve or to idle? Which is the real burden, to live for self or to live for the Kingdom of God?

I have answered the first question suggested by my theme: Who

---

48. Jl 2:28–29.

are the workers? The answer is: we all. In this age of the democracy of the Holy Spirit, the call to service is not restricted to a few men, not to the ministry, not even to those who have the gift of speech. In the great field of the Kingdom, here is a duty for all: for those with the gift of speech, and those with the gift of action; for the burning mind and for the gentle cooling hand; for the leader of men and the trainer of little children. All are called; all have the duty; all have the privilege; all may have the equipment. And our young people's movement is one of the chosen agencies of God to realize the prophecy of Joel and to bring in the day of universal service. Look down the future and see the tongue of fire leaping from heart to heart, enlisting in holy ministry all the youth of our land, till all hands are busy in building the spiritual temple of God, and all hearts repeat in unison as the dominant note of their lives: "Thy will be done on earth."

II. Three Directions of Growth

We must grow in holiness of life. Holiness is more than goodness. Eloquence has been defined as thought on fire. Holiness is goodness on fire like the burning bush that Moses saw.[49] It is goodness created by fellowship with God. Am I wrong in my impression, or is it true, that in our busy, bustling Christian life, the quiet, gentle elements of spiritual communion, the devoutness of a secret walk with God, are imperilled and to some extent lost? We do much for God, but we do not rest much in God. I have known some rare souls who breathed forth that devoutness in all their lives, and what a power they exert! They are like a personification of the still, small voice which Elijah heard.[50] I would plead for more spiritual retirement, for more moments when the door of our closet is shut behind us, and the door of our heart too is closed to the world and its exacting cares, and we enter into the secret of his presence. Is there not an element which we could adopt in the quiet Quaker meetings, in which there is no demand for speaking and no sense of failure if all are silent, but which are occasionally stirred like the pool of Be-

---

49. Ex 2:3–4.
50. 1Kgs 19:12.

thesda by a rippling touch of an angel's wing?[51] Can we not learn something from the retreats which the Catholic Church provides for her priests, in which the souls are led merely to meditation and adoration? We believe in the sanctifying power of confession and testimony. Is there not a sanctifying power in silence too?

We must grow, too, in the maturity and roundness of our moral character. Our characters are all more or less uneven and onesided, like a peach that is ripe on one side and hard on the other. In every calling in life and in every social class certain moral qualities are called for and are developed in response to that call. A man in the army may be rough, profane, and even intemperate, and yet have the full respect of his class; but if he be a coward in the face of danger, though he be a saint otherwise, his standing is gone as soon as he is found out. With ministers the reverse may be true; a minister might be physically timid and still be loved and respected but he cannot be profane or drunken and still retain his standing. As a consequence the army develops courage; the ministry develops cleanness of private morals. I might extend the proof by referring to other classes, to women, lawyers, artisans, artists, etc. I might show, too, how different nations have different standards of morals; how one nation makes a high demand in one direction and a low one in another; while another nation will exactly reverse that and despise the first nation accordingly. For instance, Mr. Bryce[52] in his *American Commonwealth* (Vol. II, page 724) expresses the judgment that Americans stand higher than Englishmen or Germans in veracity, temperance, purity, tenderness to children and the weak, and in general kindliness of behavior. But he adds in a footnote that this cannot be said as regards commercial uprightness, in which respect the United States certainly stands on no higher level than England or Germany, and possibly below France and Scandinavia. If the judgment of this fair-minded observer is correct, it would seem that we ought to lay special stress on the moral quality in which we are deficient in order to call out that quality.

Is there not one quality in which we young people of America are notably deficient and which we should study to increase in order

---

51. Jn 5:2–4.
52. James Bryce (1838–1922).

to attain to a rounded Christian character? I refer to the quality of reverence, reverence in holy places and on holy occasions; reverence for the aged, and especially reverence to our parents. In so many respects the young people of our nation stand higher than those of other countries. But it seems to be the unanimous judgment of observers that we American young people are flippant, and wanting in reverent courtesy to the aged and those in authority over us. The commandment "Honor thy father and mother" has not equal weight with some other commandments in the eyes of many. In all seriousness, I would suggest to the leaders of our great movement[53] that this be made one of the watchwords of the young people: more reverence. It is well to save others from drink, to save our cities through the good citizenship movement, but let us also save ourselves from a sin which is subtler in its nature, but which is none the less serious in the sight of God and dangerous to the rounded fulness of our Christian character.

We must grow, also, in the largeness of our views about the work. The thoughts of God are wider than the measure of a man's mind. His redemptive work is broader than we often think. We are inclined to class as work for God the things we do on Sunday and in church; attending meetings, taking part in them, giving for God's work, teaching in Sunday school, etc. But we leave out of sight the work which we do six days in the week and ten hours a day. We class that as secular work and do not consider whether we are serving God in that too. Yet unless that too is service to the Kingdom, we are giving it only the fringes of our time and strength. It must cease to be to us a mere means of earning our livelihood and advancing our station in life. It must become a conscious and voluntary contribution of service toward the Kingdom of God. A friend told me recently of a lawyer in middle life who was converted. About a year afterwards he spoke of how Christ had changed his life. Formerly he regarded his profession as a means to success; now he felt that he was called to see right done. Formerly that man's calling was a secular one; now, if he lives up to it, it is as holy as a minister's. And if all lawyers began to see their calling that way, it would certainly work a marvellous change. Instead of "Woe unto you lawyers," we

---

53. The Baptist Young People's Union of America.

should have to read: "Blessed are ye lawyers, for ye have made a dwelling place on earth for the justice of God."

Let every one of us ask himself the question: In what way does my daily work serve the Kingdom of God? If he cannot find an answer, let him consider if his conception of the Kingdom of God is as wide as the purposes of God would have it. If he cannot answer the question yet, let him consult others. And if after all this he cannot see that his daily work in any sense aids the Kingdom, serves God, and blesses humanity, but if it is merely fit to put bread and cake into his stomach, let him get out of it, for in that line of business he can never obey one of the fundamental principles of Christ's teaching: "Seek ye first the Kingdom of God." He cannot make the Kingdom the prime and central object of his life, of his desires, and of his labor, if the bulk of the energy which he puts forth is totally unconnected with the Kingdom, or perhaps even antagonistic to it.

III. Five Means of Growth

Growth is insured by consecration to Christ and the great purposes of Christ. Emerson said: "Hitch your wagon to a star." A German poet has expressed the same thought: "Man grows with his growing purposes." A man cannot truly live for the great aims of the Kingdom and remain a narrow soul or a shriveled intellect. Nor can a man devote a lifetime to selfish aims and petty ambitions without a decay of his noblest faculties—a truth nowhere expressed more heartrendingly than in Lowell's[54] *Extreme Unction*, where the old and dying man looks back across a life that has not fulfilled the possibilities of youth and has been apostate from his ideal.

> Yes, I who now with angry tears
> Am exiled back to brutish clod,
> Have borne unquenched the fourscore years
> A part of the eternal God:
> And to what end? How yield I back
> The trust for such high uses given?
> Heaven's light hath but revealed a track
> Whereby to crawl away from heaven.

---

54. James Russell Lowell (1819–91).

O glorious Youth, that once wast mine!
O high ideal! all in vain
Ye enter at this ruined shrine
Whence worship ne'er shall rise again;
The bat and owl inhabit here.
The snake nests in the altar-stone.
The sacred vessels moulder near.
The image of the God is gone.

Spiritual growth comes also by prayer and meditation; by dwelling in the ripening sunshine of God; by opening your soul to the Infinite and Eternal; by what Jeremy Taylor calls "the practice of the presence of God"; by fixing your eyes on the earthly figure of our Lord Jesus Christ and drawing strength from his risen presence. You remember the story of the giant Antaeus with whom Hercules wrestled. Hercules threw him again and again, but every time he touched the earth he bounded up with renewed vigor, for he was a son of the earth, and the touch of his mother renewed his strength and increased it. Hercules finally overcame him only by lifting him clear of the earth and strangling him in mid-air. So for us there is a renewing and life-giving touch in contact with Christ, the Source of our life. "I can do all things through him that strengtheneth me."[55]

Another means of growth lies in wisely and constantly drawing on the great storehouses of the past for spiritual sustenance and wisdom. We are all living on the heritage of the past in all departments of our life. If we had not the accumulated results of civilization and the gathered knowledge of the past, but only what we personally have wrought out and thought out, the brightest man among us would be but a mumbling savage. The same thing is true of the religious life. We have a great storehouse of thought and inspiration in the Bible, in the history of the Christian Church, in the biographies of her heroes, in the choice fruitage of her devotional literature. Let our young people strike their roots deep into the past and they grow sturdy, wise, and fit to work.

One means of growth, too, lies in fellowship with like-minded men and women. People sneer at communism. I bless God for every fractional bit of communism we have, and pray for more. Whenever

---

55. Phil 4:13.

we meet in prayer or conference meeting, we live on the principles of spiritual communism, for every man brings forth of his best and puts it at the disposal of all, is pleased if they like it, and in turn takes all he can carry away. And if refreshments are served, the communism extends to the material side of life, and then we have the two aspects in which the ''koinonia,'' the fellowship or commonship of the early Christians, expressed itself: the common meal and the exercise of spiritual gifts for the common edification. Sharing is a great thing, greater and pleasanter than giving. And it is one of the chief means of growth.

And, finally, the last means of growing fit for work is to work. The fibres of the muscles grow hard by use. So does the moral and religious fibre. Serve God and it will become easy to serve him. Lend a hand, and the hand you lent will come back suppler and stronger. If there is any one of my readers who wants to work, but doesn't know what to work at, let me present a rule which I think is quite infallible. Let my readers ask God straightforwardly to show them what he wants them to do, and I think I can promise them that they will stumble over tasks so thick that they will hardly have time to pick them all up.

''THE WELSH REVIVAL AND PRIMITIVE CHRISTIANITY''

In 1904 and 1905 a sweeping ''revival'' of religious interest and life in Wales became the subject of widespread discussion among church people in the United States. Walter Rauschenbusch shared his thoughts on the Welsh revival in The Watchman *of 15 June 1905. He regarded the revival as an example of the resurgence of primitive Christianity, the Christianity of the early church, with its main feature being the prominence of lay leadership. This he regarded as a heartening sign, and he was equally appreciative of the Welsh in having a vehicle in their singing for the expression of profound religious emotion.*

In common with all thoughtful Christians I have been deeply interested in the news of the Welsh Revival. I have no first-hand information about it, but have simply read what has been published in this country and also full reports in local papers from Wales. But I have been struck with the resemblance between the movement in Wales and the life of the primitive church in the first century. These resemblances I have not seen brought out anywhere. Perhaps a brief discussion of that aspect may be helpful.

The revival in Wales is a lay movement. It was not initiated by ministers, nor subsequently led by ministers. Pastors are doing useful work in it, but evidently their leadership has been superceded for the time being by volunteer lay workers, and the people seem to feel that it would be a relapse to the lower conditions before the revival, if the usual preaching of sermons by the ministers and their customary exclusive predominance should begin again. The people themselves have taken control.

And that is a return to primitive Christian life. The first epistle of Paul to the Corinthians gives us the most intimate insight we have into the life and worship of an apostolic church, but it would be hard to find in it anything like the exclusive leadership assumed by us ministers in our Sunday services. Read I Corinthians 14 and see how that resembles the way the meetings are governed in Wales.

All great religious movements have been uprisings of the laity. The great religious movement under the Franciscan and Dominican friars was a lay movement, for the friars mostly were not priests, but plain men who had dedicated themselves to a full Christian life as they understood it. The Reformation in one aspect was the rise of the laity to influence in the church and a breaking of the exclusive control of the priesthood. In the Puritan movement, the Quaker movement, the Methodist revival, it was always a religious uprising of the laity. The common people were drawn into the work of preaching and soul-saving and immense latent forces were immediately set free thereby.

No one will suspect a seminary professor like myself of underestimating the value of the Christian ministry. But I think it is the plain lesson of history that the ministry tends to absorb the functions of testifying and teaching, often against their own wish, and that this process chokes the spiritual powers of the church. Our congregational church polity was originally a protest against that tendency; the prayer meeting even more so.

At the beginning the church itself did the testifying and teaching. Whenever there has been a great revival, the church has resumed much of the functions assumed by the clergy and uttered its spiritual life for itself. That fact is once more demonstrated in the Welsh revival. If we want a similar revival, we must overcome the reserve of the lay members and open the draft under the smouldering fires in their hearts till they blaze up, even if the minister for the time being has to take a back seat.

A second point of similarity is the consciousness of speaking under the impulse of the Holy Spirit. The leaders of the Welsh revival recognize the Spirit as the impelling power in the simplest utterance, and are very jealous of anything that would check or quench the free impulse of the Spirit.

That was also one of the essential marks of the primitive church till the latter half of the second century. Christians did not merely in a vague way believe that the Holy Spirit was in them, but they treated their single utterances as his gift and message. Read I Corinthians 12 and 14 from that point of view. That was not without danger. The passage quoted shows that there was a good deal of disorder in the services. But there was also lots of life! They did not regard these utterances as infallible because they were inspired by the Spirit. When Paul admonished the Thessalonians not to quench the Spirit (in themselves), and not to despise prophesyings (in others), he told them also to scrutinize all things, and after such critical sifting to hold fast whatever was good (I Thess. 5: 19–21). This consciousness of personal inspiration and of an immediate impulse of the Holy Spirit in part died out with the increasing worldliness of the church, and in part it was extinguished by the leaders of the church. In the second half of the second century the Montanist movement made much of prophesying and claimed a higher type of it than even the apostles had had. In opposition to that movement the church leaders discountenanced all present-day prophesying and all claims to personal inspiration, and confined the idea of inspiration to the apostles and their writings. A high doctrine about the inspiration of the apostolic writings contributed to hush down and silence the living inspiration of the church, and to deprive the people of their consciousness of being taught and impelled by the very Spirit of God. It was still believed that the bishops as the successors of the apostles were led in their doctrine by the Spirit. Finally that prerogative was narrowed down to the Pope. He is now the only one in whom that divine gift is supposed to linger.

Doubtless the substitution of written inspiration for living inspiration was "safer," but there certainly was a profound loss in real religious life. For religion is always the living contact between the soul and God. Formerly the church claimed to furnish regeneration by administering baptism. It was a great step toward real religion when men were taught to come to God himself for the regenerating power without any intermediary. Would it not be a similar step toward real religion if we could teach men to trust God himself for spiritual enlightenment also? In all great revivals there has been a quickening of the God-consciousness in the soul and a revival of utterance which was impelled by a power higher than self. There will always be exaggerated claims by individuals in such movements, and counterfeit prophesyings in which human conceit has a larger part than divine light, but the more general the consciousness, the less chance for the conceit of a distinguished few. If we want a revival like that in Wales, we must teach our people to trust to God for a message and for power, and to honor and obey the divine voice within when they hear it.

A third point of similarity is the prevalence of deep emotional life. The "speaking in tongues," of which we have a record in I Corinthians 14, was not a speaking in foreign languages, but an utterance of profound emotions in disjointed words and ejaculations, which were not intelligible to the hearers, except to a few who could translate into rational thought what those persons utter in the language of emotion. Paul discountenanced this form of utterance in public meetings, because others got no profit from it,[56] but he says that he himself practiced it in private. Perhaps what he says in Romans 8: 26–27 about inspired prayers throws light on the profit he derived from it in his prayer-life.

There have been similar manifestations in many revivals of the past, not always to the advantage and credit of revival work. In Wales they are fortunate in having a better vehicle for this profounder emotion of the spiritual life in their singing. We all know what a feature the singing is in the Welsh revival. Now, music is the language of emotion. It expresses emotion. It awakens emotion. The in-

---

56. Rauschenbusch analyzed and discussed the biblical instances of "speaking in tongues" in "Speaking in Tongues—What Was It?" *The Watchman*, 20 Sept. 1897.

tellectual material in our hymns is often the slightest part of them. We have all joined with deep feeling in singing lines that we should regard as shallow and vapid stuff if merely recited. The singing in the Moody and Sankey revivals formerly, and still more in the Welsh revival today, occupies the same place as the "speaking with tongues" in the primitive church. Both are a pent-up emotion. But the singing is the better of the two because all can join. The primitive church probably had only the rudiments of a hymnology, and congregational singing held no such place as with us.

If we want a great revival, we must secure a medium for the emotions. The non-rational crooning would not do today. Unfortunately we have no such stock of hymns memorized as the Welsh have. Both Welshmen and Germans would probably say that American congregations don't know how to sing. If the Welsh revival will spread only as far as song will carry it, we shall be punished for our cultured laziness in not cultivating the singing in our churches as we ought to have done.

In these three points, then, the Welsh revival, like all great spiritual awakenings, has been an unconscious return to primitive Christianity. It is a movement of the people and has evoked their latent powers, thereby making the ministers less prominent and predominant. It has awakened the true religious consciousness of immediate relation to God, including a sense of spiritual enlightenment and compulsion in the utterance of faith. It has stirred the deeper emotions which transcend the ordinary methods of expression and has found a medium for them in inspired singing.

The true way for us will be, I think, not to copy slavishly the phrases and manners of the Welsh revival, but to recognize the great avenues of approach to God which are rediscovered in every revival and to take our people along these paths to meet God.

On the other hand, I have seen nothing in what has been reported about the Welsh revival to prove that it deserves in any special sense the name of "an ethical revival." That people stop swearing and drinking, that their conscience grows tender about restoring thefts and repaying debts, that they grow graver and more kindly—surely this has been the mark of every revival that was Christian at all. But that means merely that people are living better lives within the conditions previously existing. It does not change their conditions. It leaves the mine worker to toil for his bare wage.

It leaves the social classes in existence. It leaves the children to go to hard work as soon as the law permits. The exploitation of the people by rent and the wage-system will go on. Much has been made of a case where a mine boss asked a Christian miner to pray with him, as if that brought in an era of Christian equality. The loneliness of that case and the inadequacy of it show best how little the social stratification of Wales is affected. It may be that by its indirect effects, in the course of a generation, the revival may put a greater sense of worth, a stouter capacity of resistance, into the Welsh working classes, and so help them in their contest for their economic rights. But for the present the revival has merely driven home those moral teachings which were part of Christian public sentiment previous to the revival.

I think it would also be wise of the leaders in Wales to be on the lookout against an aftermath of perfectionism and of vagaries about the second coming, especially when the revival declines.

V.

MODES OF GOD'S SELF-DISCLOSURE

Two formal addresses and a Thanksgiving Day sermon provided Rauschenbusch with occasions to deal systematically with grounds for religious faith. How do people apprehend God and how does God disclose himself to them? Rauschenbusch had no single answer, and the answers he does give are phrased in differing ways according to the audience he is addressing. The first is biblical in orientation as might be expected of an address published in the University of Chicago's quarterly journal, The Biblical World. *The second, addressed to an audience with diverse religious interests, is more philosophical in approach. The stress is on innate instincts and a reconsidered argument from design. The third is not a scholarly discussion. It is a simple sermon which seeks to discern God's intention from the signs of the times, the lessons to be derived from actual historical events. In this sense, the sermon is illustrative of a long tradition in which God is believed to make known his will to the natural reason through his providential activity in history.*

"REVELATION: AN EXPOSITION"[57]

In this highly personalized discussion, Rauschenbusch moves from "general revelation" through "special revelations" to the prophets to a "culminating" and continuing revelation in Christ.

---

57. *The Biblical World* (Aug. 1897), 94–103.

The majestic and resonant exordium of the epistle to the Hebrews, "God, having of old time spoken unto the fathers in the prophets by divers portions and in divers manners, hath at the end of these days spoken unto us in his Son, whom he appointed heir of all things, through whom also he made the worlds,"[58] makes three great affirmations concerning divine revelation: first, that God has spoken to humanity; second, that this revelation in times past was fragmentary in its contents and manifold in its forms; and, third, that at the end of that epoch this historical process of revelation culminated in one who by his peculiar relations to God guarantees a perfection to which the broken and incomplete revelations of former days did not attain. We may best reach the writer's thought by considering each of these affirmations separately.

I. *The fact of revelation.*—There is a large sense in which all the universe is a revelation of God. The starry heavens tell of his infinitude; the cataracts are his voices; the sunbeams his messengers of love; the immutable laws of nature are solemn preachers of his justice; and even the eggshell thrown from the robin's nest testifies to his wisdom. Since the creation of the world, as Paul says, the invisible character of God, his everlasting power and godhead, has been discerned through his visible works. The rain that has moistened the fields, the food that has filled our hearts with gladness, have been witnesses to God. In the rulings of history he has manifested himself to men, "that they should seek him, if haply they might feel after him and find him; though indeed he is not far from each one of us; for in him we live and move and have our being."[59] The darkening of the mind and the deterioration of the passions are also mentioned in Scripture as a revelation, but a revelation of the wrath of God against all ungodliness and unrighteousness.

This general revelation of God in the structure and order of the material universe and in the moral processes of history has not been useless. The mere fact that all over the world men have had a religion of some kind, that they have groped through the darkness for a God whom they felt to be near, is a serious and pathetic fact. It is as if the race had nearly lost one of its senses or else not yet fully ac-

---

58. Heb 1:1–2.
59. Acts 17:27–28.

quired it, and was haunted by strange shadows, calling and beckon-
ing with chills of terror or thrills of blessedness, telling of a
marvelous world lying close to us, and yet almost out of reach.

Into this blindness of ours God has reached down and has revealed himself to men by a special historic process aiming toward
the establishment of the kingdom of God on earth. His revelation has
not consisted in the impartation of theoretic knowledge or of a system of truth, but in external acts and inward impressions which gave
the recipient an immediate certitude of the presence and power of the
Eternal, and some understanding of the character and purposes of
God. In many cases it was probably not so much the communication
of a new idea as rather a quickening of hopes and thoughts that had
been attained in other ways. They had been lying in the mind as sur-
mises and longings; God touched them and they became divine truth
and certainty. In other cases there was a penetration of the soul by a
divine light and faith, in which it reached out toward the future or up
toward God and saw things unseen before and knew them to be
truth. Thus did God reveal himself to men and give them knowledge
of himself; not the cold knowledge of speculation, but the burning,
overpowering knowledge of religious experience. And those who received it declared it to others with that instinct of fellowship and
communication which God has attached to the knowledge of the
truth as a spiritual instinct of propagation. Of those who heard, some
received it on the authority of the faith of those who told them, and
passed it on as moral law and traditional religion; but some were led
by these declarations to reexperience it, and perhaps to add to it by
some view from a still loftier peak of the prophetic Pisgah.[60] Thus a
kind of capital of truth has been accumulated slowly; sometimes it
has been partly lost again and blurred, then rediscovered and added
to.

We can distinguish, then, between two meanings of the word
"revelation;" the act of revelation, in which God manifests his life
and something of his character and purposes to a prophetic soul, and
second the accumulating results of such processes of revelation. The
latter are so important, so helpful to the reexperiencing of actual revelation, that this revealed sum of truth is also called revelation. So
especially the Bible, in which we have the record of the revelations

---

60. Num 23:14.

of God to holy men; their visions of the character of God; their inspired interpretations of history; and their outlooks into God's purposes for the future. But it must not be forgotten that the Bible is only in a secondary sense "revelation," it is the result of revelation and in turn an aid to revelation, but revelation in the closest sense of the word is always an act of the living God, a personal contact between his spirit and the spirit of a man, whereby the latter is quickened and enlightened.

We have probably made a mistake in regarding the act of revelation as a very rare act which happened to few men in the world's history; and by thus setting it apart as something rare we have helped to keep it rare. We have put it out of the reach of our own hopes and aspirations. It is true that there have been but few minds in the history of redemption who have been able by the revelations they received to lift the religious life of mankind perceptibly higher; but in the intervals between Abraham and Moses and Isaiah and Paul and Luther and Wesley and Carey there has been a great multitude of souls that have really received divine light from God. There were many prophets in Israel, recognized as such by their contemporaries, of whom we have only a bare trace, and doubtless more who have been quite forgotten. The influence of the great religious leaders alone would have been insufficient to keep the true knowledge of God alive in the damp and chilling atmosphere of the world if there had not been a great throng of souls whose inward life was nourished by God, not indirectly, but directly, by personal revelation. Shall we not go farther? Shall we not say that none recognizes Jesus as the Christ of God by mere hearsay or instruction; that flesh and blood never reveal him; that a revelation from God is necessary for it? Paul describes his own experience by that very word: "When it pleased God to reveal his Son in me."[61] Is it too daring to say that all really spiritual light is kindled by God himself? Paul was always anxious to cut off all human boasting by throwing us back absolutely on the grace of God for our salvation. Are we then not dependent on God for the light of God, which is one aspect of salvation?

God has spoken, not a few times, but as often as he could find a soul capable of hearing his voice; those who heard him told what they heard and thereby encouraged others to listen to the divine

---

61. Gal 1:15–16.

voice and give heed to it, thus passing on the heavenly fire on earth; also something of what they heard and experienced was added to the capital of religious thought which was handed down from generation to generation, and accepted as itself a revelation; and again some part of this knowledge was under God's providence put into writing and collected in our Bible, which we hold in reverence as a precious gift of God, as the great treasure house of revelations and religious experiences.

2. *The incompleteness of the former revelations.*—"God, having of old time spoken unto the fathers in the prophets by divers portions and in divers manners." The revelations of God in the prophets were πολυμερωσ και πολυτροπωσ, in many parts, and by many methods. They were fragmentary in their contents and varied in their manner.

The entire epistle to the Hebrews is a commentary on this expression of the incompleteness and imperfection of the revelations before Christ. There was a sense of that incompleteness not only in those who had seen perfection in Jesus, but even in those who lived before Christ. The humility expressed in the tone of expectancy, the longing for better things, for a richer outpouring of the Spirit, for a more abundant prevalence of the word of God, is splendid evidence of the real inspiration of the prophets of Israel. They had seen the vision of God and they knew there was more to come. They had sought to express what they had heard, and they knew that they were only spelling out the message laboriously and imperfectly. What a daring criticism of the religious life of his own day there is in that splendid prophecy of Jeremiah: "Behold the days come, saith Jehovah, that I will make a new covenant with the house of Israel and with the house of Judah; . . . I will put my law in their inward parts, and in their hearts will I write it; . . . and they shall no more teach every man his neighbor and every man his brother, saying, 'Know the Lord;' for they shall all know me, from the least of them to the greatest of them" (Jer. 31: 31–34). He describes there the laborious inculcation of fragments of religious knowledge, which, after all is done, still remain an external possession. The revelations of the Old Testament were fragmentary, not only to those who heard them from the prophets, but also to the prophets themselves. Their constant phrase is "the word of Jehovah came;" and then follows some brief message, and the voice ceases again. The more we search the Old Testament, the more we recognize that it is composed of fragmentary revelations put together. They came to the prophets in relation to some definite event with which they had to deal and concerning which they were assured of God's view and his will. That makes the Bible so definite, so tangible; it never floats off into religious theorizing; it builds no systems; it keeps its feet on the ground; it is intensely practical and historical. But its parts are also by that very characteristic incomplete and fragmentary. There is unity in its diversity; remarkable unity, if one considers the number of men who contributed to it and the period of time covered by their activity; but it is a unity of conviction rather than of thought; a oneness of source rather than of workmanship.

These revelations were also divers in their manner. They had to be, for those who received them were not equally receptive to the word of Jehovah. The pure in heart see God; and the purer their hearts, the clearer their vision. There is a stronger ring in some of the prophetic books than in others, a loftier view of God and of Israel's destiny in Isaiah than in Daniel.

But let us turn from the task of pointing out the limitations of the ancient revelations to the more congenial task of exalting the perfect revelation in the Son of God. The writer of Hebrews does not contrast the old with the new in order to depreciate Moses or the Aaronic priesthood, but in order to bring his hearers to a realization of the wealth of privilege in Christ. Many prophets and righteous men desired to see the things which we see and saw them not; and to hear the things which we hear and heard them not. The least in the kingdom of God is greater than the greatest before. But it humbles us to think how poorly we use our privileges. Think of what the great prophet of the exile would have seen and sung about the Servant of Jehovah if he had read the gospels, when he so described the sufferings of the Lamb of God seen dimly and far off.

3. *The culminating revelation in the Son of God.*—"God, having of old time spoken unto the fathers in the prophets by divers portions and in divers manners, hath at the end of these days spoken unto us in his Son, whom he appointed heir of all things, through whom also he made the worlds." The revelation in the Son came "at the end of these days;" it inaugurated a new epoch. It brought revelation to its culmination. Let us consider in what ways that is true.

First, the teachings of Jesus gather together the fragmentary perceptions of truth that preceded him and unite them in a grander whole, completing them where they lacked. He said of himself that he fulfilled the law, and he referred, not to his perfect obedience to the law, but to his completion and perfection of its precepts. He forbade not only murder, but also hate; not only adultery, but also lust; not only false swearing, but all swearing; not only unfair revenge, but also moderate retaliation.[62] He also perfected the previous revelations of God's will in the moral law by breaking away the deposit of ritualism and legalism that had encrusted it, and by laying bare the simple and eternal principles on which the laws rested; so, for instance, in regard to the law of the Sabbath.[63] His teaching also gathered up and brought to their culmination the previous revelations concerning the character of God. The God of Jesus Christ is as just and holy a God as the God of the Old Testament, but there is no vengeful terror in him, nothing to frighten into superstitious efforts to placate his inexplicable anger. The God of Jesus Christ is surely as loving a God as any that the most aspiring soul in olden times dared to believe in. What a marvelous cry it was that Moses heard among the crags of Sinai: "Jehovah, Jehovah, a God full of compassion and gracious, slow in anger and plenteous in mercy and truth; keeping mercy for thousands, forgiving iniquity, transgression, and sin."[64] But that and all the sweetest strains from the prophet of the exile are but as leaves of the plant, the flower whereof is the word that Christ has taught us: "Our Father in heaven." Even if we should consider nothing but the teachings of Jesus, the penetrating moral law, the views of life and the characterizations of God contained in his utterances, we should understand the deepening awe with which our Scripture passage turns from the fragmentary revelations of the past to the culminating revelation in Christ.

But the revelation of God in Christ is greater than the teachings of Jesus. Christ did not receive revelations; he was the revelation. The prophets received communications from God, and knew that they received them. To them it was the distinguishing mark of a true prophet that he received communications from Jehovah, while the

---

62. Mt 5:17–48.
63. Mk 2:27.
64. Ex 34:6–7.

false prophet spoke his own mind and fancies. Is Christ ever represented as receiving such communications? We remember several instances of a voice speaking to him from heaven, but even that is said
to have been more for the sake of confirming others in their faith
than of informing Christ. He drew from the depths of his own nature
and consciousness. His words were but expressions of himself. His
vision of God and the kingdom was not the ideal of a few hours of
exaltation, but was one with his life. The prophets distinguished between the revelation received and themselves. Christ does not. He
was one with his message. The Word of the Lord came to Jeremiah;
Christ was the Word of God. Λογσδ σὰρξ ἐλέυετο. The Word had
become human nature. The prophet could say at times: "He that
hears my words hears the words of God;" Christ could say at all
times: "He that sees me sees the Father."[65]

There is no higher revelation conceivable for us than this, that
a human life should become by nature and experience the complete
and clear expression of the will of God for men. There is nothing so
intelligible, nothing so universal as a human life.

> Where truth in closest words shall fail,
> Yet truth embodied in a tale
> Shall enter in at lowly doors.
> And so the Word had breath, and wrought
> With human hands the creed of creeds
> In loveliness of perfect deeds,
> More strong than all poetic thought.
> Which he may read that binds the sheaf,
> Or builds the house, or digs the grave,
> And those wild eyes that watch the wave
> In roarings round the coral reef.

The same poet has said: "Our little systems have their day,
They have their day and cease to be."[66] True enough; there are few
things that have so short a day as a system, and there is nothing that
lives so long as human nature. Moreover, if the revelation of God

---

65. Jn 14:9.
66. Alfred Tennyson, *In Memoriam*, XXXVI and Prologue.

was to be for babes, it must not be by a system, for a system demands a trained mind. If salvation were for those who understood a system of truth, salvation would belong to refined brain cells. If Christianity were, as some say, a religion of a book, it would be a religion of the favored classes. But it is not a religion of a book, but of a man, and a man is both the most unfathomable and the simplest object of human knowledge. It requires only a childlike heart, a limpid soul, to understand the revelation of God in Christ. "Blessed are the poor in spirit, for theirs is the kingdom."[67]

Christ excels the former revelations because he imposes no outward law. In him the daring hope of Jeremiah, to which we have referred, was fulfilled. The moral law is more incisive, more sweeping, more categorical than ever since Christ, and yet there is no legalism in him. He writes his law on our hearts. When we have come to know Christ the law is no longer a barrier without, against which we chafe, but an impulse within, which lifts us and in which we glory. The office of the rabbi who imposes truth from without is abolished. No man need say to his brother: "Sit thou down here and I will teach thee to know God." Now we take our brother by the hand and bring him to meet Jesus, and there he learns to know God by the secret intuitions of love and the molding touches of fellowship.

We have been told that when Dr. H. C. Mabie[68] was at Ongole, in India, he met a number of educated Hindus. They asked him the old question of Lessing's Nathan: "How can we know that Christianity is better than other religions, when all claim to be the best?"[69] He answered with the wisdom of a scribe who has been made a disciple to the kingdom of heaven. He did not talk about the proof by miracles and prophecies. He did not reason about the superiority of the Bible to other sacred books. He told them that Christianity was the only religion that offered to prove itself today to anyone who was willing to make a trial of it. Is not that the simplicity of truth? Other

---

67. Mt 5:5.

68. H. G. Mabie was general secretary (1890–1905) of the American Baptist Foreign Mission Society.

69. G. E. Lessing, *Nathan the Wise* (New York, 1890).

methods of proof always address themselves to the disputatious instinct in man. They demand reasoning ability and historical investigation. Those who have not that ability, or have so much of it that they grow weary of it, will succumb and accept on authority, and thus they surrender the freedom of the Christian man and enter into bondage once more. Others accept the challenge and reason; in the worst cases they lose themselves in negations that can never save; in the best cases they secure a degree of probability which always leaves room for haunting doubts. True Christianity puts a man face to face with Christ and bids him see what he can find there. And if he does not fall down at once and hail him with Thomas: "My Lord and my God,"[70] but simply tells us of a man surpassing strong and tender, we bid him keep on looking. And slowly the blurring mist of worldliness will drop from his eyes, and his soul will become capable of measuring the stature of Jesus among men, and in may be that he will echo the experience of a great disciple: "The Word became flesh and dwelt among us; and we gazed upon his glory, and found it to be a glory as of the only begotten from the Father, full of grace and truth."[71]

Thus to meet God in Christ does, it is true, presuppose the image of Christ, the record of his personality, as laid down in the gospels, or preserved in the heart of the church. Yet the spiritual impress of Christ does not depend on historical investigation, nor is it affected by historical criticism. It is the most solid and indubitable thing in the New Testament and about all Christianity. It is not the record of a dead person, whose deeds belong to history, but the manifestation of a living personality whose present life quickens the image and record of his past life, his spirit bearing witness in our hearts to the truth and grace of his earthly deeds and words.

It is a glorious truth that God has spoken to man; and every fragmentary utterance of prophetic souls, however much it may be colored by their personality and their times, should be precious in our sight if it bears the royal stamp of the divine touch and mission. But we glory in the culminating revelation of God in his Son; in the

---

70. Jn 20:28.
71. Jn 1:14.

simplicity and strength of his words; in the obedience and unbroken fellowship of his life, which made him the unsullied mirror for the effulgence of God's glory, the unblurred image of God's substance. He draws us; he masters us; he transforms us. In him we see God; in him we possess God; in him God possesses us.

"RELIGION: THE LIFE OF GOD IN THE SOUL OF MAN"[72]

The title of this essay was a favorite phrase of both Leighton Williams and Walter Rauschenbusch. The source from which it was derived was indicated by Williams in a circular letter to members of the Brotherhood of the Kingdom, "Our Duty to Cultivate the Spiritual Life," which begins with the statement: " 'The life of God in the soul of man,' wrote Henry Scougal over two hundred years ago, and thus would we also define true religion. Such is its essential character. All else—rites, ceremonies, creeds, and doctrines— are but the symbols and fruitage of it." Williams was refer- ring to Scougal's little book of the same title, The Life of God in the Soul of Man, *first published in 1677, and re- printed in many subsequent editions as a devotional classic.*

George Whitefield dated his conversion from the mo- ment he read Scougal's treatise. "I know the place. I may be superstitious but whenever I go to Oxford I cannot help run- ning to the spot where Jesus Christ first revealed himself to me and gave me a new birth." Susanna Wesley referred to it as "an excellent good book" when she commended it to her sons, Charles and John, and they too came under its spell. John Wesley reprinted it as one of the volumes of the Christian Library he assembled as suitable reading for mem- bers of his Religious Society.[73]

---

72. "Religion: The Life of God in the Soul of Man" was prepared for the New York State Conference on Religion, 20 Nov. 1900. The conference was con- vened by Leighton Williams. As Rauschenbusch notes, he was the only person asked to speak on "personal religion."

73. For Scougal's life and influence, see the Introduction to *The Life of God in the Soul of Man*, ed. Winthrop S. Hudson (Philadelphia, 1948), 12–16. Wil- liams's Circular Letter is in the Brotherhood of the Kingdom papers, American Baptist Historical Society, Rochester, N.Y.

Our theme is the personal religious life. The formula in which the theme is stated seems to call for a discussion of the deeper, philosophical aspects of the religious life. And the character of this audience both permits and demands a frank consideration of those questions concerning the religious life which weigh most heavily on the faith and thought of our own day.

The scope of our programme seems to me very significant. Doubtless those who drafted it meant to include within its circumference the most pressing religious interests of our time. But of the seven sessions this is the only one devoted to those questions that used to be the chief and almost exclusive topics of discussion in religious assemblies. All the other sessions deal with social salvation. It is another indication how profoundly the best minds of our generation are absorbed in the salvation of the common life of our nation and race. This is especially true of the religious leaders. And justly; for the farther we get beyond theories and really try to transform the social life, the more do we realize that the social problem is in the last resort a religious problem. If we are to climb over the watershed to the promised land, we need more honesty, a stiffer sense of justice, and more devotion to the public weal; we need more genuine moral heroism in the leaders of the attack, and a nobler ethical *Weltanschauung* and a livelier warmth of brotherhood in all. But whence is this increment of moral forces to come? Men do not become more moral by saying: "Go to, let us be more moral." Instinctively men turn to religion as the generator of moral force. Even the criticisms about the churches express that consciousness. No one whips a dead horse for not pulling the cart out of the mud. So we are to-day inquiring for a religious ideal large enough to include social as well as individual salvation, and for ways and means of making the latent forces of religion operative in public life.

But with this new and dominant interest in our thought the personal religious life has been somewhat overshadowed. With many, I fear, the religious habits and the intercourse with God have waned as the social interest grew. There is less personal appeal in sermons. Revivals have declined, not only because people are less susceptible, but because preachers have lost conviction. With others there is, perhaps, no loss in religious life, but their thought is deflected toward the new problems. This is in a measure my own case. When I began on the task your committee assigned to me, I found that while

I had been busy clearing the forest on the hill, the bottom-lands where my fathers raised abundant harvests had been lying fallow, and plowed hard like new-ground.

We must not neglect the personal religious life and the tremendous problems of individual destiny. There are two objects of salvation, the race and the individual. If we insist that saving the individual does not necessarily save the common life, let us remember that saving the common life does not save the individual either.

Goethe says: "Mankind is always progressing, but man is always the same." Every new soul presents a new problem of redemption. The souls filled with the life of God are the fountains from which all life-giving impulses flow out into the life of society. But a human soul is of eternal value for its own sake, and not merely for the effect it may have on society, just as our children are dear to us apart from any work they may do.

My thoughts have turned mainly to the strength and value of the religious instinct in man, and to the objective justification for that instinct in Nature; on the instinct that seeks God and on the God that satisfies the instinct.

I need not remind you of the strength of the religious instinct in the past of our race. It has been one of the driving-wheels of history. And the fact that men still go to church, in spite of the crudeness of much of the thought furnished to them, in spite of the monotony of prayer meetings, the meagerness of worship, and the wealth of attractions elsewhere, goes far to justify the assertion that man is incurably religious. Even the faintest reenforcement of the spiritual life is seized with pathetic eagerness; and when some really strong religious soul gives utterance to original experiences, the general heart-hunger is unmistakable. Even when men leave the churches they still seek religion. Find out what really moves them in the philosophy or poetry or sociology which now is their highest good, and you will find it is something at least bordering on religion. Many men are reluctant to talk of religion, not because they are indifferent to it, but because it takes hold of them so strongly that they are afraid of violating the urbanity required in our social intercourse.

The happiness felt when the religious instinct is satisfied proves and brings to our consciousness the intensity of the desire. In its supreme moments religious joy is as complete and all-possessing as the passion of love. And when it has become the permanent possession of a soul it sheds a quiet radiance over all things and gives a relish to life which is comparable, so far as I have experienced, only to the joy of doing good work, which comes at times to the intellectual and artistic worker. Other pleasures charm most in the pursuit and leave us sated soon after we have taken possession. We are always goaded on by unsatisfied desires. Love, money, and honor are fairest in the distance. It does not seem to be so with religious joy; the less so, the more purely religious it is. It does contain the desire for new and larger experiences, but not because the old have palled. There is no unrest in it. The expression "I have found peace" is, of course, a stock expression, but it does express what is the overwhelming personal feeling in first entering into religious joy. It seems to be the universal testimony of those who have made personal test of it that the joy of religious satisfaction is beyond anything else that life holds.

And as the happiness in gaining it is great, so is the pain in losing it. Doubtless many have shared the feeling of Romanes[74] in the closing words of his *Candid Examination of Theism*: "Forasmuch as I am far from being able to agree with those who affirm that the twilight doctrine of the 'new faith' is a desirable substitute for the waning splendor of 'the old,' I am not ashamed to confess that with this virtual negation of God the universe to me has lost its soul of loveliness; and although from henceforth the precept to 'work while it is day' will doubtless but gain an intensified force from the terribly intensified meaning of the words that 'the night cometh when no man can work,' yet when at times I think, as think at times I must, of the appalling contrast between the hallowed glory of that creed which once was mine, and the lonely mystery of existence as now I find it—at such times I shall ever feel it impossible to avoid the sharpest pang of which my nature is susceptible."

We have probably all felt the poignant sense of want and loss when our religious life declined and we remembered our first love from which we had fallen; or when the gray mist of doubt crept between us and the face of our God, and we feared that our faith might be lost to us forever. At such times the words of the Psalmist did not

---

74. George John Romanes, *A Candid Examination of Theism* (Boston, 1878).

seem overdrawn: "As the hart panteth after the water brooks, so panteth my soul after thee, O God! My soul thirsteth for God, for the living God."[75]

For those who have never had a vigorous and conscious religious life, there is no contrast between past and present to make them realize their loss. Hard work, good health, aesthetic pleasure, and moral enthusiasm do give a large measure of satisfaction. Yet many non-religious men probably have their hours of wistful homesickness, especially when they watch others who have what they lack. This surmise receives confirmation from the facts observable in nations or classes that have lost their religious faith. Life there seems to lose its savor; *Weltschmerz* [76] increases; there is disgust for mankind, proneness to despair, and increasing frequency in the act of suicide and the contemplation of it. The resoluteness of life is sapped.

Other powerful cravings leave a sense of degradation after they are satisfied. In our really religious moments, on the other hand, we are conscious that now our life is at its best and this impression holds good in the retrospect. There is a sinister resentment in us against those who minister to our debasing instincts. But for those who have called forth or nourished the religious life in us we cherish a peculiarly tender gratitude and devotion. If they were previously bound to us by friendship or family affection, we were conscious of the infusion of a hallowing influence that ennobled the old relation.

In the time of his religious chaos Robertson[77] of Brighton still held fast to one conviction: "It must be right to do right." That is the fixed point of modern philosophical discussions too—the sacrosanctity of the moral impulse. Whatever threaten that stands impunged. Now, however much we may lament the feebleness of the influence of religion on the social morality of our time and even doubt if there is any influence at all, we are not in doubt of its influence on our personal life. We remember that our religious dedication was synonymous with a dedication to righteousness. It raised and established our moral ideals and re-enforced our will. And any decline of our spiritual life, if it lasted long enough, brought in its train a cor-

---

75. Ps 42:1–2.
76. Weariness of life.
77. Frederic W. Robertson (1816–53).

responding decline in our moral vigor. Our ideals paled; our love for men grew chill; and selfishness and calculation took possession.

The common judgment of mankind indorses that experience. In spite of all disappointments men still believe in religion as a constitutive element in moral character and as a cause for trust. Among larger minds we observe a profound concern lest religion be lost to us. They know that we have no scientific basis for our ethics, and that if our morality should slip down from its religious basis to a merely utilitarian basis, it would be a landslide that would bury many of the most precious possessions of civilization.

So deep-seated and influential is the religious life in man. And does all this rest on an illusion? There is no other instance in organic life of a strong and general instinct pointing at nothing. There must be some objective reality to correspond to these inward motions of the soul. Can our highest joys and our deepest woes, the aspirations in us which we and others judge to be the noblest, the influence which strengthens our moral life and lifts it beyond self-seeking— can all this be adequately explained as the flickering recrudescence of aboriginal ancestor-worship?

But however deeply we may feel this instinct in ourselves and in the past and present of the race, it is not easy for the modern man to believe in the objective reality that would justify the religious life. You remember, perhaps, that exquisite passage in the diary of George Fox: "And I went into the valley of Beavor, and as I went I preached repentance to the people. And one morning, sitting by the fire, a great cloud came over me and a temptation beset me. And it was said: 'All things come by Nature.' And the elements and the stars came over me. And as I sat still and let it alone, a living God hope arose in me, and a true voice, which said: 'There is a living God who made all things.' And immediately the cloud and the temptation vanished and Life rose over all, and my heart was glad and I praised the Living God."[78] That is our condition. Even when we have preached repentance to the people, the elements and the stars come over us. And it is a vaster universe and a more relentless march of the constellations than the great Quaker knew. When the world was small, and when good and evil came without apparent cause, it

---

78. [George] *Fox's Journal*, rev. ed. J. L. Nickalls (Cambridge, 1952), 25.

was easy to believe in a tribal God, dwelling on yonder hilltop and blessing harvest and flock of those who paid him tribute. But the world has grown so large. Even the greatness of our globe would have appalled the savage, but this great sphere has come to look tiny to us. We look dizzily into the abyss of the Milky Way and our imagination flutters along the endless systems of systems like a butterfly over the combers of the Atlantic. The immensities themselves take up the cry of the ancient scoffers: "Where is now thy God?" As Vivien buried Merlin [79] in a charm "of woven paces and of waving hands," so Science seemed for a time to imprison our spirits with a rhythmic enchantment of fateful law and an inexorable web of cause and effect.

But slowly we are winning our way out. Our God has grown immeasurably larger, but our thoughts are growing great to meet Him. That universal law of causality which pressed us down, will yet lift us up. Why should there be any causing at all? In what common unity are cause and effect imbedded that they can so act on each other? And why is the law of causality universal? Whence this uniformity of law and this unity of the world? If custom had not blunted our feeling for it, we should realize that as one of the most marvelous facts in the universe. It is one of the closest approaches that science had made to the idea of God.

The old argument from design has collapsed before the doctrine of natural selection. Instead of a great Artificer sitting down to contrive and create the tiger's teeth for its prey and the squirrel's teeth for its nut, we have an incessant struggle for existence, weeding out all forms whose teeth were not well adapted for their food. The evidences of a designing mind seemed gone from nature. The grammar of the universe was without any particles expressing purpose, and only rich in causal constructions.

But further thought has shown us that the element of design has only receded and is waiting for us at the beginning of all things. Nature is a cosmos. But is it by chance that all physical causes have united in producing a general order of nature? If the tiger's and squirrel's teeth were not especially contrived for them, yet the primitive molecules and cells must have been so constituted that they fi-

---

79. Alfred Tennyson, "Merlin and Vivien," *Idylls of the King*.

nally resulted in the tiger and squirrel. Now, the persistent force which finally produced these results has run through an infinite network of physical relations. How, then, was it guided along the precise channel in which it would produce just these variations? The teleological argument has only been shifted to the immensities of nature as a whole; and though it is much harder to comprehend there, it seems to me to have tremendous power when it is comprehended.

The world is not a shifting mass of phenomena. It has its unity and coherence by resting in an ultimate Reality, which is the cause of all causation, and in that Cause there are direction, purpose, and immeasurable intelligence.

But is this Cause mind? Is it a personality in any sense like mine? In observing the fly on my window, the distance between my eyes is a sufficient base to subtend the parallax; for the moon the radius of the earth is ample; but when astronomers first tried to measure the parallax of a fixed star, the whole diameter of the earth's orbit seemed to give no result. Can our little human nature give any clew or measurement to determine the nature of the great Reality that upholds the universe? We are sensible of the audacity of the idea. Yet the human soul is the only basis we have for the parallax of God. And we remember that the attempt to measure the distance and movements of fixed stars, which failed at first, succeeded at last, and that to-day we determine even the substances composing them by the identity of their lines in the spectrum with the lines of earthly substances. Our only direct knowledge of causation is derived from our own activity when we are causes. Our senses report only time and space relations; our mind adds the conception of causality from its own consciousness. The only energy we really know is will energy. It is true, our imagination refuses to conceive an infinite personality, but on the other hand neither can this great Reality, which is a unity in the midst of change and a source of intelligent activity, be conceived by us except as in some way like our own minds.

But suppose that God is Mind, yet a new question arises to lacerate us. The old teleology directed attention to the evidences of the wisdom and goodness of God, and they were many. The doctrine of the struggle for existence has revealed the accompanying awful waste of life, the contrivances for inflicting pain, the general reign of fear in the sentient world, the precision with which violations of physical laws are punished as compared with the hesitating and uncertain retribution for moral transgressions. And so the question arises: is God moral at all, or is he extramoral? Is he an intelligence so transcending ours that what we reverence as our moral nature is of no more value to him and no more finds a counterpart in him than the functioning of our heart-valves or the transmission of our sense impressions to our brain? They tell us that our moral instinct has been bred and developed because it bound men together, and thus made those who had much of it fitter to survive than those who had little; that it is merely a protective development like the quills of a porcupine or the gregarious instinct of herbivorous animals. Balfour[80] says: "Kant compared the moral law to the starry Heavens and found them both sublime. It would, on the naturalistic hypothesis, be more appropriate to compare it to the protective blotches on the beetle's back and to find them both ingenious." If that is the origin of ethics, it derives no sanctity from the character of God. Utility for the race is its only sanction, and if the individual cares to sell out the welfare of the race for his private profit, the basis of ethics would be still further contracted from social utility to private utility.

The argument for the moral nature of God derives a powerful re-enforcement from our religious instinct. That cannot be shown to serve such a purpose for the survival of the race. If that instinct points to an objective reality corresponding in any sense to the cravings of the religious nature, then God's character must justify our adoration and love. The imperative of our moral nature and the ideals of our religious nature, taken together, are the ground of our faith that there are justice and goodness, and even love, in the Eternal. It has become a commonplace that God is love. Men take the love of God for granted as something self-evident, in order to combat the belief in the sterner retributive justice of God. But in the face of Nature as we know her, it is a tremendous affirmation to assert that God is not only just, but that he is love. For myself I need all the assurance contained in the self-consciousness of Jesus Christ to brace my faith. That popular conviction of the love of God and of the consequent goodness of the world shows how much humanity owes to Jesus. Without the historical contribution he has made to human thought and feeling, I do not see how, in the present state of scien-

---

80. Robert Gordon Balfour (1550–after 1625).

tific knowledge, that conviction could stand up against the total impression left by the natural sciences. And let any man consider what it would mean for his personal *Weltanschauung* if he were plunged into the arctic night of a world without love, and what it would mean for the social life of men if it were finally and generally understood that the moral impulse and the moral law have no other reason for their existence than utility and might be set aside if they failed to be useful, much as a man grows his beard in winter to keep warm and shaves it in summer to keep cool.

As the mist of our modern *Götterdämmerung*[81] is slowly rising, we see that the mountains of God still lift their heads on high. The worst is probably over; the future will see our religious faith strengthened and not impaired. We realize sadly that there is still a lack of confidence in our thoughts. It was when Tennyson faced these facts of the waste of life in nature that he cried:

> I falter where I firmly trod,
> And falling with my weight of cares
> Upon the great world's altar-stairs
> That slope through darkness up to God,
>
> I stretch lame hands of faith, and grope,
> And gather dust and chaff, and call
> To what I feel is Lord of all,
> And faintly trust the larger hope.[82]

And when we thus reel under the first shock of new doubts; when our own spiritual life is low and the inward oracle in our soul is almost dumb, we do well to realize how much we owe to social religion. The accumulated deposit of the spiritual life of the past, the inspired utterances of stronger souls, the institutional edifice and the history of the church, and the living contact with devoted souls reassure us and carry us safely through the vulnerable period of our spiritual metamorphosis.

And so we contemplate with profound awe this trembling compass-needle pointing out into eternity, the religious life in our souls.

---

81. Death of the gods.
82. Alfred Tennyson, "The Larger Hope," *In Memoriam*.

It contradicts our worldly common sense, crowds back our most imperious passions, thwarts our ambitions, humbles us in the dust, sets us unending tasks and rewards us with a crown of thorns. And yet we love it, reverence it, desire it; and no dearer gift could come to us than absolute certitude that all it tells us is truth.

It gives unity to our intellectual comprehension of the universe. It lends grandeur to the scattered and fragmentary purposes of our life by gathering them in a single all-comprehending aim—the Kingdom of God, which is the hallowing of his name and the doing of his will. It guarantees that our aspirations are not idle dreams nor our sacrifices fruitless toil, but that they are of God and through God and unto God, and shall have their fulfillment and reward. When the vast world numbs us with a sense of helplessness and ignorance, prayer restores our sense of worth by the consciousness of kinship with the Lord of all. Even when our strength is broken, when our hopes are frustrated and nature seems to cast us aside, a brother to the shriveling worm, we can trust and wait. By holding up the will of the Holy One as the norm of action and character, religion spurs us on to endless growth. It deepens the seriousness of our temptations by the thought that we sin not only against ourselves and our neighbors, but against the Spirit of Love and Goodness: "Against thee, thee only have I sinned."[83] And in turn it makes our victories more glories by the knowledge that in us his saving will has once more found completer expression.

The wind that blows, the birds that sing, and the crimson flood of life and nourishment that throbs in our pulses are all part of the great cosmic life. The force of God is in the movements of matter and the thrills of organic life. But they all act as they must.

In the ocean of the universe floats the little bark of human personality, part of it all, and yet an entity in itself. It knows; it wills; it is conscious of itself over against the world, and even over against God. More and more clearly the thoughts of God are mirrored by the reflecting intellect of man, illuminated by God's own mind, the light of God in the soul of man.

But to the human personality comes a faint and far call, sweeter than the rhythm of the spheres, the voice of the Father of spirits call-

---

83. Ps 51:4.

ing to his child. Our souls give answer by eternal longing and home-sickness. The husks of necessity, which we share with the beasts, drop from our hands, and we long for the bread of freedom and peace in the eternal habitations of our Father. And with that conscious turning to God, we leave slavery and enter sonship. We have realized religion. We live; yet no longer we; it is now the life of God in the soul of man.

"THE PRESENT AND THE FUTURE"[84]

On Thanksgiving day, 24 November 1898, Walter Rauschenbusch preached a sermon on "The Present and the Future" which, in closing, gave attention to the successful conclusion of the Spanish-American War. The interest in the sermon is the statement: "God thinks in acts. He speaks in events. He has made clear his will by the irresistable force of events." This is what, in the Revolutionary era, was called "natural religion." Earlier, in 1675, William Penn had referred to it as "general religion" to distinguish it from church religion.[85]

The concept was first fashioned in the 1640's by members of the Independent wing of the English Puritans who were seeking a basis for social order in a badly divided and warring nation. Their fundamental postulate was a distinction between God's two great kingdoms, the realm of nature (sometimes called the realm of God's providential government) and the realm of grace. In the first, God rules "every natural man" by the light of nature "to a civil outward good and end." In the second, God rules every Christian by his special revelation in Christ to an inward and spiritual end. Whereas the religion of grace is available only through the gift of faith, in "natural" or "general" religion the meaning of God's providential activity may be apprehended by everyone through the "natural reason." God, for example, makes clear what he requires of people and nations in their

---

84. "The Present and the Future," *Rochester Post-Express*, 25 Nov. 1898. In Rauschenbusch Scrapbook, Colgate Rochester Divinity School, Rochester, N.Y.

85. William Penn, *England's Present Interest*, reprinted in W.S. Hudson, ed., *Nationalism and Religion in America*, 140–41.

civil relationships through historical events. Blessings are meted out for their encouragement, and punishments are administered as evidence of his displeasure and thus serve as a summons to repentance and amendment of life.[86]

The concept of God's great kingdom was appropriated and utilized by many in England and America, including Roger Williams and William Penn as well as John Locke, and formed an integral part of American spirituality. It was given most luminous expression by Abraham Lincoln in his Second Inaugural Address. While William R. Williams was representative of those who kept the distinction between the two realms of God's activity relatively clear, the distinction tended to become increasingly blurred in the nineteenth century. The blurring was unconsciously present in the thought of Walter Rauschenbusch but on occasion, as in the present and some other sermons, he was able to state the lessons which, it seemed to him, God was seeking to reveal with pristine clarity through historical events.

This Thanksgiving Day stands out from many that have preceded it. . . . So far as we now can judge there has been no year since the Civil War that has been so momentous. It is probable that even to the more accurate judgment viewing it from a longer perspective, say to the historian of a hundred years hence, this year 1898 will be one of the mountain ranges in the geography of times, a great watershed from which the rivers begin to flow toward new and distant oceans. Such great eras may come to nations through great calamities or through great victories, amid weeping and rejoicing. Ours has been a year of victory . . . .

Again and again in the course of the War we have had the awed feeling that these events were not to be explained by human bravery and skill alone, but that an unseen hand was guiding and a higher will controlling. . . . There is in the heart of our people a deep sense of destiny, of a mission laid upon us by the Ruler of history. As a nation we feel the call of God just as truly as a young man chosen by

86. *The Ancient Bounds* (1645), printed in A. S. P. Woodhouse, ed., *Puritanism and Liberty* (London, 1939), 247–48. See also George L. Hunt, ed., *Calvinism and the Public Order* (Philadelphia, 1965), 115–16.

God for a great work. That consciousness came to us when we were about God's business. Ruskin[87] says that every duty that we neglect obscures some truth we ought to have known. But the reverse too is true. Every duty performed reveals truths we need to know . . . .

God thinks in acts. He speaks in events. He has made clear his will by the irrepressible force of events. We shall have to accept and obey. We may well view this new task with bated breath. If we rejoice at all in our new imperial domain, we rejoice with fear and trembling. But it is not of our seeking. We did not enter this war with the intention of annexing Puerto Rico and the Philippines. We did not even want Hawaii that begged to come in. And yet by a higher guidance than our own we now stand charged with duties the scope of which we hardly surmise. . . . The American people has but one superior. It is for us to obey. We may look back regretfully at the long period of history during which we lived in the safe isolation of our ocean walls, enjoying the undisputed supremacy of the Western hemisphere, busy in conquering our domain and building up a great nation. God calls us forward. The growth of our youth at home is ended. The life-work of manhood lies before us. The pillar of fire has lifted and moved. We must break camp and follow, though none of us have traveled the trackless future to tell us whither we are going. As a nation we must learn to walk by faith and not by sight. And if we have needed the help and light of God in the past, how much more will we need him in the future.

---

87. John Ruskin, 1819–1900.

VI.

A PUBLIC MINISTRY

What Rauschenbusch called his "public work" is generally considered to have begun in 1907 with the publication of Christianity and the Social Crisis, *which made him a national figure and was followed by addresses he was called upon to give throughout the country and by the publication of his other books. His public ministry really began, however, in 1904 with a call for a "new evangelism," a summons he issued in that year in an article in the nationally circulated and widely read interdenominational weekly* The Independent.

Even prior to the 1886 meeting in Washington of the Evangelical Alliance, there was a growing awareness among many that the old evangelism was no longer as effective as it had been. This was particularly evident in the multiplying cities where the huddled masses of the unskilled working class remained largely untouched. Also, in spite of the success of the Student Volunteer Movement in enlisting youth for foreign mission service, it seemed equally true in the first years of the new century that many of the best minds among college and university students were not being

---

88. "The New Evangelism," *The Independent* LVI (Jan.–June 1904) 1054–59.

reached by traditional evangelistic appeals. Walter Rauschenbusch's article was an analysis of the lines along which a new evangelism, to be effective, must be shaped.

The present interest in the "New Evangelism" is almost wholly an expression of dissatisfaction with the old evangelism, the waning power of which is generally conceded. There is as yet no new evangelism before us which we might adopt; we are only wishing that there might be. Our conceptions of what it ought to be are vague, as all ideas about the future necessarily are, but that is no cause for belittling the current inquiry. It is one of the most important topics that could be discussed. I shall attempt in the following discussion to apply the same method of historical investigation to this great and threatening fact of contemporary religious history which would be applied to a fact of equal importance in a past era.

The gospel of Christ is one and immutable; the comprehension and expression of it in history has been of infinite variety. No individual, no church, no age of history has ever comprehended the full scope of God's saving purposes in Jesus Christ. Neither has any proclaimed it without foreign admixtures that clogged and thwarted it. A fuller and purer expression of the evangel has therefore always been possible and desirable. It is on the face of it unlikely that the gospel as commonly understood by us is the whole gospel or a completely pure gospel. It is a lack of Christian humility to assume that our gospel and *the Gospel* are identical.

Every individual reconstructs his comprehension of life and duty, of the world and God, as he passes from one period of development to the next. If he fails to do so, his religion will lose its grasp and control. In the same way humanity must reconstruct its moral and religious synthesis whenever it passes from one era to another. When all other departments of life and thought are silently changing it is impossible for religion to remain unaffected. The gospel, to have power over an age, must be the highest expression of the moral and religious truths held by that age. If it lags behind and presents outgrown conceptions of life and duty, it is no longer in the full sense the gospel. Christianity itself lifts the minds of men to demand a better expression of Christianity. If the official wardens of the gospel from selfish motives or from conservative veneration for old statements refuse to let the Spirit of Christ flow into the larger vessels of thought and feeling which God himself has prepared for it, they are warned by finding men turn from their message as sapless and powerless. The most familiar instance is that of the revival of learning and the repudiation of medieval religion and theology in the fifteenth and sixteenth centuries.

We are to-day passing through an historical transition as thorough and important as any in history. The last 125 years have swept us through profound changes in every direction. World-wide commerce and the imperialistic policy of the Christian nations have made the problems of international and inter-racial relations urgent. The church responded by a new movement of world-wide missions, but it has failed hitherto to Christianize international politics. The monarchical system, so intimately connected with ancient religion, has crumbled and democracy has taken its place; but the church has not broadened its ethical teaching to any great extent to meet the new duties of the citizen-kings. It still confines its ethics to the *personal* and *family* life. In industry and commerce there has been a vast increase in the production of wealth and a shifting in its distribution, but the church has furnished no adequate principles either for the distribution or the consumption of wealth. We are emerging from the era of individualism. The principle of co-ordination, co-operation and solidarity is being applied in ever widening areas and is gaining remarkable hold on the spirits of men. The church is applying that principle in its organization, but its message is still chiefly on the basis of individualism.

It is not strange if the message of the church has failed to keep pace with a movement so rapid. But neither is it strange if humanity, amid the pressure of such new problems, fails to be stirred and guided by statements of truth that were adequate to obsolete conditions. The church is in the position of a mother talking to her son of seventeen, as if he were still twelve. What she says is good and loving, but it is not what the boy with his new passions and problems needs.

The present paralysis of the churches affects all Western Christendom and only a cause co-terminous with modern civilization will explain it. Communities are affected in just the degree in which they are affected by the progress of civilization—the backward countries and rural communities least, the industrial cities most. State churches and free churches alike feel the drag. It is not because the religious spirit has failed. It runs surprisingly strong, but it runs largely outside of the churches. Neither is the trouble due to lack of piety in the ministry, for, on the whole, we are as good as our fathers. We are told that the gospel has always met with indifference and hostility. But is this to-day a persecution for righteousness' sake, so that Jesus would call us blessed for enduring it, or is it a case where the salt is trodden under foot of men, because it has lost its saltness? The worst explanation is that which shrugs its shoulders and regards the present alienation of the people from the church as a mysterious dispensation of Providence against which we are helpless. Effects do not happen without causes, and God's reign is a reign of law. In short, no small or local or passing cause will explain so large a fact as the present condition of the church.

Now, apply this to evangelism. Evangelism is only the cutting edge of the church, and it is driven by the weight back of it. The evangelizing power of the church depends on its moral prestige and spiritual authority. Every evangelist banks on the accumulated moral capital of the Church Universal.

There are two kinds of evangelization. The one proclaims new truth, as Jesus did to his nation, or Paul to the Gentiles, or as a missionary does to the heathen. The other summons men to live and act according to the truth which the church has previously instilled into their minds and which they have long accepted as true. The latter is, on the whole, the kind which we have to do. To be effective, evangelism must appeal to motives which powerfully seize men, and it must hold up a moral standard so high above their actual lives that it will smite them with conviction of sin. If the motives urged seem untrue or remote, or if the standard of life to which they are summoned is practically that on which they are living, the evangelistic call will have little power. The two questions which every Christian worker should investigate for himself are these: Are the traditional motives still effective? And is the moral standard held up by the church such as to induce repentance?

The motives urged at any time will vary with the preacher and the audience, and there will always be a large measure of truth and power even in the most defective preaching that touches human nature at all. Yet there is a change in emphasis from age to age. Within our own memory the fear of hell and the desire for bliss in heaven

have strangely weakened, even with men who have no doubt of the
reality of hell and heaven. On the other hand, the insistence on present holiness and Christian living has strengthened. Good men give
less thought to their personal salvation than our fathers, but their
sympathy for the sorrows of others is more poignant. Past Christianity has developed in us a love for our fellows and a sense of solidarity so strong that they demand to be considered in every religious
appeal. On the other hand, we cannot conceal from ourselves that
the old "scheme of salvation" seems mechanical and remote, and its
effectiveness as a motive depends largely on the past teaching of it,
which is stored in our minds. The sense of great coming changes,
begotten by a better knowledge of the plastic possibilities of mankind, is strong upon us. We have a new hope for humanity such as
has long existed only where the millennial hope was a vital thing.

Even so brief an enumeration must make us feel that some motives are dropping away, because they were narrow and incom-
pletely Christian, and larger and more truly Christ-like motives are
offering themselves. It should be the scientific effort of every Christian worker to observe what motives are to-day really effective with
the young and thoughtful minds who represent the present and future. The fact that some evangelists who are determined in repudiating anything that savors of "modern thought" are so effective in
urging the old motives does not invalidate what we have said. In
every large city there are many men who belong to the old time and
are untouched as yet by the new. They respond joyfully to the ideas
in which their Christian life was nurtured and in which their holiest
memories are enshrined. But there are other men who come once
and then stay away, because they hear nothing to which they can respond. And these men are not counted. Moreover, the strong personality of the evangelist may count for more than anything he says.

What about the moral standard held up by the church in its
teaching and in its collective life? Can she summon men to repentance by it?

The moral teaching of the church in the past has dealt with private and family life. It has boldly condemned drunkenness, sexual
impurity, profanity; it has fostered gentleness and pity, and it has
been largely successful in this teaching. It has also drawn the line
against Sabbath breaking, dancing, card-playing and theater-going,

but it has not been successful in maintaining that line. In general, the community has risen toward the level of the church in private and domestic virtue, and the church has drifted toward the level of the respectable community in regard to amusements. As a result of both movements the gap has lessened. The morality of the church is not much more than what prudence, respectability and good breeding also demand. Nor is the morality of church members generally distinguished by the glow of spiritual fervor. There is less family worship and prayerful life than with our fathers. But with this moral outfit can the church authoritatively say to the world, "Repent and become like me?"

When we pass from private and domestic life to political and business life the matter is worse. About the most pressing questions arising there the church as a body is dumb. It has nothing to say about the justice of holding land idle in crowded cities, of appropriating the unearned increment in land values, of paying wages fixed by the hunger of the laborers and taking the surplus of their output as "profits," or of cornering the market in the necessaries of life. It feels restless about some glaring evils like child-labor, but only moderately so. Individuals in the church are intelligent and active, but the church both as an organized body and as a corporate spiritual force, is inert. The moral guide of humanity is silent where authoritative speech is to-day most needed. Where it does speak, it is often on the wrong side. When we consider the ideas prevalent in the churches, their personnel, and their sources of income, has the church a message of repentance and an evangel for this modern world?

One important and growing class in our population is largely alienated from the church—namely, the industrial wage-workers. The alienation is most complete where the industrial development under the capitalistic system has most completely run its course. In our country that alienation has begun within the last generation, during which this class has become a class, and the process is not yet complete. This constitutes the spiritual barrier to evangelistic efforts as soon as they go beyond the young people of the families already in the churches. Our evangelistic call strikes an invisible wall and comes back in hollow echoes. It is an untrue and cruel charge to say that the church workers have not done their best to reach the people.

The efforts of the churches in the great cities for the last generation have perhaps never been paralleled. And yet they are futile. This is one of the most stunning and heart-rending facts in all our life.

The church has passed under the spiritual domination of the commercial and professional classes. I do not mean that they alone compose its membership; but they furnish its chief support, do its work, and their ethics and views of life determine the thought of the church more than we realize. This is not due to any wrongful attempt to make the church subservient, but rather to the fact that they are the dominant classes in all industrial nations, in literature and politics, as well as in the church. Now the stratification of society is becoming more definite in our country, and the people are growing more conscious of it. The industrial conflicts make them realize how their interests diverge from those of the commercial class. As that consciousness increases, it becomes harder for the two classes to meet in the expression of Christian faith and love—in prayer meetings, for instance. When the Christian business man is presented as a model Christian, working people are coming to look with suspicion on these samples of our Christianity. I am not justifying that, but simply stating the fact. They disapprove of the Christianity of the churches, not because it is too good, but because it is not good enough. The working people are now developing the principle and practice of solidarity, which promises to be one of the most potent ethical forces of the future, and which is essentially more Christian than the covetousness and selfishness which we regard as the indispensable basis of commerce. If this is a correct diagnosis of our condition, is it strange that the church is unable to evangelize a class alienated from it by divergent class interest and class morality?

Let us sum up. The powerlessness of the old evangelism is only the most striking and painful demonstration of the general state of the churches. Its cause is not local nor temporary. It does not lie in lack of hard work or of prayer or of keen anxiety. It lies in the fact that modern life has gone through immense changes and the church has not kept pace with it in developing the latent moral and spiritual resources of the gospel which are needed by the new life. It has most slighted that part of the gospel which our times most need. It lacks an ethical imperative which can induce repentance. In private life its standard differs little from respectability. In commerce and industry, where the unsolved and painful problems lie, it has no clear message, and often claims to be under no obligation to have one. In the state churches the state has dominated; in the free churches the capitalist class dominates. Both influences are worldly—in favor of things as they are and against the ideals which animate the common people. The people are becoming daily more sensitive to the class cleavage of society. The church suffers under the general resentment against the class with which it is largely identified. To this must be added the fact that the spirit of free inquiry engendered by modern science neutralizes the dogmatic authority with which the church has been accustomed to speak.

The new evangelism which shall overcome these barriers and again exert the full power of the gospel cannot be made to order nor devised by a single man. It will be the slow product of the fearless thought of many honest men. It will have to retain all that was true and good in the old synthesis, but advance the human conception of salvation one stage closer to the divine conception. It will have to present a conception of God, of life, of duty, of destiny, to which the best religious life of our age will bow. It will have to give an adequate definition of how a Christian man should live under modern conditions, and then summon men to live so.

A compelling evangel for the working class will be wrought out only by men who love that class, share its life, understand the ideals for which it is groping, penetrate those ideals with the religious spirit of Christianity, and then proclaim a message in which the working people will find their highest self. They will never be reached by a middle class gospel preached down at them with the consciousness of superiority.

If we personally are to have a share in working out the new evangel, we shall have to be open to two influences and allow them to form a vital union in our personalities. We must open our minds to the Spirit of Jesus in its primitive, uncorrupted and still unexhausted power. That Spirit is the fountain of youth for the church. As a human organization it grows old and decrepit like every other human organism. But again and again it has been rejuvenated by a new baptism in that Spirit. We must also keep our vision clear to the life of our own time. Our age is as sublime as any in the past. It has a right to its own appropriation and understanding of the gospel. By the decay of the old, God himself is forcing us on to seek the new and higher.

This attempt at a diagnosis of our ills is not offered in a spirit of condemnation, but of personal repentance and heart-searching. We all bear our share of guilt. I have full faith in the future of the Christian church. A new season of power will come when we have put our sin from us. Our bitter need will drive us to repentance. The prophetic Spirit will awaken among us. The tongue of fire will descend on twentieth century men and give them great faith, joy and boldness, and then we shall hear the new evangel, and it will be the Old Gospel.

"CHRISTIANITY AND THE SOCIAL CRISIS"

Of Christianity and the Social Crisis *(1907), Rauschenbusch said that he wrote it with "fear and trembling." "I expected that there would be a good deal of fear and resentment." When it was published he left for a year's study in Germany. When he returned he found that it had generated great and favorable interest among many. When he reached New York City he was asked to address "a group of about 500 distinguished people at the Hotel Astor." "This," he commented, "was my first experience in that kind of thing," but it was not to be his last. A new career of "public work" opened before him.* [89]

Much of the book was prologue, a long historical study of the social aspects of religion from the Hebrew prophets, through the teachings of Jesus, the shifting character of the early church, and the institutionalized ecclesiasticism of the intervening centuries between then and the present. It is only late in the book that he turns specifically to "The Present Crisis," "The Stake of the Church in the Social Movement," and "What to Do." Portions of two of these chapters are reprinted, the one describing the crisis, the other detailing what can be done.

---

89. *Rochester Democrat and Chronicle*, 25 Jan. 1913, reprinted in *Rochester Theological Seminary Bulletin* (Nov. 1918), 52–53.

The Present Crisis[90]

The continents are strewn with the ruins of dead nations and civilizations. History laughs at the optimistic illusion that "nothing can stand in the way of human progress." It would be safer to assert that progress is always for a time only and then succumbs to the inevitable decay. One by one the ancient peoples rose to wealth and civilization, extended their sway as far as geographical conditions would permit, and then began to decay within and to crumble away without, until the mausoleums of their kings were the haunt of jackals, and the descendants of their conquering warriors were abject peasants slaving for some alien lord. What guarantee have we, then, that our modern civilization with its pomp will not be "one with Nineveh and Tyre"?[91]

The most important question which humanity ought to address to its historical scholars is this: "Why did these others die, and what can we do to escape their fate?" For death is not an inevitable and welcome necessity for a nation as it is for an individual. Its strength and bloom could be indefinitely prolonged if the people were wise and just enough to avert the causes of decay. There is no inherent cause why a great group of nations, such as that which is now united in Western civilization, should not live on in perpetual youth, overcoming by a series of rejuvenations every social evil as it arises, and using every attainment as a stepping-stone to a still higher culture of individual and social life. It has never yet been done. Can it be done in a civilization in which Christianity is the salt of the earth, the social preservative?

Of all the other dead civilizations, we have only scattered relics and fragmentary information, as of some fossil creature of a past geological era. We can only guess at their fate. But the rise and fall of one happened in the full light of day, and we have historical material enough to watch every step of the process. That was the Graeco-Roman civilization which clustered about the Mediterranean Sea.

---

90. *Christianity and the Social Crisis* (New York, 1907), 279–86.
91. From Rudyard Kipling's "Recessional."

Its golden age, which immediately preceded its rapid decline, had a striking resemblance to our own time. In both cases there was a swift increase in wealth. The Empire policed the seas and built roads. The safety of commerce and the ease of travel and transportation did for the Empire what steam transportation did for the nineteenth century. The mass of slaves, secured by the wars of conquest and organized for production in the factories and on the great estates, furnished that increase in cheap productive force which the invention of steam machinery and the division and organization of labor furnished to the modern world. No new civilization was created by these improved conditions. But the forces latent in existing civilization were stimulated and set free, and their application resulted in a rapid efflorescence of the economic and intellectual life. Just as the nations about the Seven Seas are drawing together today and are sharing their spiritual possessions in a common civilization, so the Empire broke down the barriers of the nations about the Mediterranean, gathered them in a certain unity of life, and poured their capacities and thoughts into a common fund. The result was a breakdown of the old faiths and a wonderful fertilization of intellectual life.

Wealth—to use a homely illustration—is to a nation what manure is to a farm. If the farmer spreads it evenly over the soil, it will enrich the whole. If he should leave it in heaps, the land will be impoverished and under the rich heaps the vegetation would be killed.

The new wealth created in the Roman Empire was not justly distributed, but fell a prey to a minority who were in a position to seize it. A new money aristocracy arose which financed the commerical undertakings and shouldered the old aristocratic families aside, just as the feudal aristocracies were superceded in consequence of the modern industrial revolution. A few gained immense wealth, while below them was a mass of slaves and free proletarians. The independent middle class disappeared. The cities grew abnormally at the expense of the country and its sturdy population. Great fortunes were made and yet there was constant distress and frequent hard times. The poor had no rights in the means of production, so they used the political power still remaining to them to secure state grants of land, money, grain, and pleasures. There was widespread reluctance to marry and to rear children. Education became common, and yet culture declined. There were plenty of universities, great libraries, well-paid professors, and yet a growing coarseness of taste and a decline in creative artistic and literary ability. If the yellow newspaper could have been printed, it would have "filled a long-felt want." The social conditions involved a maladjustment of political power. A strong centralized government was necessary to keep the provinces quiet while Rome taxed them and the bureaucracy grew rich on them. Government was not based broadly on the just consent of the governed, but on the swords of the praetorian guard. The old republican forms were long maintained, but Rome verged more and more toward despotic autocracy.

In a hundred ways the second century of our era seemed to be the splendid culmination of all the past. The Empire seemed imperishable in the glory of almost a thousand years of power. To prophesy its fall would have seemed like predicting the failure of civilization and humanity. The reverses which began with the death of Marcus Aurelius in A.D. 180 seemed mere temporary misfortunes. Yet they were the beginning of the end.

The German and Celtic tribes had long swirled and eddied about the northern boundary of the Empire, like the ocean about the dikes of Holland. The little Rome of Marius, a hundred years before Christ, had successfully beaten back the Cimbrians and Teutons. For two centuries the strong arm of the legions had dammed the flood behind the Rhine and Danube. Rome was so much superior in numbers, in wealth, in the science of war and all the resources of civilization, that it might have continued to hold them in check and to turn their forward movements in other directions. But the decay at the center now weakened the capacity for resistance at the borders. The farmers who had made the legions of the Republic invincible had been ruined by the competition of slave labor, crowded out by land monopoly, and sucked into the ragged proletariat of the cities. The armies had to be recruited from the conquered provinces and finally from barbarian mercenaries. The moral enthusiasm of a citizen soldiery fighting for their homes was gone. The impoverished and overtaxed provinces were unable to respond to additional financial needs. Slowly the barbarians filtered into the northern provinces by mass immigration. The civilized population did not have vitality enough to assimilate the foreign immigrants. Slowly, by gradual stages, hardly fast enough for men to realize what was going on, the ancient civilization retreated, and the flood of barbarians covered the provinces, with only some islands of culture rising above the yellow flood.

And how will it be with us? Will that vaster civilization which began in Europe and is now spreading along the shores of all the oceans, as Rome grew from Italy outward around the great inland sea, run through the same stages? If the time of our weakness comes, the barbarians will not be wanting to take possession. Where the carcass is, the vultures will gather.

Nations do not die by wealth, but by injustice. The forward impulse comes through some great historical opportunity which stimulates the production of wealth, breaks up the caked and rigid order of the past, sets free the energies of new classes, calls creative leaders to the front, quickens the intellectual life, intensifies the sense of duty and the ideal of devotion to the common weal, and awakens in the strong individuals the large ambition of patriotic service. Progress slackens when a single class appropriates the social results of the common labor, fortifies its evil rights by unfair laws, throttles the masses by political centralization and suppression, and consumes in luxury what it has taken in covetousness. Then there is a gradual loss of productive energy, an increasing bitterness and distrust, a waning sense of duty and devotion to country, a paralysis of the moral springs of noble action. Men no longer love the commonwealth, because it does not stand for the common wealth. Force has to supply the cohesive power which love fails to furnish. Exploitation creates poverty, and poverty is followed by physical degeneration. Education, art, wealth, and culture may continue to advance and may even ripen to their mellowest perfection when the worm of death is already at the heart of the nation. Internal convulsions or external catastrophes will finally reveal the state of decay.

It is always a process extending through generations or even centuries. It is possible that with the closely knit nations of the present era the resistive vitality is greater than in former ages, and it will take much longer for them to break up. The mobility of modern intellectual life will make it harder for the stagnation of mind and the crystallization of institutions to make headway. But unless the causes of social wrong are removed, it will be a slow process of strangulation and asphyxiation.

In the last resort the only hope is in the moral forces which can be summoned to the rescue. If there are statesmen, prophets, and apostles who set truth and justice above selfish advancement; if their call finds a response in the great body of the people; if a new tide of religious faith and moral enthusiasm creates new standards of duty and a new capacity of self-sacrifice—then the intrenchments of vested wrong will melt away; the stifled energy of the people will leap forward; the atrophied members of the social body will be filled with a fresh flow of blood; and a regenerate nation will look with the eyes of youth across the fields of the future.

The cry of "Crisis! crisis!" has become a weariness. Every age and every year are critical and fraught with destiny. Yet in the widest survey of history, Western civilization is now at a decisive point in its development.

Will some Gibbon[92] of Mongol race sit by the shore of the Pacific in the year A.D. 3000 and write on the "Decline and Fall of the Christian Empire"? If so, he will probably describe the nineteenth and twentieth centuries as the golden age when outwardly life flourished as never before but when that decay, which resulted in the gradual collapse of the twenty-first and twenty-second centuries, was already far advanced.

Or will the twentieth century mark for the future historian the real adolescence of humanity, the great emancipation from barbarism and from the paralysis of injustice, and the beginning of a progress in the intellectual, social, and moral life of mankind to which all past history had no parallel?

It will depend almost wholly on the moral forces which the Christian nations can bring to the fighting line against wrong, and the fighting energy of those moral forces will again depend on the degree to which they are inspired by religious faith and enthusiasm. It is either a revival of social religion or the deluge.

What to Do[93]

> *In this final chapter, the focus shifts from statesmen, prophets, apostles, and religious faith and enthusiasm, to the task of harnessing the power of a rising, upward-moving*

---

92. The reference is to the English historian Edward Gibbon and his *History of the Decline and Fall of the Roman Empire*.

93. *Christianity and the Social Crisis*, 400–422.

*working class which, if it does not turn to tyranny and des-
potism, will determine the future. But the closing word is
optimistic. What must be shall be. And one may rejoice in
sharing in the apostolate of the great day of the Lord for
which the ages have been waiting.*

The ideal of a fraternal organization of society is so splendid
that it is to-day enlisting the choicest young minds of the intellectual
classes under its banner. Idealists everywhere are surrendering to it,
especially those who are under the power of the ethical spirit of
Christianity. The influence which these idealists exert in reënforcing
the movement toward solidarity is beyond computation. They im-
pregnate the popular mind with faith and enthusiasm. They furnish
the watch-words and the intellectual backing of historical and scientific information. They supply devoted leaders and give a lofty
sanction to the movement by their presence in it. They diminish the
resistance of the upper classes among whom they spread their ideas.

But we must not blink at the fact that the idealists alone have
never carried through any great social change. In vain they dash their
fair ideas against the solid granite of human selfishness. The possessing classes are strong by mere possession long-continued. They
control nearly all property. The law is on their side, for they have
made it. They control the machinery of government and can use
force under the form of law. Their self-interest makes them almost
impervious to moral truth if it calls in question the sources from
which they draw their income. In the past they have laughed at the
idealists if they seemed harmless, or have suppressed them if they
became troublesome.

We Americans have a splendid moral optimism. We believe
that "truth is mighty and must prevail." "Truth crushed to earth
shall rise again." "The blood of the martyrs is the seed of the
Church." In the words of the great Anabaptist Balthaser Hübmaier,
who attested his faith by martyrdom, "Truth is immortal; and
though for a long time she be imprisoned, scourged, crowned with
thorns, crucified and buried, she will yet rise victorious on the third
day and will reign and triumph." That is a glorious faith. But the
three days may be three centuries, and the murdered truth may never
rise again in the nation that crucified it, but may come to victory in

some other race and on another continent. The Peasants' Rising in 1525 in Germany embodied the social ideals of the common people; the Anabaptist movement, which began simultaneously, expressed their religious aspirations; both were essentially noble and just; both have been most amply justified by the later course of history; yet both were quenched in streams of blood and have had to wait till our own day for their resurrection in new form.

Truth is mighty. But for a definite historical victory a given truth must depend on the class which makes that truth its own and fights for it. If that class is sufficiently numerous, compact, intelligent, organized, and conscious of what it wants, it may drive a breach through the intrenchments of those opposed to it and carry the cause to victory. If there is no such army to fight its cause, the truth will drive individuals to a comparatively fruitless martyrdom and will continue to hover over humanity as a disembodied ideal. There were a number of reformatory movements before 1500 which looked fully as promising and powerful as did the movement led by Luther in its early years; but the fortified authority of the papacy and clergy succeeded in frustrating them, and they ebbed away again. The Lutheran and Calvinistic Reformation succeeded because they enlisted classes which were sufficiently strong politically and economically to defend the cause of Reformed religion. It was only when concrete material interests entered into a working alliance with Truth that enough force was rallied to break down the frowning walls of error. On the other hand, the classes within which Anabaptism gained lodgement lacked that concrete power, and so the Anabaptist movement, which promised for a short time to be the real Reformation of Germany, just as it came to be the real Reformation of England in the Commonwealth, died a useless and despised death. In the French Revolution the ideal of democracy won a great victory, not simply because the ideal was so fair, but because it represented the concrete interests of the strong, wealthy, and intelligent business class, and that class was able to wrest political control from the king, the aristocracy, and the clergy.

The question is whether the ideal of coöperation and economic fraternity can to-day depend on any great and conquering class whose self-interest is bound up with the victory of that principle. It is hopeless to expect the business class to espouse that principle as a class. Individuals in the business class will do so, but the class will not. There is no historical precedent for an altruistic self-effacement of a whole class. Of the professional class it is safe to expect that an important minority—perhaps a larger minority in our country than in any country heretofore—will range themselves under the new social ideal. With them especially the factor of religion will prove of immense power. But their motives will in the main be idealistic, and in the present stage of man's moral development the unselfish emotions are fragile and easily chafe through, unless the coarse fibre of self-interest is woven into them. But there is another class to which that conception of organized fraternity is not only a moral ideal, but the hope for bread and butter; with which it enlists not only religious devotion and self-sacrifice, but involves salvation from poverty and insecurity and participation in the wealth and culture of modern life for themselves and their children.

It is a mistake to regard the French Revolution as a movement of the poor. The poor fought in the uprising, but the movement got its strength, its purpose, and its direction from the "third estate," the bourgeoisie, the business class of the cities, and they alone drew lasting profit from it. That class had been slowly rising to wealth, education, and power for several centuries, and the democratic movement of the nineteenth century has in the main been their march to complete ascendency.

During the same period we can watch the slow development of a new class, which has been called the fourth estate: the city working class, the wage-workers. They form a distinct class, all living without capital merely by the sale of their labor, working and living under similar physical and social conditions everywhere, with the same economic interests and the same points of view. They present a fairly homogeneous body and if any section of the people forms a "class," they do. The massing of labor in the factories since the introduction of power machinery has brought them into close contact with one another. Hard experience has taught them how helpless they are when they stand alone. They have begun to realize their solidarity and the divergence of their interests from those of the employers. They have begun to organize and are slowly learning to act together. The spread of education and cheap literature, the ease of communication, and the freedom of public meeting have rapidly created a common body of ideas and points of view among them.

The modern "labor movement" is the upward movement of this class. It began with local and concrete issues that pressed upon a given body of workingmen some demand for shorter hours or better wages, some grievance about fines or docking. The trades-unions were formed as defensive organizations for collective action. It is quite true that they have often been foolish and tyrannical in their demands, and headstrong and even lawless in their actions; but if we consider the insecurity and narrowness of the economic existence of the working people, and the glaring contrast between the meagre reward for their labor and the dazzling returns given to invested capital, it is impossible to deny that they have good cause for making a strenuous and continous fight for better conditions of life. If Christian men are really interested in the salvation of human lives and in the health, the decency, the education, and the morality of the people, they must wish well to the working people in their effort to secure such conditions for themselves and their dear ones that they will not have to die of tuberculosis in their prime, nor feel their strength ground down by long hours of work, nor see their women and children drawn into the merciless hopper of factory labor, nor be shut out from the enjoyment of the culture about them which they have watered with their sweat.

But the labor movement means more than better wages and shorter hours for individual workingmen. It involves the struggle for a different status for their entire class. Other classes have long ago won a recognized standing in law and custom and public opinion—so long ago that they have forgotten that they ever had to win it. For instance, the medical profession is recognized by law; certain qualifications are fixed for admission to it; certain privileges are granted to those inside; irregular practitioners are hampered or suppressed. The clerical profession enjoys certain exemptions from taxation, military service, and jury duty; ministers have the right to solemnize marriages and collect fees therefore; railways give them half fares, and these privileges are granted to those whom the clergy themselves ordain and admit to their "closed shop." A lawyer who is admitted to the bar thereby becomes a court officer; the bar association, which is his trades-union, takes the initiative in disbarring men who violate the class code, and the courts take cognizance of its action; in the state of New York the bar associations have assumed some right to nominate the judges. As for the business class, it is so completely enthroned in our social organization that it often assumes that it is itself the whole of society.

On the other hand, the working class has no adequate standing as yet. It did have in the guilds of former times, but modern industry and modern law under the *laissez-faire* principle dissolved the old privileges and reduced the working class to a mass of unrelated human atoms. Common action on their part was treated in law as conspiracy. In our country they have not yet won from their employers nor from public opinion the acknowledged right to be organized, to bargain collectively, and to assist in controlling the discipline of the shops in which they have to work. The law seems to afford them very little backing as yet. It provides penalties for the kind of injuries which workingmen are likely to inflict on their employers, but not for the subtler injuries which employers are likely to inflict on their workingmen. Few will care to assert that in the bitter conflicts waged between labor and capital the wrong has always been on one side. Yet when the law bares its sword, it is somehow always against one side. The militia does not seem to be ordered out against capital. The labor movement must go on until public opinion and the law have conceded a recognized position to the labor-unions, and until the workingmen interested in a given question stand collectively on a footing of equality with the capitalists interested in it. This means a curtailment of power for the employers, and it would be contrary to human nature for them to like it. But for the working class it would be suicidal to forego the attempt to get it. They have suffered fearfully by not having it. All the sacrifices they may bring in the chronic industrial warfare of the present will be cheap if they ultimately win through to an assured social and legal status for their class.

As long as the working class simply attempts to better its condition somewhat and to secure a recognized standing for its class organization, it stands on the basis of the present capitalistic organization of industry. Capitalism necessarily divides industrial society into two classes,—those who own the instruments and materials of production, and those who furnish the labor for it. This sharp division is the peculiar characteristic of modern capitalism which distinguishes it from other forms of social organization in the past. These two classes have to coöperate in modern production. The labor movement seeks to win better terms for the working class in striking its bargains. Yet whatever terms organized labor succeeds in winning are always temporary and insecure, like the hold which a wrestler gets on the body of his antagonist. The persistent tendency with capital necessarily is to get labor as cheaply as possible and to force as much work from it as possible. Moreover, labor is always in an inferior position in the struggle. It is handicapped by its own hunger and lack of resources. It has to wrestle on its knees with a foeman who is on his feet. Is this unequal struggle between two conflicting interests to go on forever? Is this insecurity the best that the working class can ever hope to attain?

Here enters socialism. It proposes to abolish the division of industrial society into two classes and to close the fatal chasm which has separated the employing class from the working class since the introduction of power machinery. It proposes to restore the independence of the workingman by making him once more the owner of his tools and to give him the full proceeds of his production instead of a wage determined by his poverty. It has no idea of reverting to the simple methods of the old handicrafts, but heartily accepts the power machinery, the great factory, the division of labor, the organization of the men in great regiments of workers, as established facts in modern life, and as the most efficient method of producing wealth. But it proposes to give to the whole body of workers the ownership of these vast instruments of production and to distribute among them all the entire proceeds of their common labor. There would then be no capitalistic class opposed to the working class; there would be a single class which would unite the qualities of both. Every workman would be both owner and worker, just as a farmer is who tills his own farm, or a housewife who works in her own kitchen. This would be a permanent solution of the labor question. It would end the present insecurity, the constant antagonism, the social inferiority, the physical exploitation, the intellectual poverty to which the working class is now exposed even when its condition is most favorable.

If such a solution is even approximately feasible, it should be hailed with joy by every patriot and Christian, for it would put a stop to our industrial war, drain off the miasmatic swamp of undeserved poverty, save our political democracy, and lift the great working class to an altogether different footing of comfort, intelligence, security and moral strength. And it would embody the principle of solidarity and fraternity in the fundamental institutions of our industrial life. All the elements of coöperation and interaction which are now at work in our great establishments would be conserved, and in addition the hearty interest of all workers in their common factory or store would be immensely intensified by the diffused sense of ownership. Such a social order would develop the altruistic and social instincts just as the competitive order brings out the selfish instincts.

Socialism is the ultimate and logical outcome of the labor movement. When the entire working class throughout the industrial nations is viewed in large way, the progress of socialism gives an impression of resistless and elemental power. It is inconceivable from the point of view of that class that it should stop short of complete independence and equality as long as it has the power to move on, and independence and equality for the working class must mean the collective ownership of the means of production and the abolition of the present two-class arrangement of industrial society. If the labor movement in our country is only slightly tinged with socialism as yet, it is merely because it is still in its embryonic stages. Nothing will bring the working class to a thorough comprehension of the actual status of their class and its ultimate aim more quickly than continued failure to secure their smaller demands and reactionary efforts to suppress their unions.

We started out with the proposition that the ideal of a fraternal organization of society will remain powerless if it is supported by idealists only; that it needs the firm support of a solid class whose economic future is staked on the success of that ideal; and that the industrial working class is consciously or unconsciously committed to the struggle for the realization of that principle. It follows that those who desire the victory of that ideal from a religious point of view will have to enter into a working alliance with this class. Just as the Protestant principle of religious liberty and the democratic principle of political liberty rose to victory by an alliance with the middle class which was then rising to power, so the new Christian principle of brotherly association must ally itself with the working class if both are to conquer. Each depends on the other. The idealistic movement alone would be a soul without a body; the economic class movement alone would be a body without a soul. It needs the high elation and faith that come through religion. Nothing else will call forth that self-sacrificing devotion and life-long fidelity which will be needed in so gigantic a struggle as lies before the working class.

The coöperation of professional men outside the working class would contribute scientific information and trained intelligence. They would mediate between the two classes, interpreting each to the other, and thereby lessening the strain of hostility. Their presence and sympathy would cheer the working people and diminish the sense of class isolation. By their contact with the possessing classes they could help to persuade them of the inherent justice of the labor movement and so create a leaning toward concessions. No other influence could do so much to prevent a revolutionary explosion of pent-up forces. It is to the interest of all sides that the readjustment of the social classes should come as a steady evolutionary process rather than as a social catastrophe. If the laboring class should attempt to seize political power suddenly, the attempt might be beaten back with terrible loss in efficiency to the movement. If the attempt should be successful, a raw governing class would be compelled to handle a situation so vast and complicated that no past revolution presents a parallel. There would be widespread disorder and acute distress, and a reactionary relapse to old conditions would, by all historical precedents, be almost certain to occur. It is devoutly to be desired that the shifting of power should come through a continuous series of practicable demands on one side and concessions on the other. Such an historical process will be immensely facilitated if there are a large number of men in the professional and business class with whom religious and ethical motives overcome their selfish interests so that they will throw their influence on the side of the class which is now claiming its full rights in the family circle of humanity.

On the other hand, the Christian idealists must not make the mistake of trying to hold the working class down to the use of moral suasion only, or be repelled when they hear the brute note of selfishness and anger. The class struggle is bound to be transferred to the field of politics in our country in some form. It would be folly if the working class failed to use the leverage which their political power gives them. The business class has certainly never failed to use political means to further its interests. This is a war of conflicting interests which is not likely to be fought out in love and tenderness. The possessing class will make concessions not in brotherly love but in fear, because it has to. The working class will force its demands, not merely because they are just, but because it feels it cannot do without them, and because it is strong enough to coerce. Even Bismarck acknowledged that the former indifference of the business class in Germany to the sufferings of the lower classes had not been overcome by philanthropy, but by fear of the growing discontent of the people and the spread of social democracy. Max Nordau[94] meant the same when he said, ''In spite of its theoretical absurdity, socialism has already in thirty years wrought greater amelioration than all the wisdom of statesmen and philosophers of thousands of years.'' All that we as Christian men can do is to ease the struggle and hasten the victory of the right by giving faith and hope to those who are down, and quickening the sense of justice with those who are in power, so that they will not harden their hearts and hold Israel in bondage, but will ''let the people go.''[95] But that spiritual contribution, intangible and imponderable though it be, has a chemical power of immeasurable efficiency.

We undertook in this chapter to suggest in what ways the moral forces latent in Christian society could be mobilized for the progressive regeneration of social life, and in what directions chiefly these forces should be exerted.

We saw that some lines of effort frequently attempted in the past by Christian men and organizations are useless and misleading. It is fruitless to attempt to turn modern society back to conditions prevailing before power machinery and trusts had revolutionized it; or to copy biblical institutions adapted to wholly different social conditions; or to postpone the Christianizing of society to the millennium; or to found Christian communistic colonies within the competitive world; or to make the organized church the centre and manager of an improved social machinery. The force of religion can best be applied to social renewal by sending its spiritual power along the existing and natural relations of men to direct them to truer ends and govern them by higher motives.

The fundamental contribution of every man is the change of his

---

94. Max Simon Nordau was a German (Hungarian-born) critic of the social, ethical, and religious standards of society.

95. Ex 5:1.

own personality. We must repent of the sins of existing society, cast off the spell of the lies protecting our social wrongs, have faith in a higher social order, and realize in ourselves a new type of Christian manhood which seeks to overcome the evil in the present world, not by withdrawing from the world, but by revolutionizing it.

If this new type of religious character multiplies among the young men and women, they will change the world when they come to hold the controlling positions of society in their maturer years. They will give a new force to righteous and enlightened public opinion, and will apply the religious sense of duty and service to the common daily life with a new motive and directness.

The ministry, in particular, must apply the teaching functions of the pulpit to the pressing questions of public morality. It must collectively learn not to speak without adequate information; not to charge individuals with guilt in which all society shares; not to be partial, and yet to be on the side of the lost; not to yield to political partisanship, but to deal with moral questions before they become political issues and with those questions of public welfare which never do become political issues. They must lift the social questions to a religious level by faith and spiritual insight. The larger the number of ministers who attempt these untrodden ways, the safer and saner will those be who follow. By interpreting one social class to the other, they can create a disposition to make concessions and help in securing a peaceful settlement of social issues.

The force of the religious spirit should be bent toward asserting the supremacy of life over property. Property exists to maintain and develop life. It is unchristian to regard human life as a mere instrument for the production of wealth.

The religious sentiment can protect good customs and institutions against the inroads of ruthless greed, and extend their scope. It can create humane customs which the law is impotent to create. It can create the convictions and customs which are later embodied in good legislation.

Our complex society rests largely on the stewardship of delegated powers. The opportunities to profit by the betrayal of trust increase with the wealth and complexity of civilization. The most fundamental evils in past history and present conditions were due to converting stewardship into ownership. The keener moral insight created by Christianity should lend its help in scrutinizing all claims

to property and power in order to detect latent public rights and to recall the recreant stewards to their duty.

Primitive society was communistic. The most valuable institutions in modern life—the family, the school and church—are communistic. The state, too, is essentially communistic and is becoming
increasingly so. During the larger part of its history the Christian
church regarded communism as the only ideal life. Christianity certainly has more affinity for coöperative and fraternal institutions
than for competitive disunion. It should therefore strengthen the existing communistic institutions and aid the evolution of society from
the present temporary stage of individualism to a higher form of
communism.

The splendid ideal of a fraternal organization of society cannot
be realized by idealists only. It must be supported by the self-interest
of a powerful class. The working class, which is now engaged in its
upward movement, is struggling to secure better conditions of life,
an assured status for its class organizations, and ultimately the ownership of the means of production. Its success in the last great aim
would mean the closing of the gap which now divides industrial society and the establishment of industry on the principle of solidarity
and the method of coöperation. Christianity should enter into a
working alliance with this rising class, and by its mediation secure
the victory of these principles by a gradual equalization of social opportunity and power.

The first apostolate of Christianity was born from a deep fel-
low-feeling for social misery and from the consciousness of a great
historical opportunity. Jesus saw the peasantry of Galilee following
him about with their poverty and their diseases, like shepherdless
sheep that have been scattered and harried by beasts of prey, and his
heart had compassion on them. He felt that the harvest was ripe, but
there were few to reap it. Past history had come to its culmination,
but there were few who understood the situation and were prepared
to cope with it. He bade his disciples to pray for laborers for the harvest, and then made them answer their own prayers by sending them
out two by two to proclaim the kingdom of God. That was the beginning of the world-wide mission of Christianity.[96]

---

96. Mt 9:32–10:42.

The situation is repeated on a vaster scale to-day. If Jesus stood to-day amid our modern life, with that outlook on the condition of all humanity which observation and travel and the press would spread before him, and with the same heart of divine humanity beating in him, he would create a new apostolate to meet the new needs in a new harvest-time of history.

To any one who knows the sluggishness of humanity to good, the impregnable intrenchments of vested wrongs and the long reaches of time needed from one milestone of progress to the next, the task of setting up a Christian social order in this modern world of ours seems like a fair and futile dream. Yet in fact it is not one tithe as hopeless as when Jesus set out to do it. When he told his disciples, ''Ye are the salt of the earth; ye are the light of the world,''[97] he expressed the consciousness of a great historic mission to the whole of humanity. Yet it was a Nazarene carpenter speaking to a group of Galilaean peasants and fishermen. Under the circumstances at that time it was an utterance of the most daring faith,—faith in himself, faith in them, faith in what he was putting into them, faith in faith. Jesus failed and was crucified, first his body by his enemies, and then his spirit by his friends; but that failure was so amazing a success that today it takes an effort on our part to realize that it required any faith on his part to inaugurate the kingdom of God and to send out his apostolate.

To-day, as Jesus looks out upon humanity, his spirit must leap to see the souls responsive to his call. They are sown broadcast through humanity, legions of them. The harvest-field is no longer deserted. All about us we hear the clang of the whetstone and the rush of the blades through the grain and the shout of the reapers. With all our faults and our slothfulness we modern men in many ways are more on a level with the real mind of Jesus than any generation that has gone before. If that first apostolate was able to remove mountains by the power of faith, such an apostolate as Christ could now summon might change the face of the earth.

The apostolate of a new age must do the work of the sower. When the sower goes forth to sow his seed, he goes with the certainty of partial failure and the knowledge that a long time of patience and of hazard will intervene before he can hope to see the

---

97. Mt 5:13–14.

result of his work and his venture. In sowing the truth a man may never see or trace the results. The more ideal his conceptions are, and the farther they move ahead of his time, the larger will be the percentage of apparent failure. But he can afford to wait. The powers of life are on his side. He is like a man who has scattered his seed and then goes off to sleep by night and work by day, and all the while the seed, by the inscrutable chemistry of life, lays hold of the ingredients of its environment and builds them up to its own growth. The mustard-seed becomes a tree. The leaven assimilates the meal by biological processes. The new life penetrates the old humanity and transforms it. Robert Owen[98] was a sower. His coöperative communities failed. He was able to help only a small fraction of the workingmen of his day. But his moral enthusiasm and his ideas fertilized the finest and most self-sacrificing minds among the working classes. They cherished his ultimate hopes in private and worked for realizable ends in public. The Chartist movement was filled with his spirit. The most influential leaders of English unionism in its great period after the middle of the nineteenth century were Owenites. The Rochdale Pioneers[99] were under his influence, and the great coöperative movement in England, an economic force of the first importance, grew in some measure out of the seed which Owen had scattered. Other men may own the present. The future belongs to the sower—provided he scatters seed and does not mistake the chaff for it which once was so essential to the seed and now is dead and useless.

It is inevitable that those who stand against conditions in which most men believe and by which the strongest profit, shall suffer for their stand. The little group of early Christian socialists in England, led by Maurice, Kingsley, and Hughes, now stand by common consent in the history of that generation as one of its finest products, but at that time they were bitterly assailed and misunderstood. Pastor Rudolf Todt,[100] the first man in Germany who undertook to prove

---

98. British "socialist" and reformer who expressed his views in *A New View of Society* (1813) and established communitarian societies in both England and the United States.

99. Founders in 1844 of the English network or system of cooperative societies.

100. Author of *Der radikale deutsche Socialismus und die christliche Gesellschaft* (1877).

that the New Testament and the ethics of socialism have a close affinity, was almost unanimously attacked by the church of Germany.
But Jesus told his apostles at the outset that opposition would be part
of their day's work. Christ equipped his church with no legal rights
to protect her; the only political right he gave his disciples was the
right of being persecuted.[101] It is part of the doctrine of vicarious
atonement, which is fundamental in Christianity, that the prophetic
souls must vindicate by their sufferings the truth of the truth they
preach.

> "Disappointment's dry and bitter root,
> Envy's harsh berries, and the choking pool
> Of the world's scorn, are the right mother-milk
> To the tough hearts that pioneer their kind
> And break a pathway to those unknown realms
> That in the earth's broad shadow lie enthralled;
> Endurance is the crowning quality,
> And patience all the passion of great hearts;
> These are their stay, and when the leaden world
> Sets its hard face against their fateful thought,
> And brute strength, like a scornful conqueror,
> Clangs his huge mace down in the other scale,
> The inspired soul but flings his patience in,
> And slowly that outweighs the ponderous globe,—
> One faith against a whole earth's unbelief,
> One soul against the flesh of all mankind."[102]

The championship of social justice is almost the only way left open
to a Christian nowadays to gain the crown of martyrdom. Theological heretics are rarely persecuted now. The only rival of God is
mammon, and it is only when his sacred name is blasphemed that
men throw the Christians to the lions.

Even for the social heretics there is a generous readiness to listen which was unknown in the past. In our country that openness of
mind is a product of our free intellectual life, our ingrained democ-

---

101. Martin von Nathusius, *Die Mitarbeit der Kirche* (Leipzig, 1893), 476.
[au.]

102. James Russell Lowell, "Columbus."

racy, the denominational manifoldness of our religious life, and the spread of the Christian spirit. It has become an accepted doctrine among us that all great movements have obscure beginnings, and that belief tends to make men respectful toward anything that comes from some despised Nazareth. Unless a man forfeits respect by bitterness or lack of tact, he is accorded a large degree of tolerance, though he will always be made to feel the difference between himself and those who say the things that please the great.

The certainty of opposition constitutes a special call to the strong. The ministry seems to have little attraction for the sons of rich men. It is not strange when one considers the enervating trials that beset a rich man in a pastorate. But here is a mission that ought to appeal to the rich young man if he has heroic stuff in him. His assured social standing would give him an influence with rich and poor alike which others attain but slowly if at all. The fear of being blacklisted for championing justice and mercy need have no terrors for him. To use his property as a coat of mail in fighting the battles of the weak would be the best way of obeying Christ's command to the rich young ruler to sell all and give it to the poor. When Mr. Roosevelt was still Police Commissioner in New York, he said to the young men of New York: "I would teach the young men that he who has not wealth owes his first duty to his family, but he who has means owes his to the State. It is ignoble to go on heaping up money. I would preach the doctrine of work to all, and to the men of wealth the doctrine of unremunerative work."[103] The most "unremunerative work" is the work that draws opposition and animosity.

Mr. Roosevelt implies here that a man's duty to his family is the first and dominant duty, and that this exempts him in some measure from service to the larger public. It follows that the childless have a call to the dangerous work of the kingdom of God. A man and woman who are feeding and training young citizens are performing so immense and absorbing a service to the future that they might well be exempt from taxes to the state and from sacrificial service to the kingdom of God. If nevertheless so many of them assume these duties in addition, the childless man and woman will have to do heroic work in the trenches before they can rank on the same level. It

---

103. Jacob A. Riis, *Theodore Roosevelt, the Citizen* (New York, 1903).

is not fair to ask a man with children to give his time and strength as freely to public causes as if he had none. It is still more unfair to expect him to risk the bread and the prospects of his family in championing dangerous causes as freely as if he risked only himself. The childless people should adopt the whole coming generation of children and fight to make the world more habitable for them as for their own brood. The unmarried and the childless should enlist in the new apostolate and march on the forlorn hopes with Jesus Christ.

In asking for faith in the possibility of a new social order, we ask for no Utopian delusion. We know well that there is no perfection for man in this life: there is only growth toward perfection. In personal religion we look with seasoned suspicion at any one who claims to be holy and perfect, yet we always tell men to become holy and to seek perfection. We make it a duty to seek what is unattainable. We have the same paradox in the perfectibility of society. We shall never have a perfect social life, yet we must seek it with faith. We shall never abolish suffering. There will always be death and the empty chair and heart. There will always be the agony of love unreturned. Women will long for children and never press baby lips to their breast. Men will long for fame and miss it. Imperfect moral insight will work hurt in the best conceivable social order. The strong will always have the impulse to exert their strength, and no system can be devised which can keep them from crowding and jostling the weaker. Increased social refinement will bring increased sensitiveness to pain. An American may suffer as much distress through a social slight as a Russian peasant under the knout. At best there is always but an approximation to a perfect social order. The kingdom of God is always but coming.

But every approximation to it is worth while. Every step toward personal purity and peace, though it only makes the consciousness of imperfection more poignant, carries its own exceeding great reward, and everlasting pilgrimage toward the kingdom of God is better than contented stability in the tents of wickedness.

And sometimes the hot hope surges up that perhaps the long and slow climb may be ending. In the past the steps of our race toward progress have been short and feeble, and succeeded by long intervals of sloth and apathy. But is that necessarily to remain the rate of advance? In the intellectual life there has been an unprecedented leap forward during the last hundred years. Individually we are not more gifted than our grandfathers, but collectively we have wrought out more epoch-making discoveries and inventions in one century than the whole race in the untold centuries that have gone before. If the twentieth century could do for us in the control of social forces what the nineteenth did for us in the control of natural forces, our grandchildren would live in a society that would be justified in regarding our present social life as semi-barbarous. Since the Reformation began to free the mind and to direct the force of religion toward morality, there has been a perceptible increase of speed. Humanity is gaining in elasticity and capacity for change, and every gain in general intelligence, in organizing capacity, in physical and moral soundness, and especially in responsiveness to ideal motives, again increases the ability to advance without disastrous reactions. The swiftness of evolution in our own country proves the immense latent perfectibility in human nature.

Last May a miracle happened. At the beginning of the week the fruit trees bore brown and greenish buds. At the end of the week they were robed in bridal garments of blossoms. But for weeks and months the sap had been rising and distending the cells and maturing the tissues which were half ready in the fall before. The swift unfolding was the culmination of a long process. Perhaps these nineteen centuries of Christian influence have been a long preliminary stage of growth, and now the flower and fruit are almost here. If at this juncture we can rally sufficient religious faith and moral strength to snap the bonds of evil and turn the present unparalleled economic and intellectual resources of humanity to the harmonious development of a true social life, the generations yet unborn will mark this as that great day of the Lord for which the ages waited, and count us blessed for sharing in the apostolate that proclaimed it.

"CHRISTIANIZING THE SOCIAL ORDER"

In Christianizing the Social Order *(1912), Rauschen-busch sought to provide encouragement to those whose concerns had been awakened by his first book and to answer questions that had been raised. It is his most optimistic book and his most detailed discussion of social issues. But he had a larger purpose in mind. As he wrote in the introduction: "If this book was to be written at all, it had to deal searchingly with the great social sins of our age. Evangelism always seeks to create a fresh conviction of guilt as a basis for a higher righteousness, and this book is nothing if it is not a message of sin and salvation."*

What is reprinted here is not his social analysis, but portions of two chapters which deal directly with his evangelistic concern.

Social Christianity and Personal Religion[104]

We who know personal religion by experience know that there is nothing on earth to compare with the moral force exerted by it. It has demonstrated its social efficiency in our own lives. It was personal religion which first set us our tasks of service in youth, and which now holds us to them when our body droops and our spirit flags. Religion can turn diffident, humble men like Shaftesbury[105] into invincible champions of the poor. All social movements would gain immensely in enthusiasm, persuasiveness, and wisdom, if the hearts of their advocates were cleansed and warmed by religious faith. Even those who know religious power only by observation on others will concede that.

But will the reënforcement work the other way, also? Religion strengthens the social spirit; will the social spirit strengthen personal religion? When a minister gets hot about child labor and wage slavery, is he not apt to get cold about prayer meetings and evangelistic efforts? When young women become interested in social work, do they not often lose their taste for the culture of the spiritual life and the peace of religious meditation? A hot breakfast is an event devoutly to be desired, but is it wise to chop up your precious old set of colonial furniture to cook the breakfast? Would the reënforcement of the social spirit be worth while if we lost our personal religion in the process?

---

104. *Christianizing the Social Order* (New York, 1912), 103–22.

105. The reference is to Anthony Ashley Cooper (1801–85), seventh earl of Shaftesbury, noted for his reform activities in parliament.

If this is indeed the alternative, we are in a tragic situation, compelled to choose between social righteousness and communion with God.

Personal religion has a supreme value for its own sake, not merely as a feeder of social morality, but as the highest unfolding of life itself, as the blossoming of our spiritual nature. Spiritual regeneration is the most important fact in any life history. A living experience of God is the crowning knowledge attainable to a human mind. Each one of us needs the redemptive power of religion for his own sake, for on the tiny stage of the human soul all the vast world tragedy of good and evil is reënacted. In the best social order that is conceivable men will still smolder with lust and ambition, and be lashed by hate and jealousy as with the whip of a slave driver. No material comfort and plenty can satisfy the restless soul in us and give us peace with ourselves. All who have made test of it agree that religion alone holds the key to the ultimate meaning of life, and each of us must find his way into the inner mysteries alone. The day will come when all life on this planet will be extinct, and what meaning will our social evolution have had if that is all? Religion is eternal life in the midst of time and transcending time. The explanations of religion have often been the worst possible, God knows, but the fact of religion is the biggest thing there is.

If, therefore, our personal religious life is likely to be sapped by our devotion to social work, it would be a calamity second to none. But is it really likely that this will happen? The great aim underlying the whole social movement is the creation of a free, just, and brotherly social order. This is the greatest moral task conceivable. Its accomplishment is the manifest will of God for this generation. Every Christian motive is calling us to it. If it is left undone, millions of lives will be condemned to a deepening moral degradation and to spiritual starvation. Does it look probable that we shall lose our contact with God if we plunge too deeply into this work? Does it stand to reason that we shall go astray from Jesus Christ if we engage in the unequal conflict with organized wrong? What kind of "spirituality" is it which is likely to get hurt by being put to work for justice and our fellow-men?

Some of the anxiety about personal religion is due to a subtle lack of faith in religion. Men think it is a fragile thing that will break up and vanish when the customs and formulas which have hitherto incased and protected it are broken and cast aside. Most of us have known religion under one form, and we suppose it can have no other. But religion is the life of God in the soul of man, and is God really so fragile? Will the tongue of fire sputter and go out unless we shelter it under a bushel? Let the winds of God roar through it, and watch it! Religion unites a great variability of form with an amazing constancy of power. The Protestant Reformation changed the entire outward complexion of religion in the nations of northern Europe. All the most characteristic forms in which Christianity had expressed itself and by which its strength had hitherto been gauged were swept away. No pope, no priest, no monk, no mass, no confessional, no rosary, no saints, no images, no processions, no pilgrimages, no indulgences! It was a clean sweep. What was left of religion? Religion itself! At least your Puritans and Huguenots seemed to think they had personal religion; more, in fact, than ever before. Catholics thought it was the destruction of personal religion; really it was the rise of a new type of religion. In the same way the social Christianity of to-day is not a dilution of personal religion, but a new form of experimental Christianity, and its religious testimony will have to be heard henceforth when "the varieties of religious experience" are described.[106]

Nevertheless, conservative Christian men are not frightened by their own imaginings when they fear that the progress of the social interest will mean a receding of personal religion. They usually have definite cases in mind in which that seemed to be the effect, and it is well worth while to examine these more closely.

In the first place, personal religion collapses with some individuals, because in their case it had long been growing hollow and thin. Not all who begin the study of music or poetry in youth remain lovers of art and literature to the end, and not all who begin a religious life in the ardor of youth keep up its emotional intimacy as life goes on. Take any group of one hundred religious people, laymen or ministers, and it is a safe guess that in a considerable fraction of them the fire of vital religion is merely flickering in the ashes. As long as their life goes on in the accustomed way, they maintain their religious

---

106. The reference is to William James, *The Varieties of Religious Experience* (New York, 1902).

connections and expressions, and do so sincerely, but if they move to another part of the country, or if a new interest turns their minds forcibly in some other direction, the frayed bond parts and they turn from their church and religion. If it is the social interest which attracts them, it may seem to them and others that this has extinguished their devotional life. In reality there was little personal religion to lose, and that little would probably have been lost in some other way. This would cover the inner history of some ministers as well as of church members.

In other cases we must recognize that men become apathetic about church activities in which they have been interested, because they have found something better. The Hebrew prophets turned in anger from the sacrificial doings of their people; Jesus turned away from the long prayers of the Pharisees, who were the most pious people of his day; the Reformers repudiated many of the most devout activities of medieval Catholicism. Wherever there is a new awakening of spiritual life, there is a discarding of old religious forms, and it is to the interest of personal religion that there should be. Is there nothing petty, useless, and insipid in the Catholic or Protestant church life of our day from which a soul awakened to larger purposes ought really to turn away? Is it reprehensible if some drop out of a dress parade when they hear the sound of actual fighting just across the hills?

It is also true that in this tremendous awakening and unsettlement some turn away in haste from things which have lasting value. Few men and few movements have such poise that they never overshoot the mark. When the Reformation turned its back on medieval superstition, it also smashed the painted windows of the cathedrals and almost banished art and music from its services. When mystics feel the compelling power of the inner word of God, they are apt to slight the written word. So when religious souls who have been shut away from social ideals and interests and pent up within a fine but contracted religious habitation get the new outlook of the social awakening, it sweeps them away with new enthusiasms. Their life rushes in to fill the empty spaces. Their mind is busy with a religious comprehension of a hundred new facts and problems, and the old questions of personal religion drop out of sight. In such cases we can safely trust to experience to restore the equilibrium. In a number of my younger friends the balancing is now going on. As they work their way in life and realize the real needs of men and the real values of life, they get a new comprehension of the power and preciousness of personal and intimate religion, and they turn back to the old truths of Christianity with a fresh relish and a firmer accent of conviction. We shall see that rediscovery in thousands within a few years. No doubt they are to blame for their temporary one-sidedness, but their blame will have to be shared by generations of religious individualists whose own persistent one-sidedness had distorted the rounded perfection of Christianity and caused the present excessive reaction.

The question takes a wider meaning when we turn to the alienation of entire classes from religion. There is no doubt that in all the industrialized nations of Europe, and in our own country, the working classes are dropping out of connection with their churches and synagogues, and to a large extent are transferring their devotion to social movements, so that it looks as if the social interest displaced religion. But here, too, we must remember that solid masses of the population of continental Europe have never had much vital religion to lose. Their religion was taught by rote and performed by rote. It was gregarious and not personal. Detailed investigations have been made of the religious thought world of the peasantry or industrial population of limited districts, and the result always is that the centuries of indoctrination by the church have left only a very thin crust of fertile religious conviction and experience behind. This is not strange, for whenever any spontaneous and democratic religion has arisen among the people, the established churches have done their best to wet-blanket and suppress it, and they have succeeded finely. When these people cut loose from their churches, they may not be getting much farther away from God. Usually these unchurched people still have a strong native instinct for religion, and when the vital issues and convictions of their own life are lifted into the purer light of Jesus Christ and set on fire by religious faith, they respond.

A new factor enters the situation when we encounter the influence of "scientific socialism." It is true, the party platform declares that "religion is a private affair." The saving of souls is the only industry that socialism distinctly relegates to private enterprise. If that meant simply separation of church and state, Americans could heartily assent. If it meant that the Socialist Party proposes to be the political organization of the working class for the attainment of economic ends and to be neutral in all other questions, it would be prudent tactics. But in practice it means more. The socialism of continental Europe, taking it by and large, is actively hostile, not only to bad forms of organized religion, but to religion itself. Churchmen feel that a man is lost to religion when he joins the Socialist Party, and socialist leaders feel that a socialist who is still an active Christian is only half baked. When French and German socialists learn that men trained in the democracy and vitality of the free churches of England and America combine genuine piety and ardent devotion to the Socialist Party, it comes to them as a shock of surprise. In May, 1910, about 260 delegates of the English "Brotherhoods" visited Lille in France and were received by the French trades-unionists and socialists with parades and public meetings. The crowds on the streets did not know what to make of it when they saw the Englishmen marching under the red flag of socialism and yet bearing banners with the inscriptions: "We represent 500,000 English workmen;" "We proclaim the Fatherhood of God and the Brotherhood of Man;" "Jesus Christ leads and inspires us." What were these men, Christians or socialists? They could not be both. The Frenchmen lost all their bearings when they heard Keir Hardie, the veteran English labor leader and socialist, repudiating clericalism, but glorifying the Gospel and the spirit of Christ, and declaring that it was Christianity which had made a socialist of him.

The antireligious attitude of continental socialism is comprehensible enough if we study its historical causes dispassionately. Its most active ingredient is anticlericalism. I surmise that if some of us Americans had been in the shoes of these foreign workingmen and had seen the priest from their angle of vision, we should be anticlerical too. But in the old churches religion, the church, and the priest mean the same thing; you must accept all or reject all. Men do not discriminate when they are hot with ancient wrongs.

Another ingredient in socialist unbelief is modern science and skepticism. Socialists share their irreligion with other radicals. They are unbelievers, not simply because they are socialists, but because they are children of their time. Great masses of upper-class and middle-class people in Europe are just as skeptical and materialistic, though they show no touch of red. Socialists have no monopoly of unbelief.

But in addition to this, materialistic philosophy does come to socialists embodied in their own literature as part of socialist "science.'' The socialist faith was formulated by its intellectual leaders at a time when naturalism and materialism was the popular philosophy of the intellectuals, and these elements were woven into the dogma of the new movement. Great movements always perpetuate the ideas current at the time when they are in their fluid and formative stage. For instance, some of the dogmas of the Christian church are still formulated in the terminology of a philosophy that was current in the third and fourth centuries. Calvin worked out a system of thought that is stamped with his powerful personality and with the peculiarities of his age. But after it had once become the dogmatic fighting faith of great organized bodies, it was all handed on as God's own truth. Socialism is the most solid and militant organization since Calvinism, and it is just as dogmatic. Thus we have the tragic fact that the most idealistic mass movement of modern times was committed at the outset to a materialistic philosophy with which it had no essential connection, and every individual who comes under its influence and control is liable to be assimilated to its type of thought in religion as well as in economics.

Those who fear the influence of the social interest on personal religion are not, therefore, wholly wrong. In any powerful spiritual movement, even the best, there are yeasty, unsettling forces which may do good in the long run, but harm in the short run. Atheistic socialism may influence the religious life of great classes as deforestation affects a mountain side.

On the other hand, where the new social spirit combines harmoniously with the inherited Christian life, a new type of personal religion is produced which has at least as good a right to existence as any other type. Jesus was not a good theological Christian, nor a churchman, nor an emotionalist, nor an ascetic, nor a contemplative mystic. A mature social Christian comes closer to the likeness of Jesus Christ than any other type.

In religious individualism, even in its sweetest forms, there was a subtle twist of self-seeking which vitiated its Christlikeness. Thomas a Kempis' *Imitation of Christ* and Bunyan's *Pilgrim's Progress* are classical expressions of personal religion, the one Roman Catholic and monastic, the other Protestant and Puritan. In both piety is self-centered. In both we are taught to seek the highest good of the soul by turning away from the world of men. Doubtless the religion of the monastery and of the Puritan community was far more social and human than the theory might indicate. Bunyan seems to have felt by instinct it was not quite right to have a Christian leave his wife and children and neighbors behind to get rid of his burden and reach the heavenly city. So he wrote a sequel to his immortal story in which the rest of the family with several friends set out on the same pilgrimage. This second part is less thrilling, but more wholesomely Christian. There is family life, love-making, and marriage on the way. A social group cooperate in salvation. Bunyan was feeling his way toward social Christianity.

Evangelicalism prides itself on its emphasis on sin and the need of conversion, yet some of the men trained in its teachings do not seem to know the devil when they meet him on the street. The most devastating sins of our age do not look like sins to them. They may have been converted from the world, but they contentedly make their money in the common ways of the world. Social Christianity involves a more trenchant kind of conversion and more effective means of grace. It may teach a more lenient theory of sin, but it gives a far keener eye for the lurking places of concrete and profitable sins. A man who gets the spiritual ideals of social Christianity is really set at odds with "the world" and enlisted in a lifelong fight with organized evil. But no man who casts out devils is against Christ. To fight evil involves a constant affirmation of holiness and hardens the muscles of Christian character better than any religious gymnasium work. To very many Christians of the old type the cross of Christ meant only an expedient in the scheme of redemption, not a law of life for themselves. A man can be an exponent of "the higher life"[107] and never suffer any persecution whatever from the powers that control our sin-ridden social life. On the other hand, if any man takes social Christianity at all seriously, he will certainly encounter opposition and be bruised somehow. Such an experience will throw him back on the comforts of God and make his prayers more than words. When he bears on his own body and soul the

---

107. "The higher Christian life" was a term frequently applied to a movement in the 1880's and 1890's which emphasized the centrality of the Holy Spirit in a way analogous to the stress given it by Leighton Williams and Walter Rauschenbusch. The movement, as Grant Wacker has indicated in a forthcoming study, had several affinities to the liberal "New Theology" of the same period.

marks of the Lord Jesus, the cross will be more than a doctrine to him. It will be a bond uniting him with Christ in a fellowship of redemptive love.

The personal religion created by social Christianity will stand one practical test of true religion which exceeds in value most of the proofs offered by theology: it creates a larger life and the power of growth. Dead religion narrows our freedom, contracts our horizon, limits our sympathies, and dwarfs our stature. Live religion brings a sense of emancipation, the exhilaration of spiritual health, a tenderer affection for all living things, widening thoughts and aims, and a sure conviction of the reality and righteousness of God. Devotion to the reign of God on earth will do that for a man, and will do it continuously. A self-centered religion reaches the dead line soon. Men get to know the whole scheme of salvation, and henceforth they march up the hill only to march down again. On the contrary, when a man's prime object is not his soul, but the kingdom of God, he has set his hands to a task that will never end and will always expand. It will make ever larger demands on his intellect, his sympathy, and his practical efficiency. It will work him to the last ounce of his strength. But it will keep him growing.

It is charged that those who become interested in "social work" lose interest in "personal work." Doubtless there is truth in that, and it is a regrettable one-sidedness. It is only fair to remember, however, that they share this loss of interest with the entire American church. Evangelism itself had long become so one-sided, mechanical, and superficial in its gospel and methods that the present apathy can be explained only as a reaction from it. Precisely those who have themselves gone through its experiences are now reluctant to submit young people to it. The social gospel will gradually develop its own evangelistic methods and its own personal appeals. What was called "personal work" was often not personal at all, but a wholesale regimentation of souls. It offered the same prescription, the same formula of doctrine, the same spiritual exercises and emotions for all. Those who add the new social intelligence to the old religious love of man's soul will take every man in his own social place and his own human connections, will try to understand his peculiar sin and failure from his own point of view, and see by what means salvation can effectively be brought to him. Such an evangelism would be more truly personal than the old; it would have more sense of the individuality of each man. As Robert A. Woods[108] finely says, "It calls each man by his name."

Christianity must offer every man a full salvation. The individualistic gospel never did this. Its evangelism never recognized more than a fractional part of the saving forces at work in God's world. Salvation was often whittled down to a mere doctrinal proposition; assent to that, and you were saved. Social Christianity holds to all the real values in the old methods, but rounds them out to meet all the needs of human life.

Salvation is always a social process. It comes by human contact. The word must become flesh if it is to save. Some man or woman, or some group of people, in whom the saving love of Jesus Christ has found a new incarnation, lays hold of an enfeebled, blinded human atom and infuses new hope and courage and insight, new warmth of love and strength of will, and there is a new breathing of the soul and an opening of the inner eye. Salvation has begun. That man or group of men was a fragment of the kingdom of God in humanity; God dwelt in them and therefore power could go out from them. When a lost soul is infolded in a new society, a true humanity, then there is a chance of salvation.[109] No matter what set of opinions they hold, such men and women have been one of the most precious assets of our American life, and a social theorist who scoffs at them is blind with dogmatic prejudice.

When the church insisted that it is the indispensable organ of salvation, it insisted on the social factor in redemption. The church stands for the assimilating power exerted by the social group over its members. The same influence which a semicriminal gang exerts over a boy for evil is exerted by the church for good. The advice in the Gospel to win an offending brother back by pleading with him first alone, then drawing two or three others into it, and finally bringing the matter before the church, shows a keen insight into the

---

108. Robert A. Woods was a prominent settlement worker in Boston.

109. Harold Begbie's *Twice-born Men* (New York, 1909) was "a summons to personal work," but it "proves throughout that salvation comes by social contact with religious groups." [au.]

powers of the social group over its members. More and more units of power are switched on until the current is overpowering.[110]

In a small and simple country or village community the church could follow a man in all his relations. In our modern society the social contact of the church covers only a small part of life, and the question is whether the influence it exerts on the saved man is strong and continuous enough to keep him saved. Suppose a poor "bum" leaves the Salvation Army barracks with a new light of hope in his eyes. He passes out on the streets among saloons and gambling dens, among sights and sounds and smells that call to his passions, among men and women who are not part of the saving kingdom of God, but of the carnivorous kingdom of the devil. So the poor fellow backslides. Suppose a millionaire has been at a meeting where he has caught a vision of a new order of business, in which men are not boozy with profits, but in which such as he might be brothers to all. Next morning stocks are tumbling on 'Change, and profit is calling to him. So the poor fellow backslides. The churches do save men, but so many of them do not stay saved. Even in very active churches an enormous percentage of members are in the long run swept back so that all can see the failure, and if love of money and the hardness of social pride were properly reckoned as a religious collapse, the percentage of waste would be still greater.[111] The social organism of the church becomes increasingly unable in modern life to supply the social forces of salvation single-handed. It may save, but its salvation is neither complete nor durable.

Sin is a social force. It runs from man to man along the lines of social contact. Its impact on the individual becomes most overwhelming when sin is most completely socialized. Salvation, too, is a social force. It is exerted by groups that are charged with divine will and love. It becomes durable and complete in the measure in which the individual is built into a social organism that is ruled by justice, cleanness, and love. A full salvation demands a Christian so-

---

110. Mt 18:15–20.

111. The General Conference of the Methodist Episcopal Church and the General Assembly of the Presbyterian Church, in 1912 confronted the tremendous losses by the "dropping" of members as one of the most serious questions of church life. [au.]

cial order which will serve as the spiritual environment of the individual. In the little catechism which Luther wrote for the common people he has a charmingly true reply to the question: "What is 'our daily bread'?" He says: "All that belongs to the nourishment and need of our body, meat and drink, clothes and shoes, house and home, field and cattle, money and property, a good wife and good children, good servants and good rulers, good government, good weather, peace, health, education, honor, good friends, trusty neighbors, and such like." Yes, especially "such like." In the same way "salvation" involves a saved environment. For a baby it means the breast and heart and love of a mother, and a father who can keep the mother in proper condition. For a workingman salvation includes a happy home, clean neighbors, a steady job, eight hours a day, a boss that treats him as a man, a labor union that is well led, the sense of doing his own best work and not being used up to give others money to burn, faith in God and in the final triumph and present power of the right, a sense of being part of a movement that is lifting his class and all mankind, "and such like." Therefore the conception of salvation which is contained in the word "the kingdom of God" is a truer and completer conception than that which is contained in the word "justification by faith," as surely as the whole is better than a part.

I set out with the proposition that social Christianity, which makes the reign of God on earth its object, is a distinct type of personal religion, and that in its best manifestations it involves the possibility of a purer spirituality, a keener recognition of sin, more durable powers of growth, a more personal evangelism, and a more all-around salvation than the individualistic type of religion which makes the salvation of the soul its object. I want to add that this new type of religion is especially adapted to win and inspire modern men.

It must be plain to any thoughtful observer that immense numbers of men are turning away from traditional religion, not because they have lapsed into sin, but because they have become modernized in their knowledge and points of view. Religion itself is an eternal need of humanity, but any given form of religion may become antiquated and inadequate, leaving the youngest and livest minds unsatisfied, or even repelling where it ought to attract. The real religious leaders of this generation must face the problem how they can give to modern men the inestimable boon of experiencing God as a joy and a power, and of living in him as their fathers did. I claim that social Christianity is by all tokens the great highway by which this present generation can come to God.

For one thing, it puts an end to most of the old conflicts between religion and science. The building of the kingdom of God on earth requires surprisingly little dogma and speculative theology, and a tremendous quantity of holy will and scientific good sense. It does not set up a series of propositions which need constant modernizing and which repel the most active intellects, but it summons all to help in transforming the world into a reign of righteousness, and men of good will are not very far apart on that. That kind of religion has no quarrel with science. It needs science to interpret the universe which Christianity wants to transform. Social Christianity sets up fewer obstacles for the intellect and puts far heavier tasks on the will, and all that is sound in modern life will accept that change with profound relief.

Social Christianity would also remove one other obstacle which bars even more men out of religion than the scientific difficulties of belief. The most effective argument against religion to-day is that religion has been "against the people." The people are coming to their own at last. For a century and a half at least they have been on the upgrade, climbing with inexpressible toil and suffering toward freedom, equality, and brotherhood. The spirit of Christ has been their most powerful ally, but the official church, taking Christendom as a whole, has thrown the bulk of its great resources to the side of those who are in possession, and against those who were in such deadly need of its aid. This is the great scandal which will not down. Scientific doubt may alienate thousands, but the resentment against the church for going over to the enemy has alienated entire nations. Nothing would so expiate that guilt and win back the lost respect for religion, as determined coöperation on the part of the church in creating a social order in which the just aspirations of the working class will be satisfied. Those Christian men who are the outstanding and bold friends of the people's cause are to-day the most effective apologists of Christianity.

The Christian demand for the kingdom of God on earth responds to the passionate desire for liberty which pervades and inspires the modern world. That desire is really a longing for redemption. Just as an individual may long to be free from vicious habits that enslave him and rob him of his manhood and self-respect, so great social classes now want freedom from the social unfreedom and degradation which denies their human worth and submerges their higher nature in coarseness, ignorance, and animal brutality. The theological word "redemption" originally meant the ransoming of slaves and prisoners. Christ is the great emancipator. Every advance in true Christianity has meant a broadening path for liberty. The highest Christian quality is love; but love is supreme freedom, a state in which even moral compulsion ceases because goodness has become spontaneous. This world-wide desire for freedom is the breath of God in the soul of humanity. Men instinctively know it as such, and they hate a church that would rob them of it. Social Christianity would rally that desire in the name of the kingdom of God, and help the people to a consciousness that they are really moved by religion when they love freedom. On the other hand, by its strong emphasis on social solidarity and the law of service, it will counteract that exaggerated assertion of individual rights and that selfish soul-culture which dog the steps of Freedom.

Every individual reconstructs his comprehension of life and duty, of the world and of God, as he passes from one period of his development to the next. If he fails to do so, his religion will lose its grasp and control. In the same way humanity must reconstruct its moral and religious synthesis whenever it passes from one era to another. When all other departments of life and thought are silently changing, it is impossible for religion to remain unaffected. Otherworldly religion was the full expression of the highest aspirations of ancient and medieval life. Contemporary philosophy supported it. The Ptolemaic astronomy made it easy to conceive of a heaven localized above the starry firmament, which was only a few miles up. But to-day the whole *Weltanschauung* which supported those religious conceptions has melted away irretrievably. Copernican astronomy, the conviction of the universal and majestic reign of law, the evolutionary conception of the history of this earth and of the race, have made the religious ideas that were the natural denizens of the old world of thought seem like antique survivals to-day, as if a company of Athenians should walk down Broadway in their ancient dress. When Christianity invaded the ancient world, it was a modernist religion contemptuously elbowing aside the worn-out superstitions of heathenism, and the live intellects seized it as an adequate expression of their religious consciousness. To-day the livest intellects have the greatest difficulty in maintaining their connections with it. Many of its defenders are querulously lamenting the growth of unbelief. They stand on a narrowing island amid a growing flood, saving what they can of the wreckage of faith. Is religion dying? Is the giant faith of Christianity tottering to its grave?

Religion is not dying. It is only molting its feathers, as every winged thing must at times. A new springtide is coming. Even now the air is full of mating calls and love songs. Soon there will be a nest in every tree.

As the modern world is finding itself, religion is returning to it in new ways. Philosophy in its most modern forms is tending toward an idealistic conception of the universe, even when it calls itself materialistic. It realizes spirit behind all reality. The new psychology is full of the powers and mysteries of the soul. It is no slight achievement of faith to think of God immanent in the whole vast universe, but those who accomplish that act of faith feel him very near and mysteriously present, pulsating in their own souls in every yearning for truth and love and right. Life once more becomes miraculous; for every event in which we realize God and our soul is a miracle. All history becomes the unfolding of the purpose of the immanent God who is working in the race toward the commonwealth of spiritual liberty and righteousness. History is the sacred workshop of God. There is a presentiment abroad in modern thought that humanity is on the verge of a profound change, and that feeling heralds the fact. We feel that all this wonderful liberation of redemptive energy is working out a true and divine order in which our race will rise to a new level of existence. But such a higher order can rise out of the present only if superior spiritual forces build and weave it. Thousands of young minds who thought a few years ago that they had turned their back on religion forever are full of awe and a sense of mystery as they watch the actualities of life in this process of up-building.[112] By coöperating with God in his work they are realizing God. Religion is insuppressible.

It is true that the social enthusiasm is an unsettling force which

---

112. This line of thought was worked out more fully in my little book *Unto Me*, published by the Pilgrim Press, Boston, in 1912. [au.]

may unbalance for a time, break old religious habits and connections, and establish new contacts that are a permanent danger to personal religion. But the way to meet this danger is not to fence out the new social spirit, but to let it fuse with the old religious faith and create a new total that will be completer and more Christian than the old religious individualism at its best. Such a combination brings a triumphant enlargement of life which proves its own value and which none would give up again who has once experienced it. There is so much religion even in nonreligious social work that some who had lost their conscious religion irretrievably have found it again by this new avenue. God has met them while they were at work with him in social redemption, and they have a religion again and a call to a divine ministry. Faith in a new social order is so powerful a breeder of religion that great bodies of men who in theory scorn and repudiate the name of religion, in practice show evidence of possessing some of the most powerful instincts and motives of religion. One of the most valuable achievements in the domain of personal religion which is now open to any man is to build up a rounded and harmonious Christian personality in which all the sweetness and intensity of the old religious life shall combine with the breadth, intelligence, and fighting vigor of the social spirit. Every such individuality will reproduce itself in others who are less mature, and so multiply this new species of the genus "Christian."

The Revival of Religion and the Conversion of the Strong[113]

In looking back over the field traversed in this book, it may seem to some as if our argument had fallen away from the high religious ground taken at the outset and had sagged down to the level of mere economic discussion. That impression would be superficial. This is a religious book from beginning to end. Its sole concern is for the kingdom of God and the salvation of men. But the kingdom of God includes the economic life; for it means the progressive transformation of all human affairs by the thought and spirit of Christ. And a full salvation also includes the economic life; for it involves the opportunity for every man to realize the full humanity which God

---

113. *Christianizing the Social Order*, 458–74.

has put into him as a promise and a call; it means a clean, rich, just, and brotherly life between him and his fellows; it means a chance to be single-hearted, and not to be coerced into a double life. I believe with the great historian von Ranke that "the only real progress of mankind is contained in Christianity;" but that is true only when Christianity is allowed to become "the internal, organizing force of society."[114] We have scouted around our economic system, mined under it, and aëroplaned over it, because this is the fortress in which the predatory and unbrotherly spirit still lies intrenched with flags flying. It is the strategical key to the spiritual conquest of the modern world.

But, on the other hand, no outward economic readjustments will answer our needs. It is not this thing or that thing our nation needs, but a new mind and heart, a new conception of the way we all ought to live together, a new conviction about the worth of a human life and the use God wants us to make of our own lives. We want a revolution both inside and outside. We want a moral renovation of public opinion and a revival of religion. Laws and constitutions are mighty and searching, but while the clumsy hand of the law fumbles at the gate below, the human soul sits in its turret amid its cruel plunder and chuckles. A righteous public opinion may bring the proudest sinner low. But the most pervasive scrutiny, a control which follows our actions to their fountain-head where the desires and motives of the soul are born, is exerted only by personal religion.

But here again we are compelled to turn to our economic life. What if the public opinion on which we rely is tainted and purposely poisoned? What if our religion is drugged and sick? The mammonism generated by our economic life is debilitating our religion so that its hand lies nerveless on our conscience. Jesus told us it would be so. He put the dilemma flatly before us: "Ye cannot serve God and Mammon. If ye love the one, ye will hate the other."[115] Every proof that we love Mammon with all our heart and all our soul raises the presumption that we have lost the love of God and are merely going through the motions when we worship him. We can measure the general apostasy by noting the wonder and love that follow every

---

114. Leopold von Ranke, one of the earliest "scientific" historians. The second quotation is from Johann Sottlieb Fichte.

115. Mt 6:24.

man who has even in some slight degree really turned his back on money. Men crowd around him like exiles around a man who brings them news from home.

So we must begin at both ends simultaneously. We must change our economic system in order to preserve our conscience and our religious faith; we must renew and strengthen our religion in order to be able to change our economic system. This is a two-handed job; a one-handed man will bungle it. I have discussed the economic system in many chapters. In this closing chapter I shall talk about revolutionary religion and the need of converted men for the christianizing of the social order.

When Archimedes discovered the laws of leverage, he cried Δὸσ ποῦ στῶ. He thought he could hoist the bulk of the earth from its grooves if only he had a standing place and a fulcrum for his lever. God wants to turn humanity right side up, but he needs a fulcrum. Every saved soul is a fixed point on which God can rest his lever. A divine world is ever pressing into this imperfect and sinful world, demanding admission and realization for its higher principles, and every inspired man is a channel through which the spirit of God can enter humanity. Every higher era must be built on a higher moral law and a purer experience of religion. Therefore the most immediate and constant need in christianizing the social order is for more religious individuals.

I believe in the miraculous power of the human personality. A mind set free by God and energized by a great purpose is an incomputable force. Lord Shaftesbury was naturally a man of rather narrow type and without brilliant gifts, but he gave himself with religious devotion to the cause of the oppressed classes, and so became one of the prime forces that swung England out of its carnival of capitalistic inhumanity.[116] If we in the West have been correctly informed, the emancipation of China from the Manchu oligarchy has been chiefly due to the personal teaching and persuasion of one man,

---

116. The Duke of Argyll in 1885 said: "My Lords, the social reforms of the last century have not been mainly due to the Liberal Party. They have been due mainly to the influence, character, and perseverance of one man, Lord Shaftesbury." "That," said Lord Salisbury, "is, I believe, a very true representation of the facts." [au.]

Sun Yat Sen, and the band of devoted men whom he raised up. One of the most fruitful intellectual movements in Germany[117] owes its beginning to one man, Professor Albert Eichhorn. His health has been so frail that he has published nothing but a sixteen-page pamphlet, but by personal conversations he inspired a number of able young minds, setting them new problems and fertilizing their thinking by his unselfish cooperation. The Democratic Convention of Baltimore in 1912 will stand out in our memory chiefly for the dramatic power of a single personality,[118] strong in his sincerity and the trust of his countrymen, to wrest the control of his party at least for a time from evil hands. The history of the new democracy in recent years is the history of small groups of men of conviction and courage who stood together for the new democratic measures. Often without official standing or financial backing they have shattered political redoubts that seemed impregnable. The Inquisition of the Middle Ages and the Siberian exile system alike testify to the fact that the powers of tyranny are afraid of single-handed faith.

This power of the individual rests on the social cohesion of mankind. Because we are bound together in unity of life, the good or the evil in one man's soul affects the rest. The presence of one heart that loves humanity shames the selfish spirit in others and warms the germs of civic devotion in the chilly soil, so that they grow and bear seed in turn. One brave soul rallies the timid and shakes the self-confidence of the prosperous. One far-seeing man can wake the torpid imagination of a community so that men see civic centers where they saw only real estate deals before. Hopes and convictions that were dim and vague become concrete, beautiful, and compelling when they take shape in a life that lives them out. No torch is kindled of itself, but when one man has lighted his at the altar fire of God, hundreds will take their light from him. So the faith of the pioneers becomes socialized. The belief of the few in time becomes a dogma which does not have to be proved over and over, but is a spiritual fund owned in common by a great social group. We need new dogmas that will raise the old to a new level and give them wider scope.

---

117. The so-called *religionsgeschichtliche Schule*. [au.]
118. Woodrow Wilson.

"You have heard that it was said of old time—But I say unto you."[119] Such a lifting of moral conviction comes through those who can speak with authority because they speak for God.

Create a ganglion chain of redeemed personalities in a commonwealth, and all things become possible. "What the soul is in the body, that are Christians in the world."[120] The political events of 1912 have furnished fresh proof that after individuals have preached their faith long enough, the common mind reaches the point of saturation, and moral conviction begins to be precipitated in solid layers. At such times even poor Judas thinks he would like to join the Messianic movement and be an apostle, and the rotten nobility of France follow the peasant girl:—

> "The White Maid, and the white horse, and the flapping
>   banner of God;
> Black hearts riding for money; red hearts riding for fame,
> The Maid who rides for France, and the king who rides for
>   shame;
> Gentlemen, fools, and a saint riding in Christ's high
>   name."[121]

"Force and Right rule the world; Force till Right is ready."[122] The more individuals we have who love the Right for its own sake and move toward it of their own will, the less force and compulsion do we need. Here is one of the permanent functions of the Christian church. It must enlist the will and the love of men and women for God, mark them with the cross of Christ, and send them out to finish up the work which Christ began. Is the church supplying society with the necessary equipment of such personalities? Let us grant that it can never reach all; but is it making Christian revolutionists of those whom it does teach and control? Jesus feared the proselyting efforts of the Jewish church, because it made men worse than they were before.[123] Some people to-day who carry the stamp of eccle-

---

119. Mt 5.
120. Epistle to Diognetus, chap. 6. [au.]
121. Theodore Roberts, "The Maid." [au.]
122. François de la Rochefoucauld, French moralist and coiner of maxims.
123. Mt 23:15.

siastical religion most legibly are the most hopeless cases so far as social spirit and effort are concerned. The spiritual efficiency of the church is therefore one of the most serious practical questions for the christianizing of the social order. We have shown that the American churches have been to a large extent christianized in their fundamental organization, and every step in their redemption has facilitated social progress and increased the forces available for righteousness. But the process of christianizing the church is not yet complete.

To become fully Christian the churches must turn their back on dead issues and face their present tasks. There is probably not a single denomination which is not thrusting on its people questions for which no man would care and of which only antiquarians would know if the churches did not keep these questions alive. Our children sometimes pull the clothes of their grandparents out of old chests in the attic and masquerade in long-tailed coats and crinolines. We religious folks who air the issues of the sixteenth century go through the same mummery in solemn earnest, while the enemy is at the gate.

To become fully Christian and to do their duty by society the churches must get together. The disunion of the church wastes the funds intrusted to it, wastes the abilities of its servants, and wastes the power of religious enthusiasm or turns it into antisocial directions. Civil war is always bad; it is worst when a nation is threatened by outside enemies and the very existence of the fatherland is in danger. Some churches are so far apart on essential matters that union is hopeless for the present. But the great body of Protestant Christians in America is simply perpetuating trivial dissensions in which scarcely any present-day religious values are at stake.

To become fully Christian the church must come out of its spiritual isolation. In theory and practice the church has long constituted a world by itself. It has been governed by ecclesiastical motives and interests which are often remote from the real interests of humanity, and has almost uniformly set church questions ahead of social questions. It has often built a sound-proof habitation in which people could live for years without becoming definitely conscious of the existence of prostitution, child labor, or tenement crowding. It has offered peace and spiritual tranquillity to men and women who needed thunderclaps and lightnings. Like all the rest of us, the church will get salvation by finding the purpose of its existence outside of itself, in the kingdom of God, the perfect life of the race.

To become fully Christian the church must still further emancipate itself from the dominating forces of the present era. In an age of political despotism our fathers cut the church loose from state control and state support, and therewith released the moral forces of progress. In an age of financial autocracy we must be far more watchful than we have been lest we bargain away the spiritual freedom of the church for opulent support.

We do not want to substitute social activities for religion. If the church comes to lean on social preachings and doings as a crutch because its religion has become paralytic, may the Lord have mercy on us all! We do not want less religion; we want more; but it must be a religion that gets its orientation from the kingdom of God. To concentrate our efforts on personal salvation, as orthodoxy has done, or on soul culture, as liberalism has done, comes close to refined selfishness. All of us who have been trained in egotistic religion need a conversion to Christian Christianity, even if we are bishops or theological professors. Seek ye first the kingdom of God and God's righteousness, and the salvation of your souls will be added to you. Our personality is of divine and eternal value, but we see it aright only when we see it as part of mankind. Our religious individuality must get its interpretation from the supreme fact of social solidarity. "What hast thou that thou hast not received?" Then what hast thou that thou dost not owe? Prayer ought to be a keen realization of our fellows, and not a forgetfulness of the world. A religion which realizes in God the bond that binds all men together can create the men who will knit the social order together as an organized brotherhood.

This, then, is one of the most practical means for the christianizing of the social order, to multiply the number of minds who have turned in conscious repentance from the old maxims, the old admirations, and the old desires, and have accepted for good and all the Christian law with all that it implies for modern conditions. When we have a sufficient body of such, the old order will collapse like the walls of Jericho when the people "shouted with a great shout" and "every man went straight before him" at the wall.[124] No wrong can

---

124. Jos 6:20.

stand very long after the people have lost their reverence for it and begin to say "Booh" to it.

Mending the social order is not like repairing a clock in which one or two parts are broken. It is rather like restoring diseased or wasted tissues, and when that has to be done, every organ and cell of the body is heavily taxed. During the reconstructive process every one of us must be an especially good cell in whatever organ of the social body we happen to be located. The tissues of society which it will be hardest to replace by sound growth are represented by the class of the poor and the class of the rich. Both are the product of ages of social disease. Christianizing the social order involves a sanitation of the defective and delinquent classes, and of the classes living on unearned incomes. All these need religious salvation.

Suppose that we had successfully democratized our government, made our laws just, and socialized our industries. We should still have with us a great body of people who have been crippled by war or industry, exhausted by child labor, drained of vitality in their mothers' wombs, unbalanced by alcoholism, or made neurotic by drug habits and sexual excesses. These would be the legacy bequeathed by the old order to the new, and surviving it for at least fifty years; perhaps a hundred and fifty years. To-day we have that same body of defective people, constantly replenished and increasing in proportion to the population, hanging as a dead weight on society and on the working class especially. Whatever decreases that weight will give us elbow room for constructive work. The men and women who are helping to organize the defective members of the community so that they will get the maximum enjoyment out of their life and will present the minimum of hindrance to the present social transition, are not mere ministers of mercy, but constructive agents in the christianizing of the social order. If the selfish political henchmen who have run our public institutions can be replaced by regenerate intellects, our institutions of mercy will come out of their conspiracy of silence with the workers of cruelty, and we shall begin to find out who and what is throwing all this burden on the community.

The problem of healing the social tissues is even more difficult in the case of those who break the laws. The old vindictive method of punishment has manifestly been ineffective. It is also unchristian; for nothing is Christian that is not impelled by love and the desire to redeem. It becomes increasingly intolerable as our clearer psychological knowledge reminds us that we all in youth had the same wayward and brutal instincts, and that the majority of youthful criminals are just such immature human beings as our own children. We are realizing that the social disorder which we ourselves have helped to create is responsible for a large part of our lawlessness. "Society stands in the docket with every criminal who is there."[125] We need redeemed minds to deal with the delinquents of society. The men and women who deal with offenders should be the wisest and most Christ-like persons in the community. To save the young and wayward from losing their honor and to fan the dying fire of manhood in older criminals, is a great ministry of Christ, and Christian men ought to enter the police force with the sense of enlisting for God and their country. Within this generation our prisons should become redemptive institutions. But the consciousness of doing productive and honorable work is an essential condition of true salvation. Our penal institutions must become coöperative industrial establishments, where offenders can still support their families, lay by for the day when they will be thrown on their own resources, and, if possible, make restitution to those whom they have harmed. Our prisons must cease to be slave pens where the state lends its physical compulsion to some predatory industrial concern that wants to make big profits by underselling outside labor, grafting on the state, and draining the prisoners. The participation of our states in contract prison labor is an indefensible business that ought to rob us of our sleep.

The sanitation of the wealthy classes is another problem; there we deal, not with the misery and waywardness of the poor, but with excessive material power. Some think it is idle to appeal to the rich to change their own lives; it will have to be changed for them. I do not believe it. As a class they will doubtless go their way, eating and drinking, marrying and giving in marriage till the flood comes. But individuals will respond; more of them, I believe, than in any similar situation in history before. Large groups of them have of late traveled miles in the direction of the fraternal life.

Even if there are only a few, their coming counts. Something happens when Moses leaves the palace of Pharaoh and joins the for-

---

125. Victor Hugo.

tunes of his people. At a directors' meeting a single steady voice lifted for humanity and 6 per cent and against inhumanity and 8 per cent, cannot be disregarded forever, and that voice may mean health and decency for hundreds. Socialists justly say that there is no instance in history where one of the possessing classes has voluntarily given up its privileges. But is there any case where a poor and oppressed class has made a permanent and successful advance toward emancipation without help from individuals of the higher classes?

The desire for social esteem is one of the strongest and most subtle forces in social life. The individual always toils for whatever his class regards as the game. He will collect scalps for his belt, Philistine foreskins for a bridal gift to his beloved, silver cups or wreaths of wild olive as athletic trophies, funny titles, shady millions,—it's all the same thing. Now, a few self-confident men can create a new basis of esteem in their class and therewith change the direction of effort. If a few redeemed minds in a given business community begin to yawn at the stale game of piling up and juggling money, and plunge into the more fascinating game of re-making a city, others will follow them. They cannot help it. God and the instinct of imitation will make them.

Social institutions can be hit hardest by men who have grown up inside of them and know their weak spots. Pharisaism was hit by the Pharisee Paul; monasticism by the monk Luther; the aristocracy of France by Count Mirabeau; alcoholism by John B. Gough; militarism by the ex-officer Tolstoy; frenzied finance by Lawson;[126] the traction system by the traction magnate Tom L. Johnson. Even a few renegades from the rich are invaluable. It takes a sharp blow from the outside to crack an eggshell; the soft bill of a chick can break it from within.

Every rich man who has taken the Christian doctrine of stewardship seriously has thereby expropriated himself after a fashion and become manager where he used to be owner. If a man in addition realizes that some part of his fortune consists of unearned money, accumulated by one of the forms of injustice which have been legalized by our social order, it becomes his business as a Christian and a gentleman to make restitution in some way. There is

---

126. Thomas W. Lawson.

no sincere repentance without restitution and confession of wrong. If I discovered that I or my grandfather had, knowingly or unknowingly, by some manipulation or error of the survey, added to my farm a ten-acre strip which belonged to my neighbor, could I go on harvesting the crops on it and say nothing? It is true that restitution of wealth absorbed from great communities through many years is a complicated matter, and that the giving away of large sums is dangerous business which may do as much harm as good. Yet some way must be found. Since the rich have gained their wealth by appropriating public functions and by using the taxing powers which ought to belong to the community alone, the fittest way of restitution is to undertake public service for which the state in its present impoverished condition has no means, such as the erection and running of public baths, playgrounds, and civic centers. But the moral value of such gifts would be almost incalculably increased if some acknowledgment were made that these funds were drawn from the people and belonged to them. Every time any rich man has indicated that he felt troubled in mind about his right to his wealth, the public heart has warmed toward him with a sense of forgiveness. If some eminent man should have the grace and wisdom to make a confession of wrong on behalf of his whole class, it would have a profound influence on public morality and social peace.

If a rich man has a really redeemed conscience and intellect, the best way to give away his unearned wealth would be to keep it and use it as a tool to make the recurrence of such fortunes as his own forever impossible. The Salvation Army sets a saved girl to save other girls, and that is the best way to keep her saved. By the same token a man whose forefathers made their money in breweries or distilleries ought to use it to fight alcoholism; a man who made his by land speculation should help to solve the housing question or finance the single-tax movement; a man who has charged monopoly prices for the necessaries of life should teach the people to organize coöperative societies; and so forth.

Men and women of the wealthy class who have been converted to the people as well as to God can perform a service of the highest value by weakening the resistance which their classes will inevitably offer to the equalization of property. That resistance has been by far the most important cause why humanity has been so backward in its social and moral development. The resistance of the upper classes has again and again blocked and frustrated hopeful upward movements, kept useful classes of the people in poverty and degradation, and punished the lovers of humanity with martyrdom of body or soul. The cross of Christ stands for the permanent historical fact that the men who have embodied the saving power of God have always been ill treated by those who profited by sin. Reference has been made to the work of Lord Shaftesbury.[127] In Lancashire alone he found 35,000 children under thirteen years of age, many of them only five or six years old, working fourteen and fifteen hours a day. It took Shaftesbury and his friends fourteen years of agitation to get a ten-hour bill passed, and even then it was so impeded by legal difficulties that successive Acts, chiefly instigated by him, were required to give it effect, and the ten-hour standard was not fully secured till 1874. He and his friends were loaded with denunciation and insult for years. Few clergymen stood by him; they were indifferent, or cowed by the cotton lords. Men whose names are revered because they led the fight of the capitalistic class against landed wealth, Cobden, Bright, and Gladstone,[128] were at that time the malignant opponents of the protection of the working class. Machiavelli said that men will forgive the murder of their parents more easily than the spoliation of their property.

Of course the road is smoother since democracy has leveled it. In 1567 under the Duke of Alba a man was condemned to death for the treasonable assertion that "we must obey God rather than man."[128a] It would probably be safe to say that now, especially if chapter and verse were quoted. But the opposition of the powerful classes against every movement that seriously threatens their privileges is one of the most formidable facts with which we have to reckon. All the dynasties of Europe combined against the first French Republic. All capitalistic governments would combine to trip and cripple the first Socialist Republic. If our interests found their control of government really in danger, it would be comparatively easy to embroil our nation in war; that is always the last trick of a tottering dynasty. Therewith the President would be vested with almost

---

127. See Hodder, *The Life and Work of the Seventh Earl of Shaftesbury*, 3 vols. (1866). [au.]

128. Richard Cobden, John Bright, William E. Gladstone.

128a. Acts 5:29.

dictatorial powers; martial law could be proclaimed wherever needed; state rights could be overridden; and the popular movement could be forcibly suppressed as treasonable.

A minority of wealthy men and women, who stand for the democratic American ideals and sincerely believe in the necessity and justice of the impending social changes, would do a great deal to avert the heading up of that spirit of anarchy among the rich and to prevent such a *coup d'état*, which would be the beginning of the end for our nation.

I estimate that about two thirds of my readers have read the foregoing pages about the conversion of the rich with a smiling sense of unreality, as the amiable dreams of a ''good man.'' The late Duke of Cambridge[129] had a way of talking aloud to himself even in church. One Sunday the lesson about Zacchaeus[130] was being read, who gave away half of his goods to the poor. ''Gad,'' said the Duke, ''I don't mind subscribing, but half is too much.'' The rich young ruler was asked to give the whole and went away sorrowful.[131] He wanted the goods, but the price staggered him. He missed his chance by not being game. He stood shivering on the shore and feared the plunge from which he would have come up in a tingle of life. He might have traveled day by day in the company of Jesus, with the Master's words in his memory, his eye on him, his friendship coaxing every good thing in the man's heart up and out. He might have become an apostle, one of the guiding spirits of the young church, handling growing responsibilities, seeing the world, facing kings and mobs, tasting the fullness of life. His name might to-day be a household word wherever the Gospels are read, and millions of boys might be named after him as after John and James. Instead of that he probably lived and died as the richest man of his little Galilean town, carrying in a frozen heart the dead seed of a great life, unless, indeed, some Roman official squeezed him dry or the Jewish War did for him by force what he would not do freely.

So far from being dreams these suggestions are hard sense. If I were rich myself, I could state them far more strongly. The call to

---

129. Commander-in-chief of the British army, 1856–95.
130. Lk 19:5.
131. Mt 19:21.

place unearned wealth at the service of the people's cause is to-day the daring short cut to great experiences, to the love and confidence of all good men, and almost the only way to fame open to most rich men. It is the "open but unfrequented path to immortality."[132] It is also the path to peace of heart and the joy of life. The sacrifices demanded by a religious conversion always seem sore and insuperable, but every religious man will agree that after the great surrender is made, there is a radiant joy that marks a great culmination of life. All the remaining years are ennobled. God is the great joy. Whenever we have touched the hem of his garment by some righteous action, we get so much satisfaction that we can be well content even if we get no further reward or recognition, or even if we suffer hurt and persecution for it. Not the memory of power wielded, not even the memory of love, is so sweet as the consciousness that we once suffered for a great cause. When Thomas Jefferson gave directions about his epitaph, he made no reference to having been Governor, Secretary of State, Vice President, and President of the United States. He did boast of having been the father of the University of Virginia, the author of the Declaration of Independence, and of the Virginia statute guaranteeing religious liberty.

"Now I saw in my dream, that the highway up which Christian was to go was fenced on either side with a wall, and that wall is called Salvation. Up this way therefore did burdened Christian run, but not without great difficulty, because of the load on his back. He ran thus till he came at a place somewhat ascending; and upon that place stood a Cross . . . . So I saw in my dream that just as Christian came up with the cross, his burden loosed from off his shoulders and fell from off his back . . . . Then was Christian glad and lightsome and spoke with a merry heart."[133] It is a sober fact that for many a Christian the load that burdens his soul is unearned money. If he returned it in some wise and redemptive way to the people from whom it came, he would once more own his soul, be a friend of all men, and a happy child of God. It is truly at the Cross alone that freedom of the soul is won.

---

132. John Howard died in Russian Tartary, trying to find the cause of the plague and a remedy for it. On his tombstone in St. Paul's Cathedral are the words: "He took an open but unfrequented path to immortality." [au.]

133. Bunyan's *Pilgrim's Progress.*

''A THEOLOGY FOR THE SOCIAL GOSPEL''

A Theology for the Social Gospel is not, and was not intended to be, a devotional book. Rauschenbusch's purpose was to provide social Christianity, which had grown strong as a movement, with a theology to sustain it. "We have a social gospel. We need a systematic theology large enough to match it and vital enough to back it."[134] *Although this final published volume is widely acknowledged to be Rauschenbusch's best and the most intellectually satisfying statement of his views, Rauschenbusch regarded it as a preliminary and far from complete systematic theological treatment of the Christian faith. The half-dozen chapters dealing with sin and the kingdom of evil are the most carefully argued, although he makes a telling critique of scholars who contended that the concept of the kingdom of God, as presented in the New Testament, was so thoroughly eschatological in its presuppositions that it had no relevance or useful application to any modern discussion of the social order.*

My own conviction is that the professional theologians of Europe, who all belong by kinship and sympathy to the bourgeois classes and are constitutionally incapacitated for understanding any revolutionary ideas, past or present, have overemphasized the ascetic and eschatological elements in the teachings of Jesus. They have classed as ascetic or apocalyptic the radical sayings about property and non-resistance which seem to them impractical or visionary. If the present chastisement of God purges our intellects of capitalistic and upper-class iniquities, we shall no longer damn these sayings by calling them eschatological, but shall exhibit them as anticipations of the fraternal ethics of democracy and prophecies of social common sense.[135]

The most pertinent chapter for the present collection of readings which has Christian "spirituality" as its primary

---

134. *A Theology for the Social Gospel* (New York, 1918), 1.
135. Ibid., 158.

focus is the chapter "The Social Gospel and Personal Salvation." It is apparent that Rauschenbusch's understanding of Christianity had been undergoing a subtle shift over the years. The concern for personal religion and social reform had become more and more closely interrelated until they constituted a single whole which was chiefly preoccupied with the ethical dimensions of the Christian faith. Perhaps one should ask no more of a theological treatise. Still, it is striking that, whereas the Holy Spirit loomed so large in Rauschenbusch's early writings, in A Theology for the Social Gospel *discussion of the Holy Spirit is reduced in scope to three brief paragraphs (less than a page and a half), a discussion which is limited solely to the doctrine of inspiration.*

The Social Gospel and Personal Salvation[136]

The new thing in the social gospel is the clearness and insistence with which it sets forth the necessity and the possibility of redeeming the historical life of humanity from the social wrongs which now pervade it and which act as temptations and incitements to evil and as forces of resistance to the powers of redemption. Its chief interest is concentrated on those manifestations of sin and redemption which lie beyond the individual soul. If our exposition of the superpersonal agents of sin and of the kingdom of evil is true, then evidently a salvation confined to the soul and its personal interests is an imperfect and only partly effective salvation.

Yet the salvation of the individual is, of course, an essential part of salvation. Every new being is a new problem of salvation. It is always a great and wonderful thing when a young spirit enters into voluntary obedience to God and feels the higher freedom with which Christ makes us free. It is one of the miracles of life. The burden of the individual is as heavy now as ever. The consciousness of wrongdoing, of imperfection, of a wasted life lies on many and they need forgiveness and strength for a new beginning. Modern pessimism drains the finer minds of their confidence in the world and the value of life itself. At present we gasp for air in a crushing and monstrous world. Any return of faith is an experience of salvation.

---

136. Ibid., 95–109.

Therefore our discussion can not pass personal salvation by. We might possibly begin where the old gospel leaves off, and ask our readers to take all the familiar experiences and truths of personal evangelism and religious nurture for granted in what follows. But our understanding of personal salvation itself is deeply affected by the new solidaristic comprehension furnished by the social gospel.

The social gospel furnishes new tests for religious experience. We are not disposed to accept the converted souls whom the individualistic evangelism supplies, without looking them over. Some who have been saved and perhaps reconsecrated a number of times are worth no more to the kingdom of God than they were before. Some become worse through their revival experiences, more self-righteous, more opinionated, more steeped in unrealities and stupid over against the most important things, more devoted to emotions and unresponsive to real duties. We have the highest authority for the fact that men may grow worse by getting religion. Jesus says the Pharisees compassed sea and land to make a proselyte, and after they had him, he was twofold more a child of hell than his converters.[137] To one whose memories run back twenty or thirty years, to Moody's time, the methods now used by some evangelists seem calculated to produce skin-deep changes. Things have simmered down to signing a card, shaking hands, or being introduced to the evangelist. We used to pass through some deep-soil ploughing by comparison. It is time to overhaul our understanding of the kind of change we hope to produce by personal conversion and regeneration. The social gospel furnishes some tests and standards.

When we undertook to define the nature of sin, we accepted the old definition, that sin is selfishness and rebellion against God, but we insisted on putting humanity into the picture. The definition of sin as selfishness gets its reality and nipping force only when we see humanity as a great solidarity and God indwelling in it. In the same way the terms and definitions of salvation get more realistic significance and ethical reach when we see the internal crises of the individual in connection with the social forces that play upon him or go out from him. The form which the process of redemption takes in a

---

137. Mt 23:15.

given personality will be determined by the historical and social spiritual environment of the man. At any rate any religious experience in which our fellow-men have no part or thought, does not seem to be a distinctively Christian experience.

If sin is selfishness, salvation must be a change which turns a man from self to God and humanity. His sinfulness consisted in a selfish attitude, in which he was at the centre of the universe, and God and all his fellow-men were means to serve his pleasures, increase his wealth, and set off his egotisms. Complete salvation, therefore, would consist in an attitude of love in which he would freely co-ordinate his life with the life of his fellows in obedience to the loving impulses of the spirit of God, thus taking his part in a divine organism of mutual service. When a man is in a state of sin, he may be willing to harm the life and lower the self-respect of a woman for the sake of his desires; he may be willing to take some of the mental and spiritual values out of the life of a thousand families, and lower the human level of a whole mill-town in order to increase his own dividends or maintain his autocratic sense of power. If this man came under the influence of the mind of Christ, he would see men and women as children of God with divine worth and beauty, and this realization would cool his lust or covetousness. Living now in the consciousness of the pervading spiritual life of God, he would realize that all his gifts and resources are a loan of God for higher ends, and would do his work with greater simplicity of mind and brotherliness.

Of course in actual life there is no case of complete Christian transformation. It takes an awakened and regenerated mind a long time to find itself intellectually and discover what life henceforth is to mean to him, and his capacity for putting into practice what he knows he wants to do, will be something like the capacity of an untrained hand to express artistic imaginations. But in some germinal and rudimentary form salvation must turn us from a life centered on ourselves toward a life going out toward God and men. God is the all-embracing source and exponent of the common life and good of mankind. When we submit to God, we submit to the supremacy of the common good. Salvation is the voluntary socializing of the soul.

Conversion has usually been conceived as a break with our own sinful past. But in many cases it is also a break with the sinful past of a social group. Suppose a boy has been joining in cruel or lustful actions because his gang regards such things as fine and manly. If later he breaks with such actions, he will not only have to wrestle with his own habits, but with the social attractiveness and influence of his little humanity. If a working man becomes an abstainer, he will find out that intolerance is not confined to the good. In primitive Christianity baptism stood for a conscious break with pagan society. This gave it a powerful spiritual reaction. Conversion is most valuable if it throws a revealing light not only across our own past, but across the social life of which we are part, and makes our repentance a vicarious sorrow for all. The prophets felt so about the sins of their nation. Jesus felt so about Jerusalem, and Paul about unbelieving Israel.

We call our religious crisis "conversion" when we think of our own active break with old habits and associations and our turning to a new life. Paul introduced the forensic term "justification" into our religious vocabulary to express a changed legal status before God; his term "adoption" expresses the same change in terms derived from family life. We call the change "regeneration" when we think of it as an act of God within us, creating a new life.

The classical passage on regeneration (John iii) connects it with the kingdom of God. Only an inward new birth will enable us to "see the kingdom of God" and to "enter the kingdom of God." The larger vision and the larger contact both require a new development of our spirit. In our unregenerate condition the consciousness of God is weak, occasional, and suppressed. The more Jesus Christ becomes dominant in us, the more does the light and life of God shine steadily in us, and create a religious personality which we did not have. Life is lived under a new synthesis.

It is strange and interesting that regeneration is thus connected with the kingdom of God in John iii. The term has otherwise completely dropped out of the terminology of the fourth gospel. If we have here a verbatim memory of a saying of Jesus, the survival would indicate how closely the idea of personal regeneration was originally bound up with the kingdom hope. When John the Baptist first called men to conversion and a change of mind, all his motives and appeals were taken from the outlook toward the kingdom. Evidently the entire meaning of "conversion" and "regeneration" was subtly changed when the conception of the kingdom disappeared from Christian thought. The change in ourselves was now no longer connected with a great divine change in humanity, for which we must prepare and get fit. If we are converted, what are we converted to? If we are regenerated, does the scope of so divine a transformation end in our "going to heaven"? The nexus between our religious experience and humanity seems gone when the kingdom of God is not present in the idea of regeneration.

Through the experience and influence of Paul the word "faith" has gained a central place in the terminology of salvation. Its meaning fluctuates according to the dominant conception of religion. With Paul it was a comprehensive mystical symbol and emancipation, which flooded his soul with joy and power. On the other hand wherever doctrine becomes rigid and is the pre-eminent thing in religion, "faith" means submission of the mind to the affirmations of dogma and theology, and, in particular, acceptance of the plan of salvation and trust in the vicarious atonement of Christ. Where the idea of the church dominates religion, "faith" means mainly the submission to the teaching and guidance of the church. In popular religion it may shrivel up to something so small as putting a finger on a Scripture text and "claiming the promise."

In primitive Christianity the forward look of expectancy was characteristic of religion. The glory of the coming dawn was on the eastern clouds. This influenced the conception of "faith." It was akin to hope, the forward gaze of the pioneers. The historical illustrations of faith in Hebrews xi show faith launching life toward the unseen future.

This is the aspect of faith which is emphasized by the social gospel. It is not so much the endorsement of ideals formulated in the past, as expectancy and confidence in the coming salvation of God. In this respect the forward look of primitive Christianity is resumed. Faith once more means prophetic vision. It is faith to assume that this is a good world and that life is worth living. It is faith to assert the feasibility of a fairly righteous and fraternal social order. In the midst of a despotic and predatory industrial life it is faith to stake our business future on the proposition that fairness, kindness, and fraternity will work. When war inflames a nation, it is faith to believe that a peaceable disposition is a workable international policy. Amidst the disunion of Christendom it is faith to look for unity and to express unity in action. It is faith to see God at work in the world and to claim a share in his job. Faith is an energetic act of the will, affirming our fellowship with God and man, declaring our solidarity with the Kingdom of God, and repudiating selfish isolation.

"Sanctification," according to almost any definition, is the continuation of that process of spiritual education and transformation, by which a human personality becomes a willing organ of the spirit of Christ. Those who believe in the social gospel can share in any methods for the cultivation of the spiritual life, if only they have an ethical outcome. The social gospel takes up the message of the Hebrew prophets, that ritual and emotional religion is harmful unless it results in righteousness. Sanctification is through increased fellowship with God and man. But fellowship is impossible without an exchange of service. Here we come back to our previous proposition that the kingdom of God is the commonwealth of co-operative service and that the most common form of sinful selfishness is the effort to escape from labor. Sanctification, therefore, can not be attained in an unproductive life, unless it is unproductive through necessity. In the long run the only true way to gain moral insight, self-discipline, humility, love, and a consciousness of coherence and dependence, is to take our place among those who serve one another by useful labor. Parasitism blinds; work reveals.

The fact that the social gospel is a distinct type of religious experience is proved by comparing it with mysticism. In most other types of Christianity the mystic experience is rated as the highest form of sanctification. In Catholicism the monastic life is the way of perfection, and mystic rapture is the highest attainment and reward of monastic contemplation and service. In Protestantism, which has no monastic leisure for mystic exercises, mysticism is of a homelier type, but in almost every group of believers there are some individuals who profess to have attained a higher stage of sanctification through "a second blessing," "the higher life," "complete sanctification," "perfect love," Christian Science, or Theosophy. The literature and organizations ministering to this mystical life, go on the assumption that it far transcends the ordinary way in spiritual blessings and sanctifying power.

Mysticism is a steep short-cut to communion with God. There

is no doubt that under favorable conditions it has produced beautiful results of unselfishness, humility, and undauntable courage. Its danger is that it isolates. In energetic mysticism the soul concentrates on God, shuts out the world, and is conscious only of God and itself. In its highest form, even the consciousness of self is swallowed up in the all-filling possession of God. No wonder it is absorbing and wonderful. But we have to turn our back on the world to attain this experience, and when we have attained it, it makes us indifferent to the world. What does Time matter when we can live in Eternity? What gift can this world offer us after we have entered into the luminous presence of God?

The mystic way to holiness is not through humanity but above it. We can not set aside the fundamental law of God that way. He made us for one another, and our highest perfection comes not by isolation but by love. The way of holiness through human fellowship and service is slower and lowlier, but its results are more essentially Christian. Paul dealt with the mystic phenomena of religion when he dealt with the charismata of primitive Christianity, especially with glossolalia (I Cor. xii–xiv). It is a striking fact that he ranks the spiritual gifts not according to their mystic rapture, but according to their rational control and their power of serving others. His great chapter on love dominates the whole discussion and is offered as a counter-poise and antidote to the dangers of mysticism.[138]

Mysticism is not the maturest form of sanctification. As Professor Royce well says: "It is the always young, it is the childlike, it is the essentially immature aspect of the deeper religious life. Its ardor, its pathos, its illusions, and its genuine illuminations have all the characters of youth about them, characters beautiful, but capricious."[139] There is even question whether mysticism proper, with rapture and absorption, is Christian in its antecedents, or Platonic.

---

138. I have set this forth fully in my little book, *Dare We Be Christians?* (Pilgrim Press, Boston). In my *Prayers of the Social Awakening* (Pilgrim Press), I have tried to connect the social consciousness with the devotional life by prayers envisioning social groups and movements. Professor Wilhelm Herrmann's *The Communion of the Christian with God* deals with the difference of the mystic way and the way of service. [au.]

139. Josiah Royce, *The Problem of Christianity* I (New York, 1913), 400. [au.]

I believe in prayer and meditation in the presence of God; in the conscious purging of the soul from fear, love of gain, and selfish ambition, through realizing God; in bringing the intellect into alignment with the mind of Christ; and in re-affirming the allegiance of the will to the kingdom of God. When a man goes up against hard work, conflict, loneliness, and the cross, it is his right to lean back on the Eternal and to draw from the silent reservoirs. But what we get thus is for use. Personal sanctification must serve the kingdom of God. Any mystic experience which makes our fellow-men less real and our daily labour less noble, is dangerous religion. A religious experience is not Christian unless it binds us closer to men and commits us more deeply to the kingdom of God.

Thus the fundamental theological terms about the experiences of salvation get a new orientation, correction, and enrichment through the religious point of view contained in the social gospel. These changes would effect an approximation to the spirit and outlook of primitive Christianity, going back to Catholicism and Protestantism alike.

The definitions we have attempted are not merely academic and hypothetical exercises. Religion is actually being experienced in such ways.

In the Bible we have several accounts of religious experiences which were fundamental in the life of its greatest characters. A few are told in their own striking phrases. Others are described by later writers, and in that case indicate what popular opinion expected such men to experience. Now, none of these experiences, so far as I see, are of that solitary type in which a soul struggles for its own salvation in order to escape the penalties of sin or to attain perfection and peace for itself. All were experienced with a conscious outlook toward humanity. When Moses saw the glory of God in the flaming bush and learned the ineffable name of the Eternal, it was not the salvation of Moses which was in question but the salvation of his people from the bondage of Egypt. When young Samuel first heard the call of the voice in the darkness, it spoke to him of priestly extortion and the troubled future of his people. When Isaiah saw the glory of the Lord above the Cherubim, he realized by contrast that he was a man of unclean lips. His cleansing and the dedication which followed were his preparation for taking hold of the social situation of his nation. In Jeremiah we are supposed to have the attainment of the religion of the individual, but even his intimate experiences were all in full view of the fate of his nation. Paul's experience at Damascus was the culmination of his personal struggle and his emergence into spiritual freedom. But his crisis got its intensity from its social background. He was deciding, so far as he was concerned, between the old narrow nationalistic religion of conservative Judaism and a wider destiny for his people, between the validity of the Law and spiritual liberty, between the exclusive claims of Israel on the Messianic hope and a world-wide participation in the historical prerogatives of the first-born people. The issues for which his later life stood were condensed in the days at Damascus, as we can see from his own recital in Galatians i, and these religious issues were the fundamental social questions for his nation at that time.

We can not afford to rate this group of religious experiences at a low value. As with us all, the theology of the prophets was based on their personal experiences. Out of them grew their ethical monotheism and their God-consciousness. This was the highest element in the spiritual heritage of his people which came to Jesus. He re-interpreted and perfected it in his personality, and in that form it has remained the highest factor among the various historical strains combined in our religion.

These prophetic experiences were not superficial. There was soul-shaking emotion, a deep sense of sin, faith in God, longing for him, self-surrender, enduement with spiritual power. Yet they were not ascetic, not individualistic, not directed toward a future life. They were social, political, solidaristic.

The religious experiences evoked by the social gospel belong to the same type, though deeply modified, of course, by the profound differences between their age and ours. What the wars and oppressions of Israel and Judah meant to them, the wars and exploitations of modern civilization mean to us. In these things God speaks to our souls. When we face these questions we meet God. An increasing number of young men and women—and some of the best of them—are getting their call to repentance, to a new way of life, and to the conquest of self in this way, and a good many older men are superimposing a new experience on that of their youth.

Other things being equal, a solidaristic religious experience is more distinctively Christian than an individualistic religious experience. To be afraid of hell or purgatory and desirous of a life without pain or trouble in heaven was not in itself Christian. It was self-interest on a higher level. It is not strange that men were wholly intent on saving themselves as long as such dangers as Dante describes were real to their minds. A man might be pardoned for forgetting his entire social consciousness if he found himself dangling over a blazing pit. But even in more spiritual forms of conversion, as long as men are wholly intent on their own destiny, they do not necessarily emerge from selfishness. It only changes its form. A Christian regeneration must have an outlook toward humanity and result in a higher social consciousness.

The saint of the future will need not only a theocentric mysticism which enables him to realize God, but an anthropocentric mysticism which enables him to realize his fellow-men in God. The more we approach pure Christianity, the more will the Christian signify a man who loves mankind with a religious passion and excludes none. The feeling which Jesus had when he said, "I am the hungry, the naked, the lonely,"[140] will be in the emotional consciousness of all holy men in the coming days. The sense of solidarity is one of the distinctive marks of the true followers of Jesus.

---

140. Mt 25:34–45.

VII.

PRAYERS OF THE SOCIAL AWAKENING[141]

Rauschenbusch's "favorite book" was For God and
the People: Prayers of the Social Awakening, *published in
1910. It was the product of his conviction that the new social
sensitivity within the churches would never become deeply
rooted until it found expression in the prayers of the people.
The traditional prayers were too individualistic, too general,
too archaic in language, and too infrequently voiced contemporary needs and aspirations. In the seminary chapel and
at other gatherings, Rauschenbusch sought to rectify this de-
ficiency by fashioning "models" which would be sugges-
tive to others. He also composed prayers for specific
vocational groups. Twelve of the latter were published, one
in each issue as a frontispiece, in the* American Magazine *in
1910. Each successive prayer evoked growing acclaim, and
before the year was out a small volume known in subsequent
editions as* Prayers of the Social Awakening *had been rushed
through the press to satisfy popular demand.*

*The initial response to Rauschenbusch's little manual
of devotion was astonishing. Touching letters of appreciation flooded his mail. The prayers were reprinted in the* Baltimore Sun *and other newspapers. Individual prayers were
printed on plaques to be hung in offices and homes. The
Child Labor Commission printed 13,000 copies of the
prayer "For Children Who Work." The labor press featured*

---

141. *For God and the People: Prayers of the Social Awakening* (Boston, Pilgrim Press, 1910).

the prayers "For Workingmen" and "For Women Who Toil." The prayer "For All True Lovers" was incorporated into marriage services. Other prayers were printed in books of public worship, in hymnals as aids to worship, and in manuals for private devotion. And the book itself maintained a life of its own. There were repeated printings as well as a new edition with additional prayers and the incorporation of "A Social Litany." A French translation was published in 1914, a British edition in 1927, a German translation in 1928, and a Japanese translation in 1932.

After three or four decades a curious reversal began to take place. Rauschenbusch had sought to fashion prayers that were pointed and specific, and those that were most pointed and specific were the ones that won the greatest immediate response. But these are also the ones that, because of changing circumstances, most quickly became dated and "antique." It is the more general prayers that have endured in the living liturgy of the churches, and it is mostly from among these non-vocational and less specific prayers that the present selections have been made. In some instances their sequence has been altered. The section "Prayers for Morning, Noon, and Night" has been retitled "Prayers for the Daily Round," since there are no prayers for "noon" and others are not related to a specific time of day.

PREFACE

The new social purpose, which has laid its masterful grasp on modern life and thought, is enlarging and transforming our whole conception of the meaning of Christianity. The Bible and all past history speak a new and living language. The life of men about us stands out with an open-air color and vividness which it never had in the dusky solemnity of the older theological views about humanity. All the older tasks of church life have taken on a new significance, and vastly larger tasks are emerging as from the mists of a new morning.

Many ideas that used to seem fundamental and satisfying seem strangely narrow and trivial in this greater world of God. Some of the old religious appeals have utterly lost their power over us. But there are others, unknown to our fathers, which kindle religious passions of wonderful intensity and purity. The wrongs and sufferings of the people and the vision of a righteous and brotherly social life awaken an almost painful compassion and longing, and these feelings are more essentially Christian than most of the fears and desires of religion in the past. Social Christianity is adding to the variety of religious experience, and is creating a new type of Christian man who bears a striking family likeness to Jesus of Galilee.

These new religious emotions ought to find conscious and social expression. But the church, which has brought down so rich an equipment from the past for the culture of individual religion, is poverty-stricken in face of this new need. The ordinary church hymnal rarely contains more than two or three hymns in which the triumphant chords of the social hope are struck. Our liturgies and devotional manuals offer very little that is fit to enrich and purify the social thoughts and feelings.

Even men who have absorbed the social ideals are apt to move within the traditional round in public prayer. The language of prayer always clings to the antique for the sake of dignity, and plain reference to modern facts and contrivances jars the ear. So we are inclined to follow the broad avenues beaten by the feet of many generations when we approach God. We need to blaze new paths to God for the feet of modern men.

I offer this little book as an attempt in that direction. So far as I know, it is the first of its kind, and it is likely to meet the sort of objections which every pioneering venture in religion has to encounter. I realize keenly the limitations which are inevitable when one mind is to furnish a vehicle for the most intimate spiritual thoughts of others. But whenever a great movement stirs the deeper passions of men, a common soul is born, and all who feel the throb of the new age have such unity of thought and aim and feeling, that the utterance of one man may in a measure be the voice of all. A number of the prayers in this collection were published month by month in the American Magazine. The response to them showed that there is a great craving for a religious expression of the new social feeling.

If the moral demands of our higher social thought could find adequate expression in prayer, it would have a profound influence on the social movement. Many good men have given up the habit of praying, partly through philosophical doubt, partly because they feel that it is useless or even harmful to their spiritual nature. Prayer in the past, like the hiss of escaping steam, has often dissipated moral energy. But prayer before battle is another thing. That has been the greatest breeder of revolutionary heroism in history. All our bravest desires stiffen into fighting temper when they are affirmed before God.

Public prayer, too, may carry farther than we know. When men are in the presence of God, the best that is in them has a breathing-space. Then, if ever, we feel the vanity and shamefulness of much that society calls proper and necessary. If we had more prayer in common on the sins of modern society, there would be more social repentance and less angry resistance to the demands of justice and mercy.

And if the effect of our prayers goes beyond our own personality; if there is a center of the spiritual universe in whom our spirits join and have their being; and if the mysterious call of our souls somehow reaches and moves God, so that our longings come back from him in a wave of divine assent which assures their ultimate fulfillment—then it may mean more than any man knows to set Christendom praying on our social problems.

I am indebted to my friend, Mr. Mornay Williams, who has long been the president of the New York Juvenile Asylum, for the prayer "For the Children of the Street," and "For Judges." A number of my friends have aided this book more than I can say by their advice and suggestions, and have made it in a measure the work of a group. I shall welcome suggestions from any one which would improve or enrich this little collection in some future edition.

Permission is gladly given to reprint single prayers in newspapers, church programs, and similar publications, provided no change is made in the wording except by omission or abbreviation. I should be glad if proper acknowledgment were made in every case so that the attention of others may be called to this little book and its usefulness increased.

Walter Rauschenbusch
Rochester, N.Y.

THE SOCIAL MEANING OF THE LORD'S PRAYER

The Lord's Prayer is recognized as the purest expression of the mind of Jesus. It crystallizes his thoughts. It conveys the atmosphere of his childlike trust in the Father. It gives proof of the transparent clearness and peace of his soul.

It first took shape as a protest against the wordy flattery with which men tried to wheedle their gods. He demanded simplicity and sincerity in all expressions of religion, and offered this as an example of the straightforwardness with which men might deal with their Father. Hence the brevity and conciseness of it:

"In praying use not vain repetitions, as the Gentiles do: for they think that they shall be heard for their much speaking. Be not therefore like unto them: for your Father knoweth what things ye have need of before ye ask him. After this manner therefore pray ye:

Our Father who art in heaven,
Hallowed be thy name.
Thy kingdom come.
Thy will be done, as in heaven, so on earth.
Give us this day our daily bread.
And forgive us our debts, as we also have forgiven our
    debtors.
And bring us not into temptation, but deliver us from the evil
    one."
Matthew 6:7–13.   (American Revision.)

The Lord's Prayer is so familiar to us that few have stopped to understand it. The general tragedy of misunderstanding which has followed Jesus throughout the centuries has frustrated the purpose of his model prayer also. He gave it to stop vain repetitions, and it has been turned into a contrivance for incessant repetition.

The churches have employed it for their ecclesiastical ritual. Yet it is not ecclesiastical. There is no hint in it of the church, the ministry, the doctrines of theology, or the sacraments—though the Latin Vulgate has turned the petition for the daily bread into a prayer for the "super-substantial bread" of the sacrament.

It has also been used for the devotions of the personal religious life. It is, indeed, profoundly personal. But its deepest significance for the individual is revealed only when he dedicates his personality to the vaster purposes of the kingdom of God, and approaches all his personal problems from that point of view. Then he enters both into the real meaning of the Lord's Prayer, and into the spirit of the Lord himself.

The Lord's Prayer is part of the heritage of social Christianity which has been appropriated by men who have had little sympathy with its social spirit. It belongs to the equipment of the soldiers of the kingdom of God. I wish to claim it here as the great charter of all social prayers.

When he bade us say, "Our Father," Jesus spoke from that consciousness of human solidarity which was a matter of course in all his thinking. He compels us .o clasp hands in spirit with all our brothers and thus to approach the Father together. This rules out all selfish isolation in religion. Before God no man stands alone. Before the All-seeing he is surrounded by the spiritual throng of all to whom he stands related near and far, all whom he loves and hates, whom he serves or oppresses, whom he wrongs or saves. We are one with our fellow-men in all our needs. We are one in our sin and our salvation. To recognize that oneness is the first step toward praying the Lord's Prayer aright. That recognition is also the foundation of social Christianity.

The three petitions with which the prayer begins express the great desire which was fundamental in the heart and mind of Jesus: "Hallowed be thy name. Thy kingdom come. Thy will be done, as in heaven, so on earth." Together they express his yearning faith in the possibility of a reign of God on earth in which his name shall be hallowed and his will be done. They look forward to the ultimate perfection of the common life of humanity on this earth, and pray for the divine revolution which is to bring that about.

There is no request here that we be saved from earthliness and go to heaven which has been the great object of churchly religion. We pray here that heaven may be duplicated on earth through the moral and spiritual transformation of humanity, both in its personal units and its corporate life. No form of religion has ever interpreted this prayer aright which did not have a loving understanding for the plain daily relations of men, and a living faith in their possible spiritual nobility.

And no man has outgrown the crude selfishness of religious immaturity who has not followed Jesus in setting this desire for the social salvation of mankind ahead of all personal desires. The desire for the kingdom of God precedes and outranks everything else in religion, and forms the tacit presupposition of all our wishes for ourselves. In fact, no one has a clear right to ask for bread for his body or strength for his soul, unless he has identified his will with this all-embracing purpose of God, and intends to use the vitality of body and soul in the attainment of that end.

With that understanding we can say that the remaining petitions deal with personal needs.

Among these the prayer for the daily bread takes first place. Jesus was never as "spiritual" as some of his later followers. He never forgot or belittled the elemental need of men for bread. The fundamental place which he gives to this petition is a recognition of the economic basis of life.

But he lets us pray only for the bread that is needful, and for that only when it becomes needful. The conception of what is needful will expand as human life develops. But this prayer can never be used to cover luxuries that debilitate, nor accumulations of property that can never be used but are sure to curse the soul of the holder with the diverse diseases of mammonism.

In this petition, too, Jesus compels us to stand together. We have to ask in common for our daily bread. We sit at the common table in God's great house, and the supply of each depends on the security of all. The more society is socialized, the clearer does that fact become, and the more just and humane its organization becomes, the more will that recognition be at the bottom of all our institutions. As we stand thus in common, looking up to God for our bread, everyone of us ought to feel the sin and shame of it if he habitually takes more than his fair share and leaves others hungry that he may surfeit. It is inhuman, irreligious, and indecent.

The remaining petitions deal with the spiritual needs. Looking backward, we see that our lives have been full of sin and failure, and we realize the need of forgiveness. Looking forward, we tremble at the temptations that await us and pray for deliverance from evil.

In these prayers for the inner life, where the soul seems to confront God alone, we should expect to find only individualistic religion. But even here the social note sounds clearly.

This prayer will not permit us to ask for God's forgiveness without making us affirm that we have forgiven our brothers and are on a basis of brotherly love with all men: "Forgive us our debts, as we also have forgiven our debtors." We shall have to be socially right if we want to be religiously right. Jesus will not suffer us to be pious toward God and merciless toward men.

In the prayer, "Lead us not into temptation," we feel the human trembling of fear. Experience has taught us our frailty. Every man can see certain contingencies just a step ahead of him and knows that his moral capacity for resistance would collapse hopelessly if he were placed in these situations. Therefore Jesus gives voice to our inarticulate plea to God not to bring us into such situations.

But such situations are created largely by the social life about us. If the society in which we move is rank with sexual looseness, or full of the suggestiveness and solicitations of alcoholism; if our business life is such that we have to lie and cheat and be cruel in order to live and prosper; if our political organization offers an ambitious man the alternative of betraying the public good or of being thwarted and crippled in all his efforts, then the temptations are created in which men go under, and society frustrates the prayer we utter to God. No church can interpret this petition intelligently which closes its mind to the debasing or invigorating influence of the spiritual environment furnished by society. No man can utter this petition without conscious or unconscious hypocrisy who is helping to create the temptations in which others are sure to fall.

The words "Deliver us from the evil one" have in them the ring of battle. They bring to mind the incessant grapple between God and the permanent and malignant powers of evil in humanity. To the men of the first century that meant Satan and his host of evil spirits who ruled in the oppressive, extortionate, and idolatrous powers of Rome. Today the original spirit of that prayer will probably be best understood by those who are pitted against the terrible powers of organized covetousness and institutionalized oppression.

Thus the Lord's Prayer is the great prayer of social Christianity. It is charged with what we call "social consciousness." It assumes the social solidarity of men as a matter of course. It recognizes the social basis of all moral and religious life even in the most intimate personal relations to God.

It is not the property of those whose chief religious aim is to pass through an evil world in safety, leaving the world's evil unshaken. Its dominating thought is the moral and religious transformation of mankind in all its social relations. It was left us by Jesus, the great initiator of the Christian revolution; and it is the rightful property of those who follow his banner in the conquest of the world.

PRAYERS FOR THE DAILY ROUND

Morning Prayers

O God, we thank thee for the sweet refreshment of sleep and for the glory and vigor of the new day. As we set our faces once more toward our daily work, we pray thee for the strength sufficient for our tasks. May Christ's spirit of duty and service ennoble all we do. Uphold us by the consciousness that our work is useful work and a blessing to all. If there has been anything in our work harmful to others and dishonorable to ourselves, reveal it to our inner eye with such clearness that we shall hate it and put it away, though it be at a loss to ourselves. When we work with others, help us to regard them, not as servants to our will, but as brothers equal to us in human dignity, and equally worthy of their full reward. May there be nothing in this day's work of which we shall be ashamed when the sun has set, nor in the eventide of our life when our task is done and we go to our long home to meet thy face.

Once more a new day lies before us, our Father. As we go out among men to do our work, touching the hands and lives of our fellows, make us, we pray thee, friends of all the world. Save us from blighting the fresh flower of any heart by the flare of sudden anger or secret hate. May we not bruise the rightful self-respect of any by contempt or malice. Help us to cheer the suffering by our sympathy, to freshen the drooping by our hopefulness, and to strengthen in all the wholesome sense of worth and the joy of life. Save us from the deadly poison of class-pride. Grant that we may look all men in the face with the eyes of a brother. If any one needs us, make us ready to yield our help ungrudgingly, unless higher duties claim us, and may we rejoice that we have it in us to be helpful to our fellowmen.

O God, we beseech thee to save us this day from the distractions of vanity and the false lure of inordinate desires. Grant us the grace of a quiet and humble mind, and may we learn of Jesus to be meek and lowly of heart. May we not join the throng of those who seek after things that never satisfy and who draw others after them in the fever of covetousness. Save us from adding our influence to the drag of temptation. If the fierce tide of greed beats against the breakwaters of our soul, may we rest at peace in thy higher contentment. In the press of life may we pass from duty to duty in tranquillity of heart and spread thy quietness to all who come near.

O Thou great Companion of our souls, do thou go with us today and comfort us by the sense of thy presence in the hours of spiritual isolation. Give us a single eye for duty. Guide us by the voice within. May we take heed of all the judgments of men and gather patiently whatever truth they hold, but teach us still to test them by the words and the spirit of the one who alone is our Master. May we not be so wholly of one mind with the life that now is that the world can fully approve us, but may we speak the higher truth and live the purer righteousness which thou hast revealed to us. If men speak well of us, may we not be puffed up; if they slight us, may we not be cast down; remembering the words of our Master who bade us rejoice when men speak evil against us and tremble if all speak well, that so we may have evidence that we are still soldiers of God.

O God, we who are bound together in the tender ties of love pray thee for a day of unclouded love. May no passing irritation rob us of our joy in one another. Forgive us if we have often been keen to see the human failings, and slow to feel the preciousness of those who are still the dearest comfort of our life. May there be no sharp words that wound and scar, and no rift that may grow into estrangement. Suffer us not to grieve those whom thou hast sent to us as the sweet ministries of love. May our eyes not be so holden by selfishness that we know thine angels only when they spread their wings to return to thee.

O Lord, we lift our hearts to thee in the pure light of morning and pray that they be kept clean of evil passion by the power of forgiving love. If any slight or wrong still rankles in our souls, help us to pluck it out and to be healed of thee. Suffer us not to turn in anger on him who has wronged us, seeking his hurt, lest we increase the sorrows of the world and taint our own souls with the poisoned sweetness of revenge. Grant that by the insight of love we may understand our brother in his wrong, and if his soul is sick, to bear with him in pity and to save him in the gentle spirit of our Master. Make us determined to love even at cost to our pride, that so we may be soldiers of thy peace on earth.

Evening Prayers

O Lord, we praise thee for our sister the Night, who folds all the tired folk of the earth in her comfortable robe of darkness and gives them sleep. Release now the strained limbs of toil and smooth the brow of care. Grant us the refreshing draught of forgetfulness that we may rise in the morning with a smile on our face. Comfort and ease those who toss wakeful on a bed of pain, or whose aching nerves crave sleep and find it not. Save them from evil or despondent thoughts in the long darkness, and teach them so to lean on thy all-pervading life and love, that their souls may grow tranquil and their bodies, too, may rest. And now through thee we send Good Night to all our brothers and sisters near and far, and pray for peace upon all the earth.

Our Father, as we turn to the comfort of our rest, we remember those who must wake that we may sleep. Bless the guardians of peace who protect us against men of evil, the watchers who save us from the terrors of fire, and all the many who carry on through the hours of the night the restless commerce of men on sea and land. We thank thee for their faithfulness and sense of duty. We pray for thy pardon if our covetousness or luxury makes their nightly toil necessary. Grant that we may realize how dependent the safety of our loved ones and the comforts of our life are on these our brothers, that so we may think of them with love and gratitude and help to make their burden lighter.

Accept the work of this day, O Lord, as we lay it at thy feet. Thou knowest its imperfections, and we know. Of the brave purposes of the morning only a few have found their fulfilment. We bless thee that thou art no hard taskmaster, watching grimly the stint of work we bring, but the father and teacher of men who rejoices with us as we learn to work. We have naught to boast before thee, but we do not fear thy face. Thou knowest all things and thou art love. Accept every right intention however brokenly fulfilled, but grant that ere our life is done we may under thy tuition become true master workmen, who know the art of a just and valiant life.

Our Master, as this day closes and passes from our control, the sense of our shortcomings is quick within us and we seek thy pardon. But since we daily crave thy mercy on our weakness, help us now to show mercy to those who have this day grieved or angered us and to forgive them utterly. Suffer us not to cherish dark thoughts of resentment or revenge. So fill us with thy abounding love and peace that no ill-will may be left in our hearts as we turn to our rest. And if we remember that any brother justly hath aught against us through this day's work, fix in us this moment the firm resolve to make good the wrong and to win again the love of our brother. Suffer us not to darken thy world by lovelessness, but give us the power of the sons of God to bring in the reign of love among men.

Our Father, we thank thee for all the friendly folk who have come into our life this day, gladdening us by their human kindness, and we send them now our parting thoughts of love through thee. We bless thee that we are set amidst this rich brotherhood of kindred life with its mysterious power to quicken and uplift. Make us eager to pay the due price for what we get by putting forth our own life in wholesome good will and by bearing cheerily the troubles that go with all joys. Above all we thank thee for those who share our higher life, the comrades of our better self, in whose companionship we break the mystic bread of life and feel the glow of thy wonderful presence. Into thy keeping we commit our friends, and pray that we may never lose their love by losing thee.

O God, in whom is neither near nor far, through thee we yearn for those who belong to us and who are not here with us. We would fain be near them to shield them from harm and to touch them with the tenderness of love. We cast our cares for them on thee in this evening hour, and pray thee to do better for them than we could do. May no distance have power to wean their hearts from us and no sloth of ours cause us to lag behind the even pace of growth. In due time restore them to us and gladden our souls with their sweet sight. We remember too the loved ones into whose dear eyes we cannot look again. O God, in whom are both the living and the dead, thou art still their life and light as thou art ours. Wherever they be, lay thy hand tenderly upon them and grant that some day we may meet again and hear once more their broken words of love.

Grace Before Meat

Our Father, thou art the final source of all our comforts and to thee we render thanks for this food. But we also remember in gratitude the many men and women whose labor was necessary to produce it, and who gathered it from the land and afar from the sea for our sustenance. Grant that they too may enjoy the fruit of their labor without want, and may be bound up with us in a fellowship of thankful hearts.

O God, we thank thee for the abundance of our blessings, but we pray that our plenty may not involve want for others. Do thou satisfy the desire of every child of thine. Grant that the strength which we shall draw from this food may be put forth again for the common good, and that our life may return to humanity a full equivalent in useful work for the nourishment which we receive from the common store.

Our Father, we thank thee for the food of our body, and for the human love which is the food of our hearts. Bless our family circle, and make this meal a sacrament of love to all who are gathered at this table. But bless thou too that great family of humanity of which we are but a little part. Give to all thy children their daily bread, and let our family not enjoy its comforts in selfish isolation.

O Lord, we pray for thy presence at this meal. Hallow all our joys, and if there is anything wanton or unholy in them, open our eyes that we may see. If we have ever gained our bread by injustice, or eaten it in heartlessness, cleanse our life and give us a spirit of humility and love, that we may be worthy to sit at the common table of humanity in the great house of our Father.

For a Family Reunion

O Lord, our hearts are full of gratitude and praise, for after the long days of separation thou has brought us together again to look into the dear faces and read their love as of old. As the happy memories of the years when we were young together rise up to cheer us, may we feel anew how closely our lives were wrought into one another in their early making, and what a treasure we have had in our home. Whatever new friendships we may form, grant that the old loves may abide to the end and grow ever sweeter with the ripening years.

For a Guest

Our Father, we rejoice in the guest who sits at meat with us, for our food is the more welcome because he shares it, and our home the dearer because it shelters him. Grant that in the happy exchange of thought and affection we may realize anew that all our gladness comes from the simple fellowship of our human kind, and that we are rich as long as we are loved.

Before a Parting

O God, as we break bread once more before we part, we turn to thee with the burden of our desires. Go with him who leaves us and hold him safe. May he feel that we shall not forget him and that his place can never be filled till he returns. Make this meal a sacrament of human love to us, and may our hearts divine the thoughts too tender to be spoken.

In Time of Trouble

O Lord, thou knowest that we are sore stricken and heavy of heart. We beseech thee to uphold us by thy comfort. Thou wert the God of our fathers, and in all these years thine arm has never failed us, for our strength has ever been as our days. May this food come to us as an assurance of thy love and care and a promise of thy sustenance and relief.

Morituri te salutant

O Thou Eternal One, we who are doomed to die lift up our souls to thee for strength, for Death has passed us in the throng of men and touched us, and we know that at some turn of our pathway he stands waiting to take us by the hand and lead us—we know not whither. We praise thee that to us he is no more an enemy but thy great angel and our friend, who alone can open for some of us the prison-house of pain and misery and set our feet in the roomy spaces of a larger life. Yet we are but children, afraid of the dark and the unknown, and we dread the parting from the life that is so sweet and from the loved ones who are so dear.

Grant us of thy mercy a valiant heart, that we may tread the road with head uplifted and a smiling face. May we do our work to the last with a wholesome joy, and love our loves with an added tenderness because the days of love are short. On thee we cast the heaviest burden that numbs our soul, the gnawing fear for those we love, whom we must leave unsheltered in a selfish world. We trust in thee, for through all our years thou hast been our stay. O thou Father of the fatherless, put thy arm about our little ones! And ere we go, we pray that the days may come when the dying may die unafraid, because men have ceased to prey on the weak, and the great family of the nation enfolds all with its strength and care.

We thank thee that we have tasted the rich life of humanity. We bless thee for every hour of life, for all our share in the joys and strivings of our brothers, for the wisdom gained which will be part of us forever. If soon we must go, yet through thee we have lived and our life flows on in the race. By thy grace we too have helped to shape the future and bring in the better day.

If our spirit droops in loneliness, uphold us by thy companionship. When all the voices of love grow faint and drift away, thy everlasting arms will still be there. Thou art the father of our spirits; from thee we have come; to thee we go. We rejoice that in the hours of our purer vision, when the pulse-throb of thine eternity is strong within us, we know that no pang of mortality can reach our unconquerable soul, and that for those who abide in thee death is but the gateway to life eternal. Into thy hands we commend our spirit.

PRAYERS OF PRAISE AND THANKSGIVING

For the Fatherhood of God

O Thou Great Father of us all, we rejoice that at last we know thee. All our soul within us is glad because we need no longer cringe before thee as slaves of holy fear, seeking to appease thine anger by sacrifice and self-inflicted pain, but may come like little children, trustful and happy, to the God of love. Thou art the only true father, and all the tender beauty of our human loves is the reflected radiance of thy loving kindness, like the moonlight from the sunlight, and testifies to the eternal passion that kindled it.

Grant us growth of spiritual vision, that with the passing years we may enter into the fulness of this our faith. Since thou art our Father, may we not hide our sins from thee, but overcome them by the stern comfort of thy presence. By this knowledge uphold us in our sorrows and make us patient even amid the unsolved mysteries of the years. Reveal to us the larger goodness and love that speak through the unbending laws of thy world. Through this faith make us the willing equals of all thy other children.

As thou art ever pouring out thy life in sacrificial father-love, may we accept the eternal law of the cross and give ourselves to thee and to all men. We praise thee for Jesus Christ, whose life has revealed to us this faith and law, and we rejoice that he has become the first-born among many brethren. Grant that in us, too, the faith in thy fatherhood may shine through all our life with such persuasive beauty that some who still creep in the dusk of fear may stand erect as free sons of God, and that others who now through unbelief are living as orphans in an empty world may stretch out their hands to the great Father of their spirits and find thee near.

For This World

O God, we thank thee for this universe, our great home; for its vastness and its riches, and for the manifoldness of the life which teems upon it and of which we are part. We praise thee for the arching sky and the blessed winds, for the driving clouds, and the constellations on high. We praise thee for the salt sea and the running water, for the everlasting hills, for the trees, and for the grass under our feet. We thank thee for our senses by which we can see the splendor of the morning, and hear the jubilant songs of love, and smell the breath of the springtime. Grant us, we pray thee, a heart wide open to all this joy and beauty, and save our souls from being so steeped in care or so darkened by passion that we pass heedless and unseeing when even the thornbush by the wayside is aflame with the glory of God.

Enlarge within us the sense of fellowship with all the living things, our little brothers, to whom thou hast given this earth as their home in common with us. We remember with shame that in the past we have exercised the high dominion of man with ruthless cruelty, so that the voice of the Earth, which should have gone up to thee in song, has been a groan of travail. May we realize that they live, not for us alone, but for themselves and for thee, and that they love the sweetness of life, even as we, and serve thee in their place better than we in ours.

When our use of this world is over and we make room for others, may we not leave anything ravished by our greed or spoiled by our ignorance, but may we hand on our common heritage fairer and sweeter through our use of it, undiminished in fertility and joy, that so our bodies may return in peace to the great mother who nourished them and our spirits may round the circle of a perfect life in thee.

For the Prophets and Pioneers

We praise thee, Almighty God, for thine elect, the prophets and martyrs of humanity, who gave their thoughts and prayers and agonies for the truth of God and the freedom of the people. We praise thee that amid loneliness and the contempt of men, in poverty and imprisonment, when they were condemned by the laws of the mighty and buffeted on the scaffold, thou didst uphold them by thy spirit in loyalty to thy holy cause.

Our hearts burn within us as we follow the bleeding feet of thy Christ down the centuries, and count the mounts of anguish on which he was crucified anew in his prophets and the true apostles of his spirit. Help us to forgive those who did it, for some truly thought they were serving thee when they suppressed thy light, but oh, save us from the same mistake! Grant us an unerring instinct for what is right and true, and a swift sympathy to divine those who truly love and serve the people. Suffer us not by thoughtless condemnation or selfish opposition to weaken the arm and chill the spirit of those who strive for the redemption of mankind. May we never bring upon us the blood of all the righteous by renewing the spirit of those who persecuted them in the past. Grant us rather that we, too, may be counted in the chosen band of those who have given their life as a ransom for the many. Send us forth with the pathfinders of humanity to lead thy people another day's march toward the land of promise.

And if we, too, must suffer loss, and drink of the bitter pool of misunderstanding and scorn, uphold us by thy spirit in steadfastness and joy because we are found worthy to share in the work and the reward of Jesus and all the saints.

For Discoverers and Inventors

We praise thee, O Lord, for that mysterious spark of thy light within us, the intellect of man, for thou has kindled it in the beginning and by the breath of thy spirit it has grown to flaming power in our race.

We rejoice in the men of genius and intellectual vision who discern the undiscovered applications of thy laws and dig the deeper springs through which the hidden forces of thy world may well up to the light of day. We claim them as our own in thee, as members with us in the common body of humanity, of which thou art the all-pervading life and inspirer. Grant them, we pray thee, the divine humility of thine elect souls, to realize that they are sent of thee as brothers and helpers of men and that the powers within them are but part of the vast equipment of humanity, entrusted to them for the common use. May they bow to the law of Christ and live, not to be served, but to give their abilities for the emancipation of the higher life of man. Save them from turning thy revelations into means of extortion and from checking the toilsome march of humanity till they take their toll.

But to us who benefit by their work do thou grant wisdom and justice that we may not suffer the fruit of their toil to be wrested from them by selfish cunning or the pressure of need, but may assure them of their fair reward and of the need of love and honor that is the due of those who have served humanity well. Gladden us by the glowing consciousness of the one life that thinks and strives in us all, and knit us together into a commonwealth of brothers in which each shall be heir of all things and the free servant of all men.

For Artists and Musicians

O Thou who art the all-pervading glory of the world, we bless thee for the power of beauty to gladden our hearts. We praise thee that even the least of us may feel a thrill of thy creative joy when we give form and substance to our thoughts and, beholding our handiwork, find it good and fair.

We praise thee for our brothers, the masters of form and color and sound, who have power to unlock for us the vaster spaces of emotion and to lead us by their hand into the reaches of nobler passions. We rejoice in their gifts and pray thee to save them from the temptations which beset their powers. Save them from discouragements of selfish ambition and from the vanity that feeds on cheap applause, from the snare of the senses and from the dark phantoms that haunt the listening soul.

Let them not satisfy their hunger for beauty with tricks of skill, turning the art of God into a petty craft of men. Teach them that they, too, are but servants of humanity, and that the promise of their gifts can fulfil itself only in the service of love. Give them faith in the inspiring power of a great purpose and courage to follow to the end the visions of their youth. Kindle in their hearts a passionate pity for the joyless lives of the people, and make them rejoice if they are found worthy to hold the cup of beauty to lips that are athirst. Make them the reverent interpreters of God to man, who see thy face and hear thy voice in all things, that so they may unveil for us the beauties of nature which we have passed unseeing, and the sadness and sweetness of humanity to which our selfishness has made us blind.

For Doctors and Nurses

We praise thee, O God, for our friends, the doctors and nurses, who seek the healing of our bodies. We bless thee for their gentleness and patience, for their knowledge and skill. We remember the hours of our suffering when they brought relief, and the days of our fear and anguish at the bedside of our dear ones when they came as ministers of God to save the life thou hadst given. May we reward their fidelity and devotion by our loving gratitude, and do thou uphold them by the satisfaction of work well done.

We rejoice in the tireless daring with which some are now tracking the great slayers of mankind by the white light of science. Grant that under their teaching we may grapple with the sins which have ever dealt death to the race, and that we may so order the life of our communities that none may be doomed to an untimely death for lack of the simple gifts which thou hast given in abundance. Make thou our doctors the prophets and soldiers of thy kingdom, which is the reign of cleanliness and self-restraint and the dominion of health and joyous life.

Strengthen in their whole profession the consciousness that their calling is holy and that they, too, are disciples of the saving Christ. May they never through the pressure of need or ambition surrender the sense of a divine mission and become hirelings who serve only for money. Make them doubly faithful in the service of the poor who need their help most sorely, and may the children of the workingman be as precious to them as the child of the rich. Though they deal with the frail body of man, may they have an abiding sense of the eternal value of the life residing in it, that by the call of faith and hope they may summon to their aid the mysterious spirit of man and the powers of thy all-pervading life.

For Teachers

We implore thy blessing, O God, on all the men and women who teach the children and youth of our nation, for they are the potent friends and helpers of our homes. Into their hands we daily commit the dearest that we have, and as they make our children, so shall future years see them. Grant them an abiding consciousness that they are co-workers with thee, thou great teacher of humanity, and that thou hast charged them with the holy duty of bringing forth from the budding life of the young the mysterious stores of character and ability which thou hast hidden in them. Teach them to reverence the young lives, clean and plastic, which have newly come from thee, and to realize that generations still unborn shall rue their sloth or rise to higher levels through their wisdom and faithfulness. Gird them for their task with thy patience and tranquillity, with a great fatherly and motherly love for the young, and with special tenderness for the backward and afflicted. Save them from physical exhaustion, from loneliness and discouragement, from the numbness of routine, and from all bitterness of heart.

We bless thee for the free and noble spirit that is breathing with quickening power upon the educational life of our day, and for the men and women of large mind and loving heart who have made that spirit our common possession by their teaching and example. But grant that a higher obedience and self restraint may grow in the new atmosphere of freedom. We remember with gratitude to thee the godly teachers of our own youth who won our hearts to higher purposes by the sacred contagion of their life. May the strength and beauty of Christ-like service still be plainly wrought in the lives of their successors, that our children may not want for strong models of devout manhood on whom their characters can be molded.

Do thou reward thy servants with a glad sense of their own eternal worth as teachers of the race, and in the heart of the day do thou show them the spring by the wayside that flows from the eternal silence of God and gives new light to the eyes of all who drink of it.

For All True Lovers

We invoke thy gentlest blessings, our Father, on all true lovers. We praise thee for the great longing that draws the soul of man and maid together and bids them leave all the dear bonds of the past to cleave to one another. We thank thee for the revealing power of love which divines in one beloved the mystic beauty and glory of humanity. We thank thee for the transfiguring power of love which ripens and ennobles our nature, calling forth the hidden stores of tenderness and strength and overcoming the selfishness of youth by the passion of self-surrender.

We pray thee to make their love strong, holy, and deathless, that no misunderstandings may fray the bond, and no gray disenchantment of the years may have power to quench the heavenly light that now glows in them. May they early gain wisdom to discern the true values of life, and may no tyranny of fashion and no glamor of cheaper joys filch from them the wholesome peace and inward satisfaction which only loyal love can give.

Grant them with sober eyes to look beyond these sweet days of friendship to the generations yet to come and to realize that the home for which they long will be part of the sacred tissue of the body of humanity in which thou art to dwell, that so they may reverence themselves and drink the cup of joy with awe.

PRAYERS FOR THE PROGRESS OF HUMANITY

For the Kingdom of God

O Christ, thou hast bidden us pray for the coming of thy Father's kingdom, in which his righteous will shall be done on earth. We have treasured thy words, but we have forgotten their meaning, and thy great hope has grown dim in thy church. We bless thee for the inspired souls of all ages who saw afar the shining city of God, and by faith left the profit of the present to follow their vision. We rejoice that today the hope of these lonely hearts is becoming the clear faith of millions. Help us, O Lord, in the courage of faith to seize what has now come so near, that the glad day of God may dawn at last. As we have mastered Nature that we might gain wealth, help us now to master the social relations of mankind that we may gain justice and a world of brothers. For what shall it profit our nation if it gain numbers and riches, and lose the sense of the living God and the joy of human brotherhood?

Make us determined to live by truth and not by lies, to found our common life on the eternal foundations of righteousness and love, and no longer to prop the tottering house of wrong by legalized cruelty and force. Help us to make the welfare of all the supreme law of our land, that so our commonwealth may be built strong and secure on the love of all its citizens. Cast down the throne of Mammon who ever grinds the life of men, and set up thy throne, O Christ, for thou didst die that men might live. Show thy erring children at last the way from the City of Destruction to the City of Love, and fulfil the longings of the prophets of humanity. Our Master, once more we make thy faith our prayer: "Thy kingdom come! Thy will be done on earth!"

For Those Who Come After Us

O God, we pray thee for those who come after us, for our children, and the children of our friends, and for all the young lives that are marching up from the gates of birth, pure and eager, with the morning sunshine on their faces. We remember with a pang that these will live in the world we are making for them. We are wasting the resources of the earth in our headlong greed, and they will suffer want. We are building sunless houses and joyless cities for our profit, and they must dwell therein. We are making the burden heavy and the pace of work pitiless, and they will fall wan and sobbing by the wayside. We are poisoning the air of our land by our lies and our uncleanness, and they will breathe it.

O God, thou knowest how we have cried out in agony when the sins of our fathers have been visited upon us, and how we have struggled vainly against the inexorable fate that coursed in our blood or bound us in a prison house of life. Save us from maiming the innocent ones who come after us by the added cruelty of our sins. Help us to break the ancient force of evil by a holy and steadfast will and to endow our children with purer blood and nobler thoughts. Grant us grace to leave the earth fairer than we found it; to build upon it cities of God in which the cry of needless pain shall cease; and to put the yoke of Christ upon our business life that it may serve and not destroy. Lift the veil of the future and show us the generation to come as it will be if blighted by our guilt, that our lust may be cooled and we may walk in the fear of the Eternal. Grant us a vision of the far off years as they may be if redeemed by the sons of God, that we may take heart and do battle for thy children and ours.

On the Harm We Have Done

Our Father, we look back on the years that are gone and shame and sorrow come upon us, for the harm we have done to others rises up in our memory to accuse us. Some we have seared with the fire of our lust, and some we have scorched by the heat of our anger. In some we helped to quench the glow of young ideals by our selfish pride and craft, and in some we have nipped the opening bloom of faith by the frost of our unbelief.

We might have followed thy blessed footsteps, O Christ, binding up the bruised hearts of our brothers and guiding the wayward passions of the young to firmer manhood. Instead, there are poor hearts now broken and darkened because they encountered us on the way, and some perhaps remember us only as the beginning of their misery or sin.

O God, we know that all our prayers can never bring back the past, and no tears can wash out the red marks with which we have scarred some life that stands before our memory with accusing eyes. Grant that at least a humble and pure life may grow out of our late contrition, that in the brief days still left to us we may comfort and heal where we have scorned and crushed. Change us by the power of thy saving grace from sources of evil into forces for good, that with all our strength we may fight the wrongs we have aided, and aid the right we have clogged. Grant us this boon, that for every harm we have done, we may do some brave act of salvation, and that for every soul that has stumbled or fallen through us, we may bring to thee some other weak or despairing one, whose strength has been renewed by our love, that so the face of thy Christ may smile upon us and the light within us may shine undimmed.

For Those Without Knowledge

O Thou Eternal One, we adore thee who in all ages hast been the great companion and teacher of mankind; for thou hast lifted our race from the depths, and hast made us to share in thy conscious intelligence and thy will that makes for righteousness and love. Thou alone art our Redeemer, for thy lifting arms were about us and thy persistent voice was in our hearts as we slowly climbed up from savage darkness and cruelty. Thou knowest how often we have resisted thee and loved the easy ways of sin rather than the toilsome gain of self-control and the divine irritation of thy truth.

O God, visit not upon us the guilt of the past, for our fathers have slain thy prophets. They silenced the voices that spoke thine inward thought, and generations have perished in soddenness and misery because the strong once quenched the light of truth. Do thou free humanity at last from the blood-rusted chains with which the past still binds us. Multiply the God-conquered souls who open their hearts gladly to the light that makes us free, for all creation shall be in travail till these sons of God attain their glory.

We pray thee for those who amid all the knowledge of our day are still without knowledge; for those who hear not the sighs of the children that toil, nor the sobs of such as are wounded because others have made haste to be rich; for those who have never felt the hot tears of the mothers of the poor that struggle vainly against poverty and vice. Arouse them, we beseech thee, from their selfish comfort and grant them the grace of social repentance. Smite us all with the conviction that for us ignorance is sin, and that we are indeed our brother's keeper if our own hand has helped to lay him low. Though increase of knowledge bring increase of sorrow, may we turn without flinching to the light and offer ourselves as instruments of thy spirit in bringing order and beauty out of disorder and darkness.

For a Share in the Work of Redemption

O God, thou great redeemer of mankind, our hearts are tender in the thought of thee, for in all the afflictions of our race thou hast been afflicted, and in the sufferings of thy people it was thy body that was crucified. Thou hast been wounded by our transgressions and bruised by our iniquities, and all our sins are laid at last on thee. Amid the groaning of creation we behold thy spirit in travail till the sons of God shall be born in freedom and holiness.

We pray thee, O Lord, for the graces of a pure and holy life that we may no longer add to the dark weight of the world's sin that is laid upon thee, but may share with thee in thy redemptive work. As we have thirsted with evil passions to the destruction of men, do thou fill us now with hunger and thirst for justice that we may bear glad tidings to the poor and set at liberty all who are in the prison house of want and sin. Lay thy spirit upon us with a passion of

Christ-like love that we may join our lives to the weak and oppressed and may strengthen their cause by bearing their sorrows. And if the evil that is threatened turns to smite us and if we must learn the dark malignity of sinful power, comfort us by the thought that thus we are bearing in our body the marks of Jesus, and that only those who share in his free sacrifice shall feel the plentitude of thy life. Help us in patience to carry forward the eternal cross of thy Christ, counting it a joy if we, too, are sown as grains of wheat in the furrows of the world, for only by the agony of the righteous comes redemption.

For the Church

O God, we pray for thy church, which is set today amid the perplexities of a changing order, and face to face with a great new task. We remember with love the nurture she gave to our spiritual life in its infancy, the tasks she set for our growing strength, the influence of the devoted hearts she gathers, the steadfast power for good she has exerted. When we compare her with all other human institutions, we rejoice, for there is none like her. But when we judge her by the mind of her Master, we bow in pity and contrition. Oh, baptize her afresh in the life-giving spirit of Jesus! Grant her a new birth, though it be with the travail of repentance and humiliation. Bestow upon her a more imperious responsiveness to duty, a swifter compassion with suffering, and an utter loyalty to the will of God. Put upon her lips the ancient gospel of her Lord. Help her to proclaim boldly the coming of the kingdom of God and the doom of all that resist it. Fill her with the prophets' scorn of tyranny, and with a Christ-like tenderness for the heavy-laden and down-trodden. Give her faith to espouse the cause of the people, and in their hands that grope after freedom and light to recognize the bleeding hands of the Christ. Bid her cease from seeking her own life, lest she lose it. Make her valiant to give up her life to humanity, that like her crucified Lord she may mount by the path of the cross to a higher glory.

For Ministers

O Jesus, we thy ministers bow before thee to confess the common sins of our calling. Thou knowest all things; thou knowest that we love thee and that our hearts' desire is to serve thee in faithfulness; and yet, like Peter, we have so often failed thee in the hour of thy need. If ever we have loved our own leadership and power when we sought to lead our people to thee, we pray thee to forgive. If we have been engrossed in narrow duties and little questions, when the vast needs of humanity called aloud for prophetic vision and apostolic sympathy, we pray thee to forgive. If in our loyalty to the Church of the past we have distrusted thy living voice and have suffered thee to pass from our door unheard, we pray thee to forgive. If ever we have been more concerned for the strong and the rich than for the shepherdless throngs of the people for whom thy soul grieved, we pray thee to forgive.

O Master, amidst our failures we cast ourselves upon thee in humility and contrition. We need new light and a new message. We need the ancient spirit of prophecy and the leaping fire and joy of a new conviction, and thou alone canst give it. Inspire the ministry of thy Church with dauntless courage to face the vast needs of the future. Free us from all entanglements that have hushed our voice and bound our action. Grant us grace to look upon the veiled sins of the rich and the coarse vices of the poor through thine eyes. Give us thine inflexible sternness against sin, and thine inexhaustible compassion for the frailty and tragedy of those who do the sin. Make us faithful shepherds of thy flock, true seers of God, and true followers of Jesus.

For Our City

O God, we pray thee for this, the city of our love and pride. We rejoice in her spacious beauty and her busy ways of commerce, in her stores and factories where hand joins hand in toil, and in her blessed homes where heart joins heart for rest and love.

Help us to make our city the mighty common workshop of our people, where every one will find his place and task, in daily achievement building up his own life to resolute manhood, keen to do his best with hand and mind. Help us to make our city the greater home of our people, where all may live their lives in comfort, unafraid, living their lives in peace and rounding out their years in strength.

Bind our citizens, not by the bond of money and of profit alone, but by the glow of neighborly good will, by the thrill of common joys, and the pride of common possessions. As we set the greater aims for the future of our city, may we ever remember that her true wealth and greatness consist, not in the abundance of the things we possess, but in the justice of her institutions and the brotherhood of her children. Make her rich in her sons and daughters and famous through the lofty passions that inspire them.

We thank thee for the patriot men and women of the past whose generous devotion to the common good has been the making of our city. Grant that our own generation may build worthily on the foundation they have laid. If in the past there have been some who have sold the city's good for private gain, staining her honor by their cunning and greed, fill us, we beseech thee, with the righteous anger of true sons that we may purge out the shame lest it taint the future years.

Grant us a vision of our city, fair as she might be: a city of justice, where none shall prey on others; a city of plenty, where vice and poverty shall cease to fester; a city of brotherhood, where all success shall be founded on service, and honor shall be given to nobleness alone; a city of peace, where order shall not rest on force, but on the love of all for the city, the great mother of the common life and weal. Hear thou, O Lord, the silent prayer of all our hearts as we each pledge our time and strength and thought to speed the day of her coming beauty and righteousness.

For Our Nation, A Cooperative Commonwealth

O God, we praise thee for the dream of the golden city of peace and righteousness which has ever haunted the prophets of humanity, and we rejoice with joy unspeakable that at last the people have conquered the freedom and knowledge and power which may avail to turn into reality the vision that so long has beckoned in vain.

Speed now the day when the plains and the hills and the wealth thereof shall be the people's own, and thy freemen shall not live as tenants of men on the earth which thou hast given to all; when no babe shall be born without its equal birthright in the riches and knowledge wrought out by the labor of the ages; and when the mighty engines of industry shall throb with a gladder music because the men who ply these great tools shall be their owners and masters.

Bring to an end, O Lord, the inhumanity of the present, in

which all men are ridden by the pale fear of want while the nation of which they are citizens sits throned amid the wealth of their making; when the manhood in some is cowed by helplessness, while the soul of others is surfeited and sick with power which no frail son of the dust should wield.

O God, save us, for our nation is at strife with its own soul and is sinning against the light which thou aforetime hast kindled in it. Thou hast called our people to freedom, but we are withholding from men their share of the common heritage without which freedom becomes a hollow name. Thy Christ has kindled in us the passion for brotherhood, but the social life we have built denies and slays brotherhood.

We pray thee to revive in us the hardy spirit of our forefathers that we may establish and complete their work, building on the basis of their democracy the firm edifice of a cooperative commonwealth, in which both government and industry shall be of the people, by the people, and for the people. May we, who now live, see the oncoming of the great day of God, when all men shall stand side by side in equal worth and real freedom, all toiling and all reaping, masters of nature but brothers of men, exultant in the tide of the common life, and jubilant in the adoration of Thee, the source of their blessings and the Father of us all.

PRAYERS OF WRATH

Against War

O Lord, since first the blood of Abel cried to thee from the ground that drank it, this earth of thine has been defiled with the blood of man shed by his brother's hand, and the centuries sob with the ceaseless horror of war. Ever the pride of kings and the covetousness of the strong has driven peaceful nations to slaughter. Ever the songs of the past and the pomp of armies have been used to inflame the passions of the people. Our spirit cries out to thee in revolt against it, and we know that our righteous anger is answered by thy holy wrath.

Break thou the spell of the enchantments that make the nations drunk with the lust of battle and draw them on as willing tools of death. Grant us a quiet and steadfast mind when our own nation clamors for vengeance or aggression. Strengthen our sense of justice and our regard for the equal worth of other peoples and races. Grant to the rulers of nations faith in the possibility of peace through justice, and grant to the common people a new and stern enthusiasm for the cause of peace. Bless our soldiers and sailors for their swift obedience and their willingness to answer the call of duty, but inspire them nonetheless with a hatred of war, and may they never for love of private glory or advancement provoke its coming. May our young men still rejoice to die for their country with the valor of their fathers, but teach our age nobler methods of matching our strength and more effective ways of giving our life for the flag.

O thou strong Father of all nations, draw all thy great family together with an increasing sense of our common blood and destiny, that peace may come on earth at last, and thy sun may shed its light rejoicing on a holy brotherhood of peoples.

Against the Servants of Mammon

We cry to thee for justice, O Lord, for our soul is weary with the iniquity of greed. Behold the servants of Mammon, who defy thee and drain their fellowmen for gain; who grind down the strength of the workers by merciless toil and fling them aside when they are mangled and worn; who rack-rent the poor and make dear the space and air which thou hast made free; who paralyze the hand of justice by corruption and blind the eyes of the people by lies; who nullify by their craft the merciful laws which nobler men have devised for the protection of the weak; who have made us ashamed of our dear country by their defilements and have turned our holy freedom into a hollow name; who have brought upon thy church the contempt of men and have cloaked their extortion with the Gospel of thy Christ.

For the oppression of the poor and the sighing of the needy now do thou arise, O Lord; for because thou art love, and tender as a mother to the weak, therefore thou art the great hater of iniquity and thy doom is upon those who grow rich on the poverty of the people.

O God, we are afraid, for the thunder cloud of thy wrath is even now black above us. In the ruins of dead empires we have read how thou hast trodden the wine-press of thine anger when the measure of their sin was full. We are sick at heart when we remember that by the greed of those who enslaved a weaker race that curse was fastened upon us all which still lies black and hopeless across our land, though the blood of a nation was spilled to atone. Save our people from being dragged down into vaster guilt and woe by men who have no vision and know no law except their lust. Shake their souls with awe of thee that they may cease. Help us with clean hands to tear the web which they have woven about us and to turn our people back to thy law, lest the mark of the beast stand out on the right hand and forehead of our nation and our feet be set on the downward path of darkness from which there is no return forever.

PRAYERS FOR CONFERENCES AND CONVENTIONS

O God, we praise thy holy name, for thou has brought us from afar, drawn together by the splendor of thy kingdom, to take counsel for thy work. Be with us through all the strain of the days that are before us. Brood over our assemblies with thy Holy Spirit. Give us vision beyond the range of worldly prudence, and by thy wisdom make us wise, lest all our planning be futile. If difficulties confront us, give us the courageous faith that bids the mountains melt away. Smite a pathway even across the impassable sea for thy people. Hush all spirit of contention and self-will. Make us peaceful through love and through the unity of our desire. May this gathering set the standard of our Lord high up where in coming years we may see it and take courage to fulfil the vows we here make . . . .

Thy peace be upon this city, and upon all who love the Lord Jesus. In His name we pray.

As we look across the vast field of our work, O Master, we feel the challenge of thy call and turn to thee for strength. So much to do for thee, and so little wherewith to do it.

O Christ, thou who art touched with a feeling of our infirmities and hast been tempted even as we, look with thy great sympathy on thy servants. Thou knowest the drain of our daily work and the limitations of our bodies. Thou knowest that we carry but a little candle of knowledge to guide the feet of the erring amid the mazes of modern life. Thou knowest that our longing for holiness of heart is frustrated by the drag of our earthliness and the weight of ancient sins.

Fit us for our work, lest we fail thee. We lean on thee, thou great giver of life, and pray for physical vigor and quiet strength. We call to thee, thou fountain of light, to flood our minds with thy radiance and to make all things clear and simple. We submit our inmost desires to thy holy will, and beseech thee to make thy law sweet to our willing hearts.

Give, Lord, what thou askest, and then ask what thou wilt. We make our prayer, O God by faith in Christ, our Lord.

We praise thee, O God, for our friends and fellow workers, for the touch of their hands and the brightness of their faces, for the cheer of their words and the outflow of good will that refreshes us.

Grant us the insight of love that we may see them as thou seest, not as frail mortals, but as radiant children of God who have wrought patience out of tribulation and who bear in earthen vessels the treasures of thy grace.

May nought mar the joy of our fellowship here. May none remain lonely and hungry of heart among us. Let none go hence without the joy of new friendships. Give us more capacity for love and a richer consciousness of being loved. Overcome our coldness and reserve that we may throw ajar the gates of our heart and keep open house this day.

Lift our human friendships to the level of spiritual companionship. May we realize thee as the eternal bond of our unity. Shine upon us from the faces of thy servants, thou all-pervading beauty, that in loving them we may be praising thee. Through Christ, our Lord.

Our Father, as we come to the parting, we humbly give thanks for the days of our gathering. We thank thee for the real work accomplished, for the plans laid, for the officers chosen. . . . Make us worthy to bear thy message. May every word and act be the simple pulsing of a Christian heart.

We thank thee for the voices that have interpreted thy will and summoned us to thy work. We praise thee for the hours of holy quiet in which we crossed the threshold of thy presence and listened to the inner voice in the most holy place. Fix on the sensitive film of our spirits the image and splendor of Christ which shone upon us in the great moments of these past days.

And now, as we turn our faces homeward toward the toil and care, the trials and temptations of our work, we feel our utter need of thee, thou great companion of our souls. Be thou the strength of our weakness, the wisdom of our foolishness, the triumph of our failures, the changeless unity in our changing days. Knowing the brevity of our years, help us to work resolutely while it is day. Shine upon us, thou sun of our life, even in the valley of the shadow, and may the sun of faith never die in our hearts. We make our petition through Jesus Christ, our Saviour and Lord.

THE AUTHOR'S PRAYER

O thou who art the light of my soul, I thank thee for the incomparable joy of listening to thy voice within, and I know that no word of thine shall return void, however brokenly uttered. If aught in this book was said through lack of knowledge, or through weakness of faith in thee or of love for men, I pray thee to over-rule my sin and turn aside its force before it harm thy cause. Pardon the frailty of thy servant, and look upon him only as he sinks his life in Jesus, his Master and Saviour. Amen.

SELECT BIBLIOGRAPHY

Books by Walter Rauschenbusch listed in chronological order. Subsequent editions and translations of his books have been omitted.

Neue Lieder, with Ira D. Sankey. Authorized translation of *Gospel Hymns Number 5*. New York: Biglow and Main, 1889.
Das Leben Jesu: Ein sytematisher Studiengang für Jugendvereine und Bibelklassen. Cleveland: P. Ritter, 1895.
Evangeliums-Lieder 1 und 2, with Ira D. Sankey. New York: Biglow and Main, 1897.
Evangeliums-Sanger 3, 150 Neue Lieder für abendgottesdienste und besondere versammlungen, with Ira D. Sankey. Kassel: J.G. Oncken, 1907.
Christianity and the Social Crisis. New York: Macmillan, 1907.
For God and People: Prayers of the Social Awakening. Boston: Pilgrim Press, 1910.
Unto Me. Boston: Pilgrim Press, 1912.
Christianizing the Social Order. New York: Macmillan, 1912.
Dare We Be Christian? Boston: Pilgrim Press, 1914.
The Social Principles of Jesus. New York: Association Press, 1916.
A Theology for the Social Gospel. New York: Macmillan, 1917.
The Righteousness of God, a reconstructed text by Max L. Stackhouse of an early unpublished manuscript. Nashville: Abingdon Press, 1968.

Articles by Walter Rauschenbusch listed in chronological order. Many fugitive items having no direct bearing on the theme have been omitted, as have those that are reprinted in the text.

"The Tuition of the Spirit." *Second Annual Report of the Amity Missionary Conference* (1892): 9.
"The Coming of the Lord." *Fifth Annual Report of the Amity Missionary Conference* (1895): 3.
"The New Apostolate." *Sixth Annual Report of the Amity Missionary Conference* (1896): 29–30.
"The Ideals of the Social Reformers." *American Journal of Sociology* 2 (1896): 202–19.
"The Stake of the Church in the Social Movement." *American Journal of Sociology* 3 (1897): 18–30.

"Jesus as an Organizer of Men." *Biblical World,* New Series 9 (1898): 102–11.
"Christian Socialism." In *A Dictionary of Religion and Ethics,* edited by Shailer
    Mathews and Gerald B. Smith, 90–91. New York: Macmillan, 1921.

Articles or pamphlets by Leighton Williams related to the thrust of the Brotherhood of the Kingdom, listed in chronological order.

The Baptist Position: Its Experimental Basis. Amity Tracts No. 1. New York: E.
    Scott, 1892.
The Powers of the Kingdom. Amity Tracts No. 8. Prepared for the Eleventh Annual
    Conference of the Brotherhood of the Kingdom, August 3–7, 1903.
"The Brotherhood of the Kingdom and Its Work." *The Kingdom* 1 (August 1907):
    no pagination.
"The Reign of the New Humanity." A paper read at the Conference of the Brotherhood of the Kingdom, August 8, 1907. *The Kingdom* 1 (December 1907): no
    pagination.
"Our Duty to Cultivate the Spiritual Life." A circular letter addressed by request to
    the Brotherhood of the Kingdom, April 19, 1913.

Secondary works which provide an introduction to Walter Rauschenbusch and
his times.

Bodein, Vernon P. *The Social Gospel of Walter Rauschenbusch and Its Relation to
    Religious Education.* New Haven: Yale University Press, 1944.
Handy, Robert T. *The Social Gospel in America, 1870–1920.* New York: Oxford
    University Press, 1966.
Hopkins, C. Howard. *The Social Gospel in American Protestantism.* New Haven:
    Yale University Press, 1940.
Hudson, Frederic M. "The Reign of the New Humanity." Ph.D. diss., Columbia
    University, 1968.
Johnson, Carl E. "Walter Rauschenbusch as Historian." Duke University, 1976.
Robins, Henry B. "The Religion of Walter Rauschenbusch." *Colgate Rochester
    Divinity School Bulletin* 1 (1928): 37–43.
Sharpe, Dores R. *Walter Rauschenbusch.* New York: Macmillan, 1942.
Smucker, Donovan E. "The Origins of Walter Rauschenbusch's Social Ethics."
    Ph.D. diss., University of Chicago, 1957.

INDEX TO INTRODUCTION

INDEX TO TEXTS